Why Be Good?

Why Be Good?

A Historical Introduction to Ethics

DUNCAN RICHTER

Virginia Military Institute

New York — Oxford
OXFORD UNIVERSITY PRESS
2008

Oxford University Press, Inc., publishes works that further Oxford University's
objective of excellence in research, scholarship, and education.

Oxford   New York
Auckland   Cape Town   Dar es Salaam   Hong Kong   Karachi
Kuala Lumpur   Madrid   Melbourne   Mexico City   Nairobi
New Delhi   Shanghai   Taipei   Toronto

With offices in
Argentina   Austria   Brazil   Chile   Czech Republic   France   Greece
Guatemala   Hungary   Italy   Japan   Portugal   Singapore
South Korea   Switzerland   Thailand   Turkey   Ukraine   Vietnam

Published by Oxford University Press, Inc.
198 Madison Avenue, New York, New York 10016
http://www.oup.com.

Oxford is a registered trademark of Oxford University Press

Library of Congress Cataloging-in-Publication Data
Richter, Duncan.
   Why be good? : a historical introduction to ethics / Duncan Richter.
   p. cm.
   Includes bibliographical references and index.
   ISBN 978-0-19-532505-8 (pbk. : alk. paper)—ISBN 978-0-19-532504-1 (hardcover : alk. paper)
1. Ethics—History. I. Title.
   BJ71.R48 2008
   170.9—dc22   2007019011

Printed in the United States of America
On acid-free paper

To Isabel and Henry

Contents

Acknowledgments

I have many people to thank for their help with this book. My wife Stephanie Wilkinson gave me an intelligent non-philosopher's perspective on what I was trying to get across as well as a good eye for punctuation and style. My colleague Kirby Arinder kindly looked over some draft chapters and suggested possible improvements. Jeremy Pierce helped my understanding of a common criticism of Thomas Aquinas. At Oxford University Press, Robert Miller, Andrew Fargnoli, and Andrew Pachuta have helped make the book possible and saved me from many errors.

I am grateful also to numerous philosophy instructors from other schools who read the manuscript and gave invaluable advice from the point of view of people who might use the book in teaching. My thanks to Joel Whittemore of McMurry University, Robert Lane of the University of West Georgia, Brian Stern of the University of Colorado at Boulder, Natasha Mohr of the University of Nebraska, Omaha, John G. Messerly of the University of Texas at Austin, Rodger Jackson of Richard Stockton College of New Jersey, Anton Tupa of the University of Florida, Robert Hollinger of Iowa State University, Greg Peterson of South Dakota State University, Christopher G. Griffin of Northern Arizona University, Ed Sherline of the University of Wyoming, and several anonymous reviewers. Finally, I would like to thank the VMI cadets on whom I have tried out versions of this text in my own course on ethics. Any remaining flaws in the book are my fault.

Why Be Good?

Introduction

This book is all about answers to one question: Why be good? It might seem a simple question to answer. There are obvious reasons for obeying the law when the police are watching or for obeying your parents when they are around, and you might believe that God is watching you all the time and will punish or reward you according to how well you obey his rules. But what if you could make sure that no one was watching, that you would definitely get away with any bad or illegal act that you committed? Would you have any reason then not to do whatever you wanted? And, you might wonder, does it make any difference what it is that you want to do?

Imagine three people in New Orleans in the aftermath of Hurricane Katrina, in a part of the city that has not been flooded but where order has broken down completely. One of these people goes wild, not only taking necessary supplies from stores that have been looted but pushing around anybody he comes across, taking whatever he likes and hurting people for the fun of it. Another wants to join in but fears that she will be caught and punished by someone bigger and more powerful than her. The third has no such fear but simply does not want to bully other people. Which of these people would you want to be? Which one has the best future ahead of him or her? Which one is the best person?

Let's assume for the sake of argument that the man who runs riot has a really good time doing so and that he never gets caught. He is not punished by other rioters, innocent bystanders, the police, or even God. Now does being in his shoes appeal to you? Perhaps you think he is a good man, in the sense of being smart and strong. Even if you do not—even if you think the person who leaves others alone is good—you still might not see the value of being good in this way yourself. That is, you can recognize someone as being good in the sense of being moral without thinking it is good in the sense of being smart or worthwhile to be like that.

There are different senses of the word "good," in other words. Calling something good can be like giving it a thumbs-up, but the word can also be used to characterize something in a specific way, without endorsing it. Saying "He's a good football player but not a good man" describes the man's abilities without giving him the overall thumbs-up. Saying "I hate her, she's always so *good*" characterizes the woman's moral qualities but again refuses to endorse her. We all want to be good in the sense of being worthy of endorsement, of earning a big thumbs-up (if not two); but we don't necessarily all want to be good in the ethical sense. So then the question arises, Why be morally good? Why respect other people and their property if there is no profit in it for you? Why care about truth and justice if there is no profit in it for you? And what profit could there possibly be in truth and justice?

Questions like these have been around for thousands of years, but some people believe they are more pressing today than ever before. Part of the reason for this might be that we seem to live in a culture that values results over everything else. The end is everything and the means do not matter. Some of the biggest villains think this way, stealing from their employees' pension funds just to help their bottom line or even murdering thousands of innocent civilians in cold blood in order to get their way. But we make heroes of people who think along these lines too, as long as we share their ends. Television sports commentators praise players who commit "good" fouls, breaking the rules and possibly hurting other athletes in order to help their team win a game. This is reflected in our novels and television shows as well as in real life. Many of the heroes of police dramas and spy stories are mavericks who don't play by the rules but always get results. Rules, we often hear, were made to be broken, so why not moral rules? People have always cared about results, but it sometimes seems that today, unlike in past times, that is *all* we care about.

The idea that only the results or consequences of actions matter—that there is nothing you can think of that is absolutely off-limits as the means to your end—is called **consequentialism**. This name was given in 1958 by the British philosopher Elizabeth Anscombe in a paper called "Modern Moral Philosophy."[1] She identified it as a striking development in thinking about ethics that started, she thought, some time in the nineteenth century. According to consequentialists, we cannot say in advance that it will never be right to kill an innocent person deliberately. If terrorists threaten to unleash a deadly biological weapon unless the government frames, convicts, and executes someone, consequentialists would say we must at least consider the possibility that such an injustice is the right thing to do. Many people today would agree, and that is Anscombe's complaint. We lack the respect for justice that people used to have, she thinks, and would be better off returning to ancient ways of thinking about ethics. There are modern ethical theories that reject consequentialism, but each of these faces problems of its own. We will look at these theories in later chapters, and you can decide for yourself whether Anscombe is right on this point. I want simply to allow for the possibility that she is right and so investigate theories both ancient and modern in an attempt to find the best answers to questions about what it means to be good and why anyone should try to be a person of good character.

Anscombe's paper made waves. It was an attack on all modern theories of ethics. She argued that all such theories are badly flawed, either morally or philosophically. Either they were not well thought out, and thus bad philosophically, or else they worked perfectly well intellectually but were not morally acceptable.[2] Not surprisingly, most ethicists begged to differ. But others were persuaded that she was right and that we should go back to ancient ideas about how to live. In particular, the ancient ideas that appealed most to these people were the views of Aristotle. Aristotle did not talk much about right and wrong as such but instead about character traits. Good traits are called **virtues** (and bad ones are called **vices**), so this kind of approach to ethics is called **virtue ethics**. We will return to the question of virtue and character throughout the book, especially in the chapters on Plato and Aristotle.

Before we go on, though, let us get some terminology straight. **Moral philosophy** is a British name for ethics, the philosophical study of good and evil, right and wrong. **Philosophical** means rational or logical and serious or careful—not, as some people might think, pointless, divorced from reality, or unconstrained by any standards so that any opinion is as good as any other. This book is all about moral philosophy, so you will see what it means for yourself. For now, let us say that **philosophy** is the attempt to use reason to solve problems that cannot be solved in other ways—mathematically, say, or in a chemistry lab. Faced with problems that we do not know how to solve otherwise, philosophers think very carefully about them in the hope that this will make clear how they can be solved or at least what it is that we are puzzled about. This is how almost all academic disciplines have come about. People wondering about living things, for instance, figured out what they had in common and what it was that they wanted to know about them and devised the field we call "biology" in order to study them. Psychology—whose relevance to ethics we will explore in Chapter 10—did not separate itself from philosophy until the nineteenth century. Ethics is not like this. It is still a branch of philosophy and quite possibly always will be. This does not mean that there is anything wrong with ethics, but it does mean that we do not have an established method of proven reliability for cranking out solutions to ethical problems. Without such a method, all we can do is either keep ethical problems from our minds (which seems a bit irresponsible) or else think very carefully about them. The second road is the one we will take in this book.

But isn't it all just a matter of personal opinion? Surely, you might think, there is no objective, absolute, timeless, universal truth about good and bad or right and wrong? Throughout the book we will come across reasons for thinking otherwise—for believing that ethics is not all relative—but here are a few for now. The simplest form of relativism says that there is no such thing as absolute truth. But that very statement seems to present itself as an absolute truth, so it contradicts itself. If any form of relativism is true, it must be something more sophisticated or subtle than that. What about the idea that each culture's ethics are right for that culture? Well, again, that is itself a universal judgment about what is right, not a relative one. And why should it be right for one society to oppress women, for instance, if this is not right in other cultures? Why should it be right for a society to enslave people or to commit genocide? Even if you really believe that what the Nazis did was right "for them," why should this have been right for those people but wrong for others? Just because they believed it was right? If simply believing something ("Murdering these people is right," say) makes it true, then there is no possibility of being wrong about ethics. Ethics would be a realm where illusion and reality were one and the same. Nobody's beliefs (or no culture's beliefs, at least) could conceivably be wrong, and sentences such as "The culturally accepted slave trade was wrong" or "The Nazis were wrong" could not possibly be true.

Those sentences do seem to make sense though, even to people who disagree with them. It does seem at least *possible* that they are true. We do distinguish between mere belief (which might be false) and true belief or belief that is right. If I say that I used to support (or oppose) capital punishment or abortion, for instance, but now I have seen that I was wrong, then you will have no trouble understanding what I mean. (Of course, you might not agree, but that is another matter.) And if the United States of America were to say "We used to accept slavery and racial segregation, but now we see that they are intolerably wrong," then this makes perfect sense. Relativism must be false, therefore, because it says that the United States in the days of slavery was right to accept it and right after the emancipation of the slaves *not* to accept it. It goes further than this, in fact. It says that *whatever* the United States (or any other society) accepted at any time *must* have been right. This, surely, cannot be true.

Relativism is such a tempting position for so many people that you might well not be convinced by this. As I said, we shall return to it later. For now, though, let me just quickly summarize the reasons for rejecting the kind of cultural relativism that I have been talking about here.

1. Relativism seems to be arbitrary. If slavery was right in the United States (and not just legal) before, say, January 1, 1863 (the date of Abraham Lincoln's Emancipation Proclamation), but wrong after that, what possible reason could there be for this change? Did God perhaps change his mind about the ethics of slavery on that day? Or are ethics simply dictated by governments, whether they be of the United States, the Confederate States, the Taliban, or Nazi Germany?

2. Relativism seems to be false. If cultural relativism is correct, then every culture at every time is right, whatever it believes. In that case, though, while there could certainly be change in ethics, there could never be improvement or decline. Instead of saying "Society is much better now that we no longer officially sanction racial segregation" or "Society has gone downhill since the 1950s," we could only say that society was right in the 1950s; right in the 1960s; right in the 1970s, 1980s, 1990s; and right today. But it surely is not true that this is all we can say on such subjects. As an individual, I might express a preference for some particular time or culture; but if I am a relativist, I cannot regard this preference as right in any absolute sense. This creates problems of coherence, as we will see in point 4.

3. Relativism seems to be **immoral** (ethically bad) or at least **amoral** (ethically neutral). What kind of person honestly believes that the Holocaust was right,

in any sense of the word? Or that slavery or segregation could ever be right? Or that women should, in any time or place, not have had the same rights as men? The short answer is "A Nazi." But Nazis are not relativists. They are not live-and-let-live types who think that every culture is just as good as every other. This brings up a final objection.

4. Relativism seems to be incoherent or impossible to believe. Relativism tells you that the Nazis were *right* to murder millions of Jewish people and invade the countries around Germany in the name of the Third Reich. It also tells you that the people attacked by the Nazis were *right* to fight against the Nazis, in line with their cultural beliefs. Nazism is right, communism is right, Islamism is right, free market democracy is right, equal rights are right, unequal rights are right, and so on. Who has right on their side? Everybody! You have to root equally for every team at once, including your own and the ones that are against yours. This seems to be impossible, unless by "rooting for all teams" we really mean rooting for none. In the end, perhaps relativism is just another name for the belief that nothing is right or wrong. There is no distinction between an illusion that something is right and a true belief that something is right because the whole *idea* of right and wrong is an illusion. That is not relativism, though. It is what we might call "amoralism." If you believe that, or suspect that it might be true, or want a way to prove that it is not true, then this book is for you. It is precisely what this book is about.

Relativism raises the question whether "right" and "wrong" are just meaning-less words. Even if we reject relativism, there are other reasons that we need to think about what "wrong" and "right" mean. If they mean "tending to make people unhappy (or happy)," then one set of acts will turn out to be wrong (or right), while if they mean "forbidden (or commanded) by God," then a different set will emerge. Philosophers like to distinguish between **applied ethics**, which focuses on particular practical issues, perhaps taking a theory like consequentialism and seeing what it implies about abortion or animal rights, say, and **normative ethics**, which examines the strengths and weaknesses of competing ethical theories (one that says you should always do whatever produces the most happiness, say, versus another that says you should never violate anybody's natural human rights), and **meta-ethics**, which focuses on the meaning of words such as "good" and "right." This kind of distinction can be very useful, especially in seeing what a given philosopher is trying to do; but it can arguably go only so far. What meta-ethical theory we support is likely to shape the normative theory we support, and vice versa. For instance, those who think that "good" refers to something subjective are likely to think that good acts will somehow feel good. Those who define "good" in terms of something (thought to be) objective and independent, such as the will of God, on the other hand, will not necessarily think that good acts will feel good. In a similar way, our intuitions about applied ethics will both shape and be shaped by our preferred normative theory. In this book we will come across issues in meta-ethics and applied ethics because they are hard to separate from questions of normative ethics and because, as a result, they are important to the work of the various philosophers we are going to discuss. Indeed, our search will take us into other branches of philosophy too, including **metaphysics** (investigation into the ultimate nature of reality) and **epistemology** (investigation into the nature of knowledge). So this book could possibly serve as a general introduction to philosophy. Its focus, though, is on ethics and specifically on the main answers that have been offered throughout the history of Western philosophy to the question "Why be good?"

Why take a historical approach? Partly because contemporary virtue ethics begins with Anscombe's call to return to Aristotle. Aristotle himself, who lived in the fourth century BCE, was responding in part to the work of his teacher Plato; and it was Plato who most famously raised the question we are trying to answer in his classic work the *Republic*. That book begins with a lively argument between the philosopher Socrates and a character called Thrasymachus, who rejects the idea that we should be good. His skepticism about ethics will be the major theme of this book, which gives us another reason to start with Plato before moving on to Aristotle. Virtue theory, the kind of normative ethical theory that emphasizes character, began with the Greeks; and its history is the history of various responses to their work. These include the work of consequentialists and others that Anscombe criticized. Modern theories of ethics did not just spring up out of nowhere. They belong to a tradition and are best understood as responses to what their authors believed were flaws in that tradition. If we are going to judge these modern theories, then, we need to understand the ancient theories that they were reacting against or trying to improve.

History is also an important part of Anscombe's original thesis. Concepts of duty, obligation, right and wrong, and so on, she argued, have a history and belong in a particular kind of historical context. This context, she says, is religious. Anscombe, who was a Christian, claims that we cannot simply reject belief in God while keeping Christian or Jewish ethics. (The anti-Christian Friedrich Nietzsche—whom we will meet in Chapter 9—thought the same thing.) If God has told us not to lie, then that is a kind of reason not to lie. We might ask what reason we have to do what God tells us, but then various answers to that question can be given too. Most simply, perhaps even crudely, we can talk about promises of eternal reward and threats of punishment in hell. You might not believe in heaven and hell, and you might think that self-interest is a questionable motive for doing the right thing; but *if* heaven and hell are real and *if* God has commanded that we not lie, then this certainly does give us a reason not to lie. Believers in God and God's commandments might also talk about God's gift of life as a reason to be grateful to him and to do what he asks, without making any reference to self-interest. If we think of God as our father, then the relationship becomes still more subtle; and our reasons for obeying him likewise. If we do not believe in God, on the other hand, then the biblical story of the Ten Commandments will be just a story to us. It gives us no reason whatsoever not to tell lies.

Nor, for that matter, does the way we were raised. Or so philosophers as diverse as Aristotle and Nietzsche seem to think. We might have been raised well or badly, so the fact that we were raised not to lie is not in itself a reason not to lie. Most people are raised with fairly traditional values ("traditional" means handed on, and we get our values mostly from the previous generation), and these tend to be religious. So, of course, our values are likely to be the same as those of the major religious traditions. But those traditions are rooted in certain beliefs about God. Without those beliefs, the values lack a foundation or a rationale. Anscombe's complaint is that most nonconsequentialist modern philosophers have wanted to keep their religiously grounded values but to jettison the religious foundation itself without seeing that the values lose their sense when this is done. Similar claims have been made by Arthur Schopenhauer, Fyodor Dostoevsky (in his great novel *The Brothers Karamazov*), Nietzsche, and Anscombe's teacher, Ludwig Wittgenstein.

Of course, these people might all be wrong. I do not think they are, but what follows in this book will not assume that they are right. I mention their view here simply to make you aware of it and to explain one reason this book takes the approach that it does. In what follows, I will look at how the question "Why be good?" arises in Plato's work. I will then look at Aristotle's response and move from there through the questions of whether God exists, how we might know, and what this might mean and then on to distinctively modern theories based on agnosticism and atheism, before bringing us up to date with a final look at contemporary ideas about virtue and the relation between ethics and the rest of philosophy. As we go, we will see some of the reasons philosophers moved away from the theories of the Greeks and questioned faith in God. Whether the ideas developed since then are any better I will leave you to decide for yourself. I do offer criticisms of most of the ideas that I talk about, but I have tried to keep the criticism separate from the presentation of the ideas themselves. The chapters that follow all take the same basic shape, beginning with an explanation of the main ethical ideas of (usually) one philosopher, drawing out what that philosopher might say to Thrasymachus about why we should be good, and then ending with some objections and a brief conclusion. If you find yourself thinking that something is wrong with the ideas presented, you might find your suspicions confirmed in the Objections section.

This is a fairly short book. It cannot possibly tell you everything there is to know about ethics in general or even the specific question "Why be good?" I have therefore had to leave out references not only to some great individual philosophers but also to some entire traditions of thought. This book is about Western philosophy, not world philosophy; and it focuses on a fairly small number of big-name philosophers from the Western tradition, most of whom came from Europe.[3] Antarctica excepted, there is not a continent on earth that has not produced wisdom, and this has been expressed in various forms. Some of these are recognizable as philosophy, with clearly stated arguments in favor of their conclusions. We find this in the Buddhist tradition, for instance.[4] In other cases, wisdom is treated as something less clear-cut, more mystical. That makes it hard to discuss in a book like this but hardly worthless. For the sake of clarity and brevity, I have limited myself to the Western tradition, but there is wisdom enough in this tradition for our introductory purposes. In this or any other tradition, there have been few minds greater than Plato's, and it is with him that we will begin.

Notes

1. Anscombe's paper was originally published in the journal *Philosophy* 53 (1958). It has since been reprinted in *The Collected Philosophical Papers of G. E. M. Anscombe: Ethics, Religion and Politics*, vol. 3 (Oxford: Blackwell, 1981), and Mary Geach and Luke Gormally, eds., *Human Life, Action and Ethics: Essays by G. E. M. Anscombe* (Exeter, UK: Imprint Academic, 2005).
2. For an example of the latter kind of problem, see the discussion of Peter Singer in Chapter 10.
3. If you want a book on world philosophy, I recommend David E. Cooper, *World Philosophies: An Historical Introduction* (Oxford: Blackwell Publishing, 2002).
4. A nice introduction to Buddhism is Steve Hagen, *Buddhism Plain and Simple* (New York: Broadway Books, 1999).

Suggestions for Further Reading

I will make specific suggestions about other books you might want to read at the end of each of the following chapters. At the end of the Conclusion, I list some good introductory ethics books, which you might want to use as a supplement to this. Even better as a supplement would be a collection of works by the philosophers under discussion so that you can read what they thought in their own words. Steven M. Cahn and Peter Markie (eds.), *Ethics: History, Theory, and Contemporary Issues*, 3rd ed. (New York: Oxford University Press, 2005) would be a good choice, including extracts from the works of all the main philosophers covered here.

Often, the easiest way to find out more on a subject is to go online. Lawrence M. Hinman, at the University of San Diego, edits an excellent site called "Ethics Updates," which covers ethical theory and applied ethics. There are links to videos, PowerPoint slideshows, essays, recommendations for further reading, discussion questions, and much more. Robert Cavalier of Carnegie Mellon University also has a good "Online Guide to Ethics and Moral Philosophy." Web sites can move, and their addresses can easily be mistyped; but searching by the name of each site should get you there quite simply.

For philosophy generally, the most useful sites are the Stanford Encyclopedia of Philosophy and the Internet Encyclopedia of Philosophy.

CHAPTER 1

Plato

As the first philosopher ever to explore the question "Why be good?" Plato can almost be said to have invented ethics, at least as an academic discipline. This alone would make him one of the greatest philosophers there has ever been. But there is more to him and his work than this. In this chapter, we will see how the question arises in his greatest work, the *Republic,* and how it leads into discussion of a host of other philosophical questions. First of all, though, it might be worth getting some idea of just who this man was.

Plato (ca. 427–347 BCE) was the greatest student of Socrates (ca. 470–399 BCE) and the teacher of the great philosopher Aristotle (384–322 BCE). Since Socrates wrote none of his philosophy down, most of what we know about him comes from Plato. In fact, it is sometimes hard to tell where Socrates ends and Plato begins.[1] This is because Plato didn't write books. Instead, he wrote dialogues, like scripts for plays, almost all of them featuring a character called Socrates, who generally wins every argument. Some of these dialogues are thought to be fairly accurate reports of conversations that Socrates actually had. Others, such as the *Republic,* are believed to present Plato's views, or perhaps what Plato believed Socrates would have said if he had thought about things a bit more. It is clear that Socrates had an enormous influence on Plato, and much of Plato's philosophical work can be thought of as an attempt to provide reasons for believing various ideas that Socrates professed.

Socrates himself did not provide such reasons. Instead, he mostly argued against other people, often in public. A typical Socratic dialogue involves Socrates talking with someone we might expect to be an expert. Through careful questioning, Socrates reveals the expert's ignorance about the very things he ought to know most about. Thus, a self-righteous man is shown to be unable to give an account of righteousness, a general fails to say what courage is, and so on. Socrates himself never claims to be able to say what righteousness or courage is either, but at least he admits that he knows nothing. It is in this, he says, that his wisdom lies.

This kind of teasing irony must have made Socrates unpopular with some influential people. So did his connections with some hated political figures, such as the treacherous Alcibiades. Socrates was also accused of being a sophist, one of the professional teachers who were thought to encourage skepticism about traditional values. For all these reasons, Socrates was accused of impiety and the corruption of the young. A jury of 501 Athenians found him guilty and voted for the death penalty.

This popular vote for the death of a great and innocent man confirmed Plato's opposition to unrestrained democracy. One of the goals of his *Republic* is to set out a better alternative form of government. It also outlines a system of education. The word "academic" comes from the school that Plato founded called the "Academy" at which Aristotle (the subject of our next chapter) was the star student. In this chapter, though, the focus will be on Plato and his ideas about ethics.

The Challenge

Virtue theory, the idea that ethics is primarily about having a good character, begins with Plato's *Republic*. In this book, Plato tries to answer the challenges of Thrasymachus, Glaucon, and Adeimantus, which I will describe shortly. Strictly speaking, this original challenge is about justice, rather than goodness in general; but I think Plato's arguments are more interesting if we apply them to this broader question, and this can be done with little distortion to the arguments of Plato himself or those who challenge him.[2]

Plato begins the *Republic* with the character Cephalus, whom Socrates and his young friend Glaucon are visiting. Cephalus is a successful businessman, who in real life lost all his money when Athens was overthrown by Sparta. He is a decent man, but his main interest is in making money, not in thinking about right and wrong. He thinks of ethics in terms of rules one has to follow in order to avoid punishment, in this life or the next. This kind of negative (or medicinal) view of ethics, as something that offers nothing positive itself but merely helps us avoid bad things, is one that Socrates finds interesting. But before arguing this point, Socrates argues with Cephalus' son Polemarchus, who also thinks of ethics as a set of rules or principles (especially the rule that we should help our friends and harm our enemies), and, most importantly, Thrasymachus, a sophist.

Thrasymachus says various contradictory things about justice, and there is some disagreement about what exactly his opinion is. The most interesting idea he seems to have is what I will focus on here. Thrasymachus argues that morality or ethics or trying to do the right thing is all a mug's game. In other words, ethics are for fools. "In any and every situation, a moral person is worse off than an immoral one" (343d).[3] The "right thing," he says, is simply what those in power want others to do. "My claim is that morality is nothing other than the advantage of the stronger party."[4] These people (the stronger) are not necessarily the government, although they are surely likely to include politicians. Rather, they are members of the slightly mysterious classes sometimes referred to today as the "power elites" or "social elites."

To see Thrasymachus' point, it will help to think about how we train animals (he offers an analogy with a shepherd and his flock) and how we raise children.

What do we teach dogs to do, for instance? Whatever we want. When a dog does what we want it to do, we say "Good dog!" and give it a reward. When it does something bad, we punish it and say "Bad dog!" But what are "good" and "bad"? Are they good and bad for the dog itself? They might be, if we happen to want what is best for the dog. But the defining characteristic of "good" in doggy ethics is "whatever your trainer or owner wants." And the defining characteristic of "bad" in doggy ethics is "whatever your trainer or owner does *not* want." In fact, it is even more precise than this. When, after all, is the dog told that it has been bad? Not when it does any random thing that its owner does not want it to do. Dogs do not behave randomly. "Bad" behavior for dogs is behavior that dogs like and their owners do not like. A well-trained dog is one that acts in accordance with its owner's wishes, not its own.

Why would it do this? There are two reasons. The first is the threat of punishment for "bad" behavior and the promise of reward for "good" behavior. The second is that eventually the dog internalizes the owner's rules and behaves as the owner wants even when there is no likelihood of either punishment or reward. Acting for the first kind of reason makes perfect sense to Thrasymachus—who wouldn't want to avoid punishment? But acting for the second kind is a sure sign that the dog has lost. It is either a sucker or a victim, depending on how much intelligence or free will you credit dogs with. If such conditioning cannot be resisted, then the dog is a victim. Its will has been taken over, if not destroyed. If the conditioning could be resisted but is not, then the dog is a fool.

So far you might be on Thrasymachus' side. But, you might say, surely it is different for human beings. Well, consider children. What do parents try to get their children to do? What the parents want. This is likely to include behavior that we would recognize as ethical. After all, few parents would want their children to lie to them, steal from them, or murder them. Few parents, too, would want their children to be regarded as weird or difficult by other adults, such as their friends and their children's teachers. But the particular behavior that will be encouraged by any given parent is going to be whatever behavior that parent wants his or her child to engage in (whether it be for selfish, moral, aesthetic, or other reasons). As with dogs, "bad" behavior is going to be behavior that the child wants to engage in but the parent opposes. Children who learn to be "good" when their parents are around are probably smart. Those who continue to be "good", especially those who avoid "bad" behavior (i.e., doing what they want to do), even when nobody is around to see them, are fools or victims. This is Thrasymachus' view.

Now what about adults? Well, where do our values come from? Largely from our parents but also from teachers, our peers, and the government that makes the laws. From whomever has power or influence over us. What then should we do? Usually, it is smart to bear in mind the power these people have and to behave accordingly. If there is a cop on the road, slow down. But if there isn't? Do what you want, Thrasymachus would say! The extent to which you refrain from "bad" acts (i.e., things that you want to do but others do *not* want you to do) is the extent to which you are either a fool (if you do not see what is going on) or a victim (of conditioning or simply a power imbalance). Thrasymachus' conclusion is that it is good to be "bad" and bad to be "good," although he cannot quite bring himself to say this explicitly. Perhaps even he has some shame, and perhaps this is a clue to the answer to our question.

Thrasymachus especially admires those who are very bad indeed. So bad, that is, that they get away with it, like the most successful gangsters and dictators:

> This is the person you should consider, if you want to assess the extent to which immorality rather than morality is personally advantageous—and this is something you'll appreciate most easily if you look at immorality in its most perfect form and see how it enhances a wrongdoer's life beyond measure, but ruins the lives of its victims, who haven't the stomach for crime, to the same degree. It's dictatorship I mean, because whether it takes stealth or overt violence, a dictator steals what doesn't belong to him—consecrated and unconsecrated objects, private possessions, and public property—and does so not on a small scale, but comprehensively. Anyone who is caught committing the merest fraction of these crimes is not only punished, but thoroughly stigmatized as well: small-scale criminals who commit these kinds of crimes are called temple-robbers, kidnappers, burglars, thieves, and robbers. On the other hand, when someone appropriates the assets of the citizen body and then goes on to rob them of their very freedom and enslave them, then denigration gives way to congratulation, and it isn't only his fellow citizens who call him happy, but anyone else who hears about his consummate wrongdoing does so as well. The point is that immorality has a bad name because people are afraid of being at the receiving end of it, not of doing it.[5]

In Plato's dialogue, Socrates (here speaking for Plato himself) combats Thrasymachus with arguments of his own[6] and Thrasymachus storms off in a huff, sulking but still convinced that he is right. Indeed, he does seem to have a point. We might well wonder why anyone but a loser would actually believe in the goodness of being "good." Going all out to be the next Stalin might not be a very good idea (in terms of self-interest as well as ethics), but a more moderate version of Thrasymachean cynicism can still seem like the smart position to adopt.

After Thrasymachus has left, the more moderate Glaucon and his brother Adeimantus raise a similar problem. Thrasymachus, as we have seen, makes a challenging point but loses the debate because he goes too far in insisting that the extreme of injustice is the best goal. Now, Socrates' friends try to salvage the point worth considering that lies behind this silly (and evil) ideal. Most people, Glaucon says, think of goodness as a pain in the neck. Ideally, we could do whatever we liked, rampaging through the world, pillaging and murdering anyone who stood in our way. But real life isn't that much fun. Those who pillage and murder (even those who merely lie, cheat, and steal) are ostracized and punished. There is also the problem that a universal freedom to maim, kill, etc. brings with it the very unpleasant possibility of being maimed or killed oneself. So we compromise with reality and with each other and abide by a set of ethical principles and government-enforced laws. Doing the right thing is the lesser of two evils, the price we must pay in order to make the world as little bad as possible.

To show that this is how most people think, Glaucon invites us to consider the story of Gyges and his magic ring. This ring turns its wearer invisible and allows Gyges to get away with any crime he cares to commit.[7] Let us assume for the sake of argument that it makes him not just invisible but completely undetectable so that he is safe even from the gods. Unconstrained by fear of any punishment, Gyges seduces the queen and, with her help, murders the king and takes his place. Now, we might not go that far, but surely very many of us would take some advantage of this kind of freedom. Perhaps we wouldn't hurt anybody (and why is that?), but we might well commit "victimless" crimes—spying on people, say, or (if we stretch the story to include additional powers) using our magically gained knowledge to make money on the stock market or by gambling.[8] And, of course, we might also steal or interfere with people in other ways, playing tricks on our enemies or doing whatever else takes our fancy. Glaucon puts it this way:

> [E]veryone thinks the rewards of immorality far outweigh those of morality—and they're right, according to the proponent of this view. The sight of someone with that kind of scope refusing all those opportunities for wrongdoing and never laying a finger on things that didn't belong to him would lead people to think that he was in an extremely bad way, and was a first-class fool as well—even though their fear of being wronged might make them attempt to mislead others by singing his praises to them in public.[9]

His claim is not that this kind of behavior is good but simply that even normally just and good people would likely give way to temptation in such circumstances. After all, it is often said, absolute power corrupts absolutely. If you can get away with it (a big "if", admittedly), why should you not want to be corrupt? Glaucon presses Socrates to explain why justice (or simply being good) is such a good thing. What is the value of justice in itself? His brother Adeimantus wants to know what the value of justice is for the just person, what good it brings to its possessor. Having brushed off Thrasymachus' extreme immoralism, Socrates agrees to answer the milder challenge offered by Glaucon and Adeimantus. In effect, Glaucon is suggesting that most people think of ethics as a kind of social contract. It is a set of rules that we all agree to live by.

Social contract theories of various kinds have been popular throughout the ages. Socrates himself offers another one in Plato's dialogue *Crito*, which is thought to represent Socrates' actual views more than Plato's. The dialogue is set in Socrates' prison cell, where he is waiting to be executed. In effect, he is on death row. Friends of his try to help him escape, but although he is confident that the attempt would be successful, he refuses to go. His reasons for staying, and dying, are these: (1) if everyone disobeyed the laws, there would be chaos, which is bad, and so he should not disobey the laws; (2) the state of Athens has given him an education, protection from criminals and enemy powers, and much else besides, so to disobey the state would be unacceptably ungrateful; and (3) by living in Athens all his life when he could have left, he has implicitly agreed to live by the laws of the state, so to break these laws now would be to violate this social contract.

Fairly obvious objections can be made to the first two of these arguments (Will there really be chaos if one man—Socrates—breaks the law on this one occasion? Is it really ungrateful to refuse to submit to execution?), but they have their defenders still. The one that concerns us here is the third. It, too, faces serious problems. Some laws, after all, are seriously immoral. Think of what would be involved in obeying all the laws in a country like Nazi Germany or the United States in the days of slavery. Is it really morally better to return an escaped slave to her "owner" than to break an implicit contract with the state? And what kind of contract is this anyway? If a verbal contract is not worth the paper it is written on, how much can an implicit contract be worth, one that is never explicitly agreed to and that quite likely never even crosses most people's minds? Obviously, we are not talking about a literal contract here, but exactly what we should make of the analogy is open to question. Alasdair MacIntyre objects to all theories of this kind for this reason:

> The minimum conditions for the word *consent* to have meaningful application include at least that the man alleged to have consented shall somehow have signified his consent and that he shall have sometime indicated his understanding of what he has consented to. But neither of these conditions is satisfied by the doctrine of tacit [i.e., implicit] consent.[10]

Bear in mind also that the kind of contract that the *Crito* mentions is a contract to obey the law, not any ethical rule. So even if this argument still appeals to you, and it does to many people, it will need to be modified at least to bring in ethical rules if we are going to use it to answer Thrasymachus. Perhaps Glaucon's thoughts are a step in this direction. We will look more closely at some modern versions of social contract theory in Chapter 5.

To sum up: Thrasymachus thinks that being "good" is the opposite of being good and that it is best to be a corrupt political tyrant. Glaucon thinks that most people (not himself, or so he claims) think that being "good" is not completely bad and might even be good, but it is not the best that one could hope for. The best would be to have magical powers that would enable one to do whatever one liked and get away with it. But we don't have magical powers, so we're stuck with boring old ethics.

Plato's job then is to have Socrates (who was a real person but here is more of a fictional character speaking on Plato's behalf) come up with a defense of goodness. He must show that being good is not just a matter of doing what other people happen to want for their own selfish reasons. He must show also that being good is not just a matter of doing what each of us happens to want. And to answer Glaucon, he must show that being good is not just something we should grudgingly settle for but the best conceivable way to be. It's a tall order, and most people think that Plato fails in his attempt. But let's see for ourselves.

What Is Good?

The first thing that Plato tries to do is to define what it means to be good. Only then, he thinks, can he attempt a justification of such a life. He says (through the character Socrates) that the best way to see what goodness is would be to look at it on a large scale, so he proposes to look at what makes for a good society rather than a good individual. His answer is that a good society will need people to do productive work, people to defend its citizens from criminals and external enemies, and people to govern. Each job, he argues, should be done not by everybody, nor by just anybody, but only by those best suited to work of that kind. So the wisest people should govern (not the most popular of those who want the job, as in a modern democracy). The bravest, most loyal, and toughest should do the military and police work. And the rest should do the productive work. The society will work best if it has each of these classes in the right proportion and if each sticks to its own job. Thus, roughly speaking, the wise will make the laws, the brave will enforce them, and the lower types will obey them.

We do not need to catalogue all the faults we can see in a society of this kind, but it is probably worth pointing out some of the more glaring ones. There is minimal freedom in Plato's "ideal" state. People do not choose which class they belong to but instead must do whatever job they are deemed most cut out for. Thus, the rulers do not want to rule, and anyone from another class who would like to try his or her hand at governing is out of luck. Nor is this society at all democratic. The wise are not elected but recognized as wise during the process of their education. In fact, which class one belongs to is determined largely by heredity, or so Plato imagines things would work out. That is to say, while he is describing an unreal ideal, and so cannot know how it would work in practice, Plato seems to expect that some people would belong to one class rather than another purely because of their genetic makeup.[11] He describes other restrictions, concerning censorship of the arts and sexual relations, for instance. There would be no marriage or family life as we know it in the republic.

It is also worth wondering whether this republic could ever exist in reality. Its members are supposed to have grown up with a specific kind of education (or indoctrination) and to have been taught a "noble lie" about the naturalness of their society's social arrangements. The combination of censorship, propaganda, and armed enforcement of the status quo might keep a Platonic republic in existence; but it is hard to see how it could ever get off the ground in the first place. How could a society be persuaded (or forced) to give up its institutions, customs, and freedoms and adopt Plato's ideal instead? We might again stop at this point and consider the parallel with the individual. If no society on earth would be likely to agree to adopt Plato's model, would any individual agree to adopt his ethics? Or is it necessary to be shaped the appropriate way in the first place? The only way to answer such questions is to leave politics behind and focus on what Plato recommends for the individual. It is ethics after all, not politics, that Thrasymachus and Glaucon are primarily interested in and that Socrates is supposed to be concerned with.

Socrates' main point with regard to ethics is that being good is not mainly about doing what you or anyone else wants (so Thrasymachus was wrong). It is not about *doing* anything, as Cephalus and Polemarchus think. It is about *being* a certain way. Just as an ideal state can be described, or so Plato thinks, in terms of its constitution or structure, without having its particular laws or policies detailed, being good, for Plato, is about having certain qualities of character, which we call "virtues."

But which way should we be? What kind of character should we have? Plato divides the mind or soul into three parts, just as he divides his republic into three classes, and argues that the way to be good is to have these parts working harmoniously together. So, what are the three parts? At one point he likens them to a (rational) man, a (spirited) lion, and a (hungry) monster.[12] The rational part is clearly meant to be something like an inner Socrates, the "real you," almost its own being, independent of the body. The monster is more like the bodily appetites, almost the body itself, but with a primitive kind of mental life (think of an empty stomach or a dry tongue—physical objects imbued with a kind of blind desire) that can develop more sophisticated emotions such as a desire for money. Trickiest is the spirited part, which lies, as it were, between the other two. In the republic, it corresponds with the paramilitary Auxiliaries, a class that rules over the productive class but in accordance with rules made by the philosopher–king Guardians. Indeed, the Auxiliaries start out in the same class as the Guardians and are basically those who do not make it to the required level of wisdom for rulers. Plato likes to compare the Guardians with dogs,[13] and this analogy seems to fit the spirited part of the soul quite well.

So, what is the proper role of each part? Plato says we should be ruled by the rational part. And how should the rational part be? It should be wise. The rational part should rule over the lower part (the bodily appetites and animal drives) with the help of the "spirited" part. How should this part be? It should be brave and loyal, like a good dog. And how should the appetitive part be? It should be temperate, that is, moderate in its tastes. If we have all three parts in the right proportion, each being as it should, then (by Plato's proposed definition) we will be good.

Why is this good? Why should we accept Plato's definition of what it means to be good? Surely not just because it isn't Thrasymachus' definition. We want the truth, after all, not just a convenient theory to wave at our enemies. Plato offers two kinds of answer to the question of why it would be good to be good in his sense.

Goodness as Self-Interest

The first reason that Plato offers for being good in his sense is that it will get you what you want more reliably than any alternative will. Think of it this way. The rational part of your mind—which I will call "reason"—is like a person. It might even be the "real you." For instance, if you say something in the heat of the moment to a friend and think it over later, what you "really meant" or "really thought" is what your reason supports. What you actually said, that is, might not be what you now believe you really meant. Your real meaning is the one you think of when you have calmed down and are being more rational. So there is some justification for thinking that you (the real you) are your reason. (As well as some justification, let us remember, for thinking on the contrary that what you really meant is what you *actually said* and that the real you is *not* so rational or so nice as we might all like to think.) The spirited part of your mind—which I will call "spirit"—is like a trusty dog or bodyguard. And the appetitive part of your mind is like a monster, roaring with instinctual lusts. Now, which should be in charge?

If the monster gets out of hand, then you and your dog are in trouble. Everyone (or virtually everyone) has a monster inside, but people whose lives are ruled by their bodily appetites, unchecked by reason or spirit (which might include conscience), are likely to end up miserable. Consider the main bodily appetites for food, drink, and sex. If you are not rational about what you eat, you are likely to end up either too fat or too thin for your own good. At the extreme, if the monster is really in complete control, you will end up dead, or at least too fat to move, in a very short space of time. If you are not rational about what you drink you might drown yourself or drink poison. More realistically, the irrational use of alcohol or other drugs can, of course, lead to addiction. Again, of course, the danger of death is very real here too. Even an addiction to nonlethal drugs is likely to be expensive and to exclude you from large parts of society (e.g., you might lose your job or become trapped in the limited social and intellectual world of the stereotypical cannabis smoker). If you do not control your sexual appetites, you are likely to have trouble maintaining a monogamous relationship, others (especially of the sex you are attracted to) will tend to look down on you, you might find yourself seriously ill, and you could be arrested. All in all, rule by the monster is clearly undesirable, solely in terms of getting the satisfaction we all want out of life. That is to say, even leaving aside moral considerations (which we must do in order to stop our defense of moral goodness from being pointlessly circular), there is good reason not to allow our lives to be ruled by the monster within but instead to keep a leash on these appetites.

Rule by the dog would be little better. This, Plato suggests, is the psychological equivalent of living in a police state. You are true to the dictates of your spirit, which includes conscience but also a strong sense of loyalty to friends and family. It is not a life of reflection or independent thought. Plato describes the person dominated by spirit as living above all for honor and glory. In practice, this means bowing to those with more power (respecting the honorable) and bullying those with less (to gain "honor" for oneself). Such people also lack the psychological resources to stop themselves being taken over by financial greed. Reason is needed to distinguish between what is really good and what merely seems good.

This might not convince you, and unfortunately Plato does not really provide any proof that this is how such a person would be or that the corresponding kind of state would inevitably, as he claims, decline into oligarchy. However, a political state that despises reason and hence all rational principles, that prizes the physical prowess of well-trained warriors and the glory gained by successful military campaigns does sound familiar from twentieth-century history. Fascist Italy was much like this. *The Doctrine of Fascism*, written by Giovanni Gentile but attributed to Benito Mussolini (1883–1945), states that "War alone brings up to their highest tension all human energies and puts the stamp of nobility upon the peoples who have the courage to meet it."[14] Mussolini's fascists reveled in Italy's glorious past during the days of the Roman Empire and saw themselves as spirited patriots. In reality, Mussolini was subservient to the more powerful Adolf Hitler and bullied both his own people and those of Ethiopia, which he invaded at least partly for the "glory" of it.

Being dominated by your spirit, then, can be seen as the psychological equivalent of fascism. Lacking much reason, you are a kind of zombie, slavish to the rules your parents imposed on you, or brainlessly loyal to the code of your tribe. You are a good dog. You might make a good servant (of a religious movement or of the Mafia) but never a good leader. If this does not appeal, then what is left but the rule of reason?

Rule by the inner human being, the real you, allows you to think for yourself and decide what to do. You might indeed decide to do what your spirit urges, but you might also decide to let the monster have its way for a while. It is all up to you. And if the dog (spirit) is on the person's side, then the monster can be brought under control—or let loose—just as much or as little as you choose. Isn't this obviously the best way to live?

It might be. But it might not be, for two reasons. One is that part of the appeal of this life as I have so far presented it is that it allows for a fairly immoral life, as ordinary morality would see it. It is the life of self-interest, not ethics. And we have yet to prove that self-interest, even enlightened self-interest, is in favor of a morally good life. So the life of reason might well seem insufficiently moral. That will be a problem with any kind of ethics based on self-interest alone. After all, mainstream ideas about goodness hold that someone who only ever acts from the motive of self-interest is not a wholly good person. Most ideas about ethics value **altruism**, doing things for the sake of others. One need not be a complete altruist, although this is the ideal of some religions; but total self-interest sounds an awful lot like selfishness, which few people count as a good thing.[15]

The second problem is that the mind might not have the parts that Plato describes, so the choices he presents might not be real options at all, or at least not the only options. Plato treats the mind as if it were a mysterious nonphysical object, of which, presumably, reason, spirit, and appetites are meant to be parts. Few philosophers or psychologists today think of the mind in these terms. The only *object* that seems relevant to the mind is the brain, and it is not divisible into parts neatly corresponding with Plato's parts.

However, it does not follow that Plato is wrong, even if we give up the idea of the mind as an object. As long as we accept that we do have minds (whatever this might mean), we can think of these minds in Plato's terms. Those terms would have to be thought of as optional or metaphorical rather than literal or scientifically based, but that need not be a problem. We can and do think of reason and appetite as part of our psychological makeup. Spirit is a more foreign notion, but conscience isn't; and we are familiar with emotions such as individual pride, patriotism, and school spirit (even if these are only things we reject), which all belong to Plato's category of spirit. We do not have to think of the mind in Plato's terms, but we can do so. And if we do, then his idea that reason should rule, with spirit at its side, seems quite attractive. It comes fairly naturally to us to think of a "true" inner self that is noble and rational, a set of bodily appetites and animal desires, and something else that might be called "heart" or "spirit."

That such thoughts come naturally to us by no means proves that they are correct, of course. However, Plato's interest is in how we should live, not how we *do* live. He is interested in values more than facts. In other words, if we take his analysis of the mind or a person as a factual claim, a psychological theory, then things look bad for Plato. But if we focus, as I think we should, on his ethics, on his ideas about how one *ought* to live, then contemporary philosophical and psychological ideas about the mind are pretty much irrelevant. Such theories not only are designed to answer a different kind of question (about how things are rather than about how things should be) but also do not really conflict with what Plato wants to say. A (not very original) poet who talks about the sea lapping at the shore need not worry if oceanographers report that the sea does not actually have a tongue to lap with so long as the facts do not make it impossible to think of what the sea does as being *like* a cat, say, lapping at a saucer of milk. Similarly, Plato's "theory" of the soul can be thought of, and perhaps must be if we are not to reject it completely, as a poetic metaphor, designed perhaps to inspire us but certainly also to help us understand how he is recommending that we ought to be.

The problem now is how to show that the rational life that he describes would be the life of a good person and not that of an evil genius hatching fiendish plots. Plato considers this problem (although not quite in those terms) and has an answer to it.

The first part of this answer also appeals to self-interest. In the dialogue *Phaedo*, Plato argues that if we are good, then after death our minds will live on in a kind of heaven. If we are bad, a worse fate awaits us, although Plato is not quite sure what this is. One possibility is that we will be reincarnated as an animal of an appropriate sort.[16] If you live like a pig, you might come back as a pig. If you live like a dog, you might come back as a dog. And so on. Another possibility is that if the bodily appetites gain too much control over your mind, then it might become too bodily to enter the purely intellectual realm of perfect goodness that awaits those who live as they should. In this case, Plato imagines body-infected minds haunting the earth as ghosts.[17] Finally, he suggests that the plight of the damned might be nothing so subtle. Perhaps they are just plunged into a river of fire.[18] Whatever it is, the afterlife of the bad is bad, he assures us, and the afterlife of the good is good.

Obviously, this all depends on the rather controversial idea that there is an afterlife, but first we should consider whether it helps Plato's case at all. If the life that gets the heavenly rewards Plato refers to here is just a life dominated by reason and not necessarily a very moral life, then his whole theory about the afterlife gives us no motive at all to be morally good. But the life he has in mind might be more moral than that. If you rationally choose to "feed the monster" too much, then you run the risk of a bad afterlife. Furthermore, the good life presented in the *Phaedo* is not just a life lived rationally, that is, prudently. It is a life in which the monster is kept down as much as possible (for the reason just given) and in which the mind yearns for purely intellectual things. These things are Plato's "forms" or "ideas." Since they are completely nonphysical and abstract, they are hard to describe. Roughly speaking, they are pure essences that physical objects can only ever approximate. To give a very down-to-earth example, the "form of table" would be what all tables have in common. We might call it "tableness." If you believe in God, you might think of the form of human being as the idea that God had in his mind when he decided to create human beings. That is roughly what forms are, but they are not actually shapes or ideas at all. Being a table might involve having a certain kind of shape (although you might wonder exactly what this shape would be), but being human does not necessarily require having a particular shape. Nor is a form an idea in anyone's mind. Even if there were no minds, Plato believes, the forms would live on.

The form of table or human being might sound absurd and not like any-thing that reason would yearn for. Think about mathematical reasoning though. When we think about numbers or triangles, we are not thinking about physi-cal objects. We know what right-angled triangles are but not because we have found them in a jungle somewhere or out in space. They have no particular size, mass, or color, for instance. For this reason, it is impossible to draw one exactly since the drawing we make will always have some thickness to its lines, some color, and so on. The triangles with which geometry is concerned have no color at all, nor thickness to their lines. We might think that triangles are imaginary entities, but we do not seem simply to have made them up. After all, it is pos-sible to discover objective properties that they have, such as angles that add up to 180°. So triangles, circles, and the like seemed to Plato to be real objects that exist in a nonphysical world and that can be known not through the senses but really only through reasoning. That is the kind of thing that forms are, and perhaps they do not seem quite so absurd now.

These are very humble forms in the scheme of things though. The big ones, what the rational mind truly loves, are the forms of truth, beauty, and, above all, good-ness. The form of truth is basically just Truth. It is what all true things (mostly state-ments) resemble, partake of, or point toward. Beauty is what all beautiful things have in common. And the form of the Good is the pure essence of goodness itself. Think of goodness as an ingredient in all good things. This is not actually quite right since forms are not physical, but it is close enough for now. Without good-ness, there can be no good things. Knowledge is good, and so is truth; thus, these depend on goodness, on the form of the Good, for their existence. In fact, reality itself is good, so it depends on the form of the Good. The form of the Good, good-ness itself, is thus a kind of ultimate reality, or something beyond reality. Some people after Plato identified it with God. If the rational mind loves forms, and the form of the good is the highest of all forms, then the rational mind should love the form of the Good above all else. And if the rational life is the life of one who loves goodness above all else, then it will be a good life, not just a well-calculated life of selfish indulgence. The question now is whether a rational person would believe in and strive for any such thing as the form of the good.

The Forms

Plato discusses the forms in various places, sometimes seeming (via the characters in his dialogues) to be rejecting the idea. So it is difficult, if not impossible, to get a consistent and clear idea of exactly what it was he had in mind when he talked about forms.[19] Even within the *Republic* itself, Plato gives us more metaphors than definitions or arguments to explain what the forms are or why we should believe in them. Still, he clearly does believe in something that he calls "forms," and I hope I have said enough to give you some idea of what he has in mind. Now, why should anyone believe in such things?

If we combine what he says in the *Republic* with what he says in other dialogues, such as the *Phaedo*, we can see that Plato offers basically three reasons for believing in the forms. The first has to do with **epistemology**, or the theory of knowledge. Plato believes that there is such a thing as true knowledge. But, he also believes, it is impossible to have true knowledge of things that are in flux. What is to be known must, as it were, stay still and unchanging. Physical objects are not like this, though. Their constituent atoms swirl around and interchange with those of neighboring objects. Plato did not believe in atoms, but he would agree that physical objects change, grow, and decay all the time. If they keep changing, then the mind can never completely grasp them. So we cannot know them. But knowledge *is* possible. So there must be objects that are not physical, that do not change. These unchanging metaphysical entities are the forms. Queer as they might seem, they must exist.

This, of course, is no proof at all. Why accept that a very slowly changing object cannot be known? Why insist on such an idealized conception of knowledge? And even if unchanging, nonphysical objects exist (e.g., numbers), why accept that these must be Plato's forms? Why, for instance, must goodness be one of them? Remember that Plato refers to many different forms, but the key one for him is the form of the Good, a nonphysical object that is pure goodness through and through. Even if we accept his thinking about knowledge, so that what we know must be nonphysical, pure, and eternal (and there is good reason not to accept this), why should we also accept that one such object is goodness (or the Good)? After all, what is good is precisely the kind of thing that many people deny can be known at all. If judgments of quality are subjective or merely matters of opinion, then they are not matters of knowledge. I might like vanilla more than chocolate, but I do not, so the argument goes, *know* that vanilla shakes taste better. That is just my opinion. The same is said about religious, political, and ethical matters. Plato wants to deny this kind of subjectivism or relativism, but he has not so far given us a reason to reject it.

Fortunately, he has another argument to fall back on. Rightly or wrongly, we do seem to have certain idealized notions or conceptions of perfection. To use an example from the *Phaedo*, if we see two sticks, we will see that they are not exactly the same length.[20] Even if we cut them carefully, they will never be exactly the same length. No two things are. So where did we get this idea of exact equality or sameness? Consider also the truism "nobody's perfect." How do we know? It seems to Plato that we must compare people against a standard of perfection and find that they all fall short of the ideal. But where did we get the ideal from if nothing in this world is it? There must be another world, and in order to have ideas about its contents, we must have existed previously in this world of ideal things. These are the forms. And, if we lived there before this life, Plato reasons, there's a good chance that we will live there again once this life is over.

Plato assumes that the only way to get an idea is from experience. If we have an idea of perfect goodness, say, or perfect equality, then we must have experienced perfect goodness (i.e., the form of the good) or perfect equality. It is tempting to reject this assumption, but then we would have to come up with an alternative origin of human concepts. This is not easy, so Plato's argument this time is quite good.

One possibility is that we derive our concepts of perfection by extrapolation, that is, by extending (in imagination) a series of objects of different levels of goodness. Take a lousy cheeseburger (raw, rotten meat on a burnt bun, moldy cheese, no ketchup, etc.), then a pretty bad burger (undercooked meat on a charred bun, cheap cheese, too much ketchup, etc.), then an OK burger (cooked about right, nothing special), and so on and so on. Eventually, you will find yourself imagining the perfect cheeseburger, even if nobody in reality has ever experienced such a culinary delight. We could do the same for sticks of roughly equal length, politicians of various degrees of integrity, and so on. No need for a world of forms.

Plato would object though. This extrapolation depends on our ability to put in order the burgers, politicians, or whatever in a series from the worse to the better. But doesn't this presuppose that we have a standard of goodness to begin with? And won't this standard be perfect since it is the standard against which everything else is to be judged? Possibly, but there are other alternatives. One is that we order negatively. We know what we do not like (there's plenty of that to experience in this world), and we call "perfect" whatever has the fewest or least flaws. Plato might object that the very idea of the least flaws (flawlessness) is an ideal not to be found in this world, but he strains credulity at this point. Surely, we do rank things without reference to Platonic forms and might easily imagine something that would outrank (or be outranked by) everything else of its kind. The question of how we order our ideas or apply general standards to multiple particular cases is ongoing in philosophy today, and it would take us too far afield to get into it here. So I will leave this argument of Plato's behind now, damaged but still afloat. In other words, I will take it that you *probably* disagree with Plato but not assume that you do.

Finally, Plato's theory of forms provides a tidy answer to the age-old problem of universals. Universals are things like goodness, beauty, humanity, and tableness. They are properties shared by more than one object. The problem of universals is what their ontological status is, that is, what kind of reality (if any) do they have, what sort of things are they? Beauty seems to be real (some things really are beautiful, really do possess beauty), but how can something be real, in what sense can it be real, if it is not actually an existing physical object? And surely beauty is not a physical object, not something that could be measured or painted or cut in half. Plato's answer to what kind of reality something like beauty can have is that such universals are actually existing *nonphysical* objects. They are forms. This is neat but, again, not very plausible. Can't properties be real without being objects? And is beauty, say, really real and not just a name we apply to certain things?

For instance, I am a little less than six feet tall. This really is a property of mine, or so I would say. It is an objective fact that I am that tall (or short, depending on your point of view). But there is surely no *object* that is just-under-six-feet-tallness or six-feet-tallness or even just tallness. (Plato suggests in the *Phaedo*, on the contrary, that tallness and shortness are objects, only not physical objects: they are forms.[21]) It is hard to take seriously the idea that a species of objects including such things as tallness and beauty really exists, even in another, more perfect world than this one.

Some people would even go so far as to deny that there is an objective property of tallness or beauty. I mentioned above that whether I am tall or short depends on your point of view. To a giraffe all human beings probably look small. To cats we are big. These are relative terms, and we are likely to apply them relative to our own size. Tall people, I might well think (consciously or unconsciously), are those who are taller than me. This is debatable though. Basketball players really do tend to be tall, and we might want to call this an objective fact. Doing so does not commit us to the existence of an actual object, physical or Platonic, that is pure tallness. What about beauty? Are (many) models and movie stars really, objectively beautiful, in the way that (most) basketball players are tall? We can measure height, after all, but not looks. Judgments of beauty seem to be more subjective, more relative, than judgments of tallness; but there is still quite a bit of agreement. Few people think that warthogs are beautiful. Few people think Will Smith and Salma Hayek are ugly. So we might want to say that beauty is objective, even if it is not an actual object, as Plato claims.

To this day, some people support Plato on these issues, and I do not claim to be able to prove him wrong. But it does not look as though it would be irrational to deny that there is such a thing as the form of the good (or of the beautiful, or of tallness, etc.), let alone to refuse to spend one's life striving for it. So his argument looks weak. This is not quite the end of Plato's interest, however.

It is possible that his world of forms was never meant to be as metaphysically bizarre as it sounds. People talk about the world of sports, for instance, without being accused of metaphysical speculation. And the world of forms is not physical, so it cannot be in time or space; and it is not meant to be thought of as existing out in space somewhere. Perhaps Plato means little more than that there are such things as beauty, truth, justice, and so on. He would still have critics, of course, but he would not seem crazily unrealistic if he stuck to this claim.

He would face other problems though. One of the questions we were trying to answer, after all, was precisely what it means to say that there is such a thing as justice. If Plato's theory of forms is not taken literally, then what good is it at all? If the world of forms is not in fact a world but just a metaphorical way of speaking, then how could the souls of good people inhabit it after death? Is a nonreal world of forms much more appealing or inspiring than a sort of theoretical dictionary, an abstract set of abstract concepts (e.g., justice, beauty, tableness, and the rest)? There's the rub. The idea of the forms, and of the form of the good especially, is meant to inspire. Plato famously compares the form of the good with the sun and the lives of the unenlightened with those of prisoners chained up in a cave who see only shadows. He means us to want to escape the darkness of our own cave of ignorance and seek the light. For him to be able to get us to want such a thing, we have to think of the forms in somewhat romantic, not "realistic" terms. Otherwise, they just will not do what Plato wants them to do. They will not inspire us to change our lives. Philosophers have been interested in gaining understanding of truth and beauty for thousands of years. If Plato's words concerning forms, concerning the Good and Truth, are to add anything to the appeal of philosophy, then they cannot be understood as nothing but a flowery and obscure way of talking about what all philosophers are looking for already. The metaphor must be taken as somehow true. Knowing what that would really mean seems to be no easier than knowing what "true" means in the first place though, which is one thing that the theory of forms is supposed to explain. Perhaps if we are sufficiently moved by his imagery, then we will feel that we understand him, at least enough to want to make a quest out of the cave and toward the light. And it is precisely this that seems to be his primary goal.

In effect, then, Plato is a kind of poet. His arguments do not prove that his theories are correct. They do prove that an intelligent person can believe them though. Even if the arguments contain mistakes, they are not stupid mistakes. But the real power lies in the images. Plato does not prove that Thrasymachus and Glaucon are wrong. What he does is to show that it is not necessarily foolish to think that they are wrong and to invite us to take a different view of life and, indeed, of the world. This view cannot be proved right (there is no such thing as proving a poetic view right or wrong), but it has captured more imaginations than Thrasymachus or Glaucon ever did.

Is Plato therefore a sophist? Does he offer a view that is just as good as any other? I don't think so. It does, after all, capture the imagination. It is noble and inspiring. Thrasymachus' view has a kind of rebellious appeal, but rebellion itself can be tiresome and juvenile (just like Thrasymachus, if Plato is to be believed). In the end, though, Plato has not answered the challenge. He has distracted us from it with a poetic vision which, if adopted, would make us lose interest in the challenge. That is quite an achievement, but it is not what Plato was asked to do. In the next chapter, we will consider whether Plato's student Aristotle could do any better.

Why Be Good?

Before we turn to Aristotle, it is worth recalling what we have said about Plato's answer to the question "Why be good?" We have seen that the question means something like "Why try to do anything that you do not want to do if you can get away with not doing it?" Plato's response is, in part, to question who "you" are in this question. If you want to eat something, say, is it really all of you, the whole you, that wants it? Or is it only your appetitive part or, for that matter, only your taste buds or your stomach? His point is not so much the prudential one that we should think not only in terms of immediate gratification but also take long-term consequences into account. It is also that we want different, sometimes incompatible, things. I might want the honor of fighting for my country. I might also, though, want to avoid any kind of danger. And I might have moral doubts about some of the fights my country gets itself into. In a case like this, what is it that I want to do? Which is my real desire? Presumably, all three (the desire to fight, the desire to stay safe, and the desire to do what I think is right) are real. Which one is most truly my desire depends, Plato suggests, on which part of myself, on which *kind* of desire, I most identify with. It makes sense to identify with the rational part, rather than, say, with any part that has irrational, self-destructive desires; but even Thrasymachus might agree with that. The question is, is it rational to try to be good or to do the right thing? If it is good to be rational (or rational to be good), does this kind of goodness translate into moral goodness as we know it? And here Plato gets into difficulties.

Objections

Plato wants us to believe that the rational person will come to believe in the forms. Since the top form of all is the form of the good, the rational person will value the good above all else. So the rational person will indeed strive to be good. And this will include being morally good, Plato believes. What exactly that will entail Plato does not claim to know. Only the enlightened person might know whether, for instance, abortion is ever compatible with goodness. But since our ordinary ideas about goodness do come, in some shadowy way, from real goodness, presumably the Good will not be *radically* different from what we ordinarily think of as good. So, Plato says, it is good to be good.

The problem is that he has not given us good reason to believe in the forms in general or the form of the good in particular. Instead, he seems to presuppose something like belief in the forms. As Julia Annas says, "In Books 5 and 10 [of the *Republic*] Forms are quite explicitly brought in as being already accepted by all the interlocutors, though they are new to the reader."[22] What then follows is more a series of poetic images than a sustained logical proof of the existence of an entire metaphysical realm of mysterious and wonderful forms. So if Plato persuades you that you should be good after all, he might have saved you from being another Thrasymachus but he has not done so by giving you any reasons not to be bad. Instead, he has turned around your way of thinking. Even if Plato succeeds in one way, he does not really answer the challenge that was originally set. And if he does not move you with his images of sunlight and shadows, then he has not succeeded at all. So we must move on if we want a rational, philosophical answer to our question.

Conclusion

Plato has introduced our question for us, first through the extreme Thrasymachus and then through the more moderate Glaucon. He might even have persuaded you that you ought to be good. However, what he was supposed to be doing was something other than mere persuasion. He was supposed to prove rationally that it is good to be good. His attempt to prove this, though, depends on the rather vague and implausible theory of forms. Some people do believe this theory, especially as it applies to mathematics, where it is hard to say what numbers and geometric shapes are. Most do not. Instead, Plato's imagery of the Good as being like the sun and of ignorant people being like prisoners in a dark cave captures the imagination and, possibly, inspires us to live for what is good, enlightened, beautiful, and true. In the course of the *Republic,* he also set the agenda for almost all of Western philosophy after him. This is no mean feat. For rational proof that it is really in one's own interest to be good, though, it seems that we have to look elsewhere.

Questions for Further Thought

1. As far as ethics is concerned, does it matter whether there is life after death?
2. How accurate is the claim that most people think of ethics as a burdensome necessity? If you had the ring of Gyges, what would you do?
3. How much truth is there in the theory of forms?
4. Can goodness be objective without being an object?
5. Is politics just ethics on a bigger scale?

Notes

1. Although there is good reason to believe that the dialogue we will focus on in this chapter, Plato's *Republic,* does represent Plato's own ideas. On this, see Terence Irwin, *Plato's Ethics* (New York: Oxford University Press, 1995), 4–7.
2. The Greek word that Plato uses is *dikaiosune.* This is usually translated as "justice" but sometimes simply as "morality." Julia Annas gives good reason for preferring

the usual translation (see Julia Annas, *An Introduction to Plato's* Republic [Oxford: Oxford University Press, 1981], 11–13), but Plato makes so much of the concept of justice that for him it plays almost the same role as the concept of morality does for most people. For our purposes, it scarcely matters whether we think of virtue or justice as what needs to be justified since justice is the part of virtue that is hardest to justify. Anthony Rudd points out in his *Kierkegaard and the Limits of the Ethical* (Oxford: Clarendon Press, 1993), 102, that the three other cardinal virtues—courage, temperance or self-control, and wisdom—are obviously desirable from a purely self-interested point of view. Justice is the most obvious virtue that requires one to sacrifice one's own (apparent) interests for the sake of others. Whether this sacrifice is merely apparent is what is at issue between Socrates and people like Thrasymachus.

3. Translation by Robin Waterfield (Oxford: Oxford University Press, 1993). All quotations from the *Republic* will use this translation.

4. Ibid., 338c.

5. Ibid., 344a–c.

6. See Annas, *An Introduction*, 49–57, and Irwin, *Plato's Ethics*, 176–180, for what these arguments are and why they are not very good.

7. It was this ring of Gyges' that gave J. R. R. Tolkein the idea for the ring in *The Lord of the Rings*. The story is meant to show that it is bad to be bad and good to be good, that this kind of ring gives us nothing we should want. Whether the story succeeds in showing this is debatable, but the character Gollum, who is addicted to the ring, is hardly enviable.

8. These crimes are not really victimless at all, but we would probably be more likely to commit them if we *thought* of them that way. Hence my use of quotation marks around the word "victimless."

9. Plato, *Republic*, 360c–d.

10. Alasdair MacIntyre, *A Short History of Ethics* (New York: Collier Books, 1966), 160.

11. See Annas, *An Introduction*, 175–176 for details, as well as an explanation of why Plato would have improved his argument by leaving out his eugenic fantasies.

12. See Plato, *Republic*, Book 9, 588b–589b.

13. See Ibid. 375a, 416a–b, 422d, 451d, 459a ff., and 537a. Annas, *An Introduction*, comments on this, 80–81.

14. Benito Mussolini "The Doctrine of Fascism" in John Somerville and Ronald E. Santoni, eds., *Social and Political Philosophy* (New York: Anchor Books, 1963), 431.

15. A notable exception is Ayn Rand (1905–1982), author of *The Virtue of Selfishness* and other books. Rand, however, does believe in respecting the rights of other people. She champions "selfishness" mostly because the only form of altruism she recognizes is the all-out kind and because she wants to support capitalism against the oppressive communism under which she lived for much of her life. This is not to say that there are no flaws in her philosophy.

16. Plato *Phaedo* 81e–82b in G. M. A. Grube, ed., *Five Dialogues: Euthyphro, Apology, Crito, Meno, Phadeo* (Indianapolis: Hackett Publishing Company, 1981).

17. Ibid., 81c–d.

18. Ibid., 113e–114b.

19. See Anthony Kenny, *A Brief History of Western Philosophy* (Oxford: Blackwell, 1998), 37–39, for five different things Plato says about forms or ideas, not all of them

compatible with each other, and four contemporary notions that are at least somewhat similar to the kind of thing he seems to have had in mind. Since Plato's claims are not mutually compatible, it is impossible to derive from them a coherent doctrine of forms. This makes it impossible to be anything other than either wrong or somewhat vague about what they are meant to be. I will opt here for vagueness.

20. See Plato, *Phaedo*, 74a–75c.
21. Ibid., 102b–e.
22. Annas, *An Introduction*, 234.

Suggestions for Further Reading

The dialogues by Plato that I have concentrated on here are his *Crito*, *Phaedo*, and, especially, the *Republic*. Many good translations are available, but I recommend G. M. A. Grube's version of Plato's *Five Dialogues: Euthyphro, Apology, Crito, Meno, Phaedo* (Indianapolis: Hackett Publishing Company, 1981) and Robin Waterfield's translation of Plato's *Republic* (Oxford: Oxford University Press, 1993).

For commentary on Plato, see Terence Irwin, *Plato's Ethics* (New York: Oxford University Press, 1995), and Julia Annas, *An Introduction to Plato's Republic* (Oxford: Oxford University Press, 1981). Annas' book is aimed more at beginners and so is probably the better book to start with.

Also see Richard Kraut, ed., *The Cambridge Companion to Plato* (Cambridge: Cambridge University Press, 1992) and Gail Fine, ed., *Plato 2: Ethics, Politics, Religion, and the Soul* (New York: Oxford University Press, 2000).

CHAPTER 2

Aristotle

Aristotle's theory of ethics is a direct response to Plato's. We might think, then, that he answers the same challenge that Plato sets out to answer: Why be good? Unfortunately for our purposes, he does not. Instead, he focuses on what it means to be good or to live a good life. Aristotle believes that being good is the best way to get what we want and that it is simply right or fitting. Whereas Plato considered the good life to be one of reaching for a beautiful, supernatural ideal, Aristotle sees it as being one that is appropriately in harmony with nature.

The Meaning of Life

Aristotle begins his *Nicomachean Ethics* with the supposition that life is meaningful. He does not say this explicitly, so let me explain why I interpret the opening of his book in this way. Every action and decision, he says, seems to aim at some good:

> Every craft and every line of inquiry, and likewise every action and decision, seems to seek some good; that is why some people were right to describe the good as what everything seeks.[1]

For instance, if I decide to start jogging, it will probably be because I see health as a desirable goal. Health itself might be my ultimate goal, or it might be more of a means to some further end, such as long life. And I might want a long life for some other reason too, such as my desire to attend a New Year's Eve party in 2100. We could keep going like this forever, with every goal being not an end in itself but a means to some other end. In this case, if we go on forever, then there will be no end, no ultimate goal. What seemed to give each means a meaning, in other words, would really not do so at all. If every apparent end (purpose) is really just a means, then there is no purpose to anything we do. It is all, ultimately, pointless.

Aristotle does not prove that life is not pointless in this way. Instead, he says the following:

> Suppose, then, that the things achievable by action have some end that we wish for because of itself, and because of which we wish for the other things, and that we do not choose everything because of something else—for if we do, it will go on without limit, so that desire will prove to be empty and futile.[2]

In effect, Aristotle is saying that we should *assume* that life has meaning because otherwise we will think of it as meaningless. Is this a huge blunder? Is Aristotle simply making a groundless assumption because it is a nicer idea than the alternative (that life is meaningless)? Some modern philosophers would think so. Aristotle's pagan philosophy was made acceptable to the Christian world by St. Thomas Aquinas in the thirteenth century (see Chapter 4) and has since had a considerable impact on Western thinking, especially via the Catholic Church. Part of the rejection of traditional and religious ways of thinking has been the rejection of the comforting idea that life has a meaning of its own. The new vision is memorably set out in Jean-Paul Sartre's novel *Nausea*, whose main character (closely modeled on Sartre himself) is literally sickened by his "realization" of the pointlessness of all things (except, perhaps, art) in the godless world that Sartre takes us to be living in.

One can, therefore, think that Aristotle was wrong to be so optimistic. But even if he is wrong, he has not made a *mistake*. He is quite explicit that what he is doing is making a supposition, an assumption; and he makes it for quite practical reasons. There is no point in reasoning about how we should live if everything we do is in fact quite pointless. So a book like the *Nicomachean Ethics* necessarily presupposes that there is some goal toward which we should aim. Writing about how we ought to live presupposes that there is a right or good way, that not all ways of life are completely futile. It is also, of course, much more pleasant to take Aristotle's view rather than Sartre's, but that is not his concern. Aristotle would no more choose a pleasant illusion than Sartre would. Both seek the truth.

Aristotle makes a similar kind of argument with regard to God's existence. This is relevant because, while life might be able to have meaning without God, philosophers as diverse as Aristotle and Sartre have at least suspected that in fact the two go together. Aristotle's god is not the God of the Judeo–Christian tradition that Sartre has in mind, but neither is he the classic Greek superhero-on-Olympus kind of deity. Aristotle's god is not the creator of the world and has no discernible personality. Rather, he is the prime mover of all things, who moves without moving. How is this done? According to Aristotle, events can happen because they are caused (in the sense, roughly, of being pushed or pulled) but they can also happen (and generally do) because of some *reason*. If you wonder why peacocks have such colorful feathers, for instance, a causal explanation might be offered: a peacock's plumage acquires its various colors through the complex processes of biochemistry. Or you might get an evolutionary account of how random genetic changes and the constant struggle for survival led drab peacocks to die out. But it is quite likely that you will also be told that peacocks have bright feathers in order to help them attract mates. This is explanation in terms of purposes or ends, reasons rather than causes. "To attract a mate" is not a cause of anything; it is not an object or event that pushes or pulls any part of the peacock's body. But we still might think that this is the reason peacocks have their distinctive tail feathers. Aristotle believes in something like this. As well as causes of events, there are reasons. And indeed, he believes, there is a reason for everything. He assumes then not only that human life has some ultimate purpose or goal but that the entire universe does. God is this goal, the reason that everything happens.

God

If you believe in God, it does not follow that you believe in what Aristotle calls "gods." Like most other Greeks of his time, Aristotle talked about gods in the plural, but in fact he really believed in only one god. This god is a purely intellectual being, thinking all the time of his own intellectual activity. He is so good he is above even the things that we commonly regard as good acts. Instead all he does is think. Aristotle's reasoning as to why his readers should not believe that a god would engage in nonintellectual activities is as follows:

> In another way also it appears that complete happiness is some activity of study. For we traditionally suppose that the gods more than anyone are blessed and happy; but what sorts of actions ought we to ascribe to them? Just actions? Surely they will appear ridiculous making contracts, returning deposits, and so on. . . . When we go through them all, anything that concerns actions appears trivial and unworthy of the gods. Nonetheless, we all traditionally suppose that they are alive and active, since surely they are not asleep like Endymion.[3] Then if someone is alive, and action is excluded, and production even more, what is left but study? Hence the gods' activity that is superior in blessedness will be an activity of study. And so the human activity that is most akin to the gods' activity will, more than any others, have the character of happiness.[4]

Before we see why Aristotle thinks we should do as god does and why he thinks that this means practicing intellectual virtues more than moral ones, we need to understand why he believes that there is any god at all. We might well ask "Why must there be an ultimate reason for all things?" There need not be, but Aristotle assumes that events are explicable. This is a key assumption for any scientist and perhaps for anyone who wants to avoid Sartre's nauseating nihilism. It might be psychologically unavoidable to try to make sense of the world and thus to go on the assumption that there is some sense to be found. Certainly, science must work on this assumption (even if it turns out to be unjustified). Modern science has tended to explain events, though, much more in terms of causes than reasons, and in this sense it is quite different from Aristotle's **teleological** (from the Greek word for end or purpose: **telos**) way of thinking.

So, we might persist, why could the ultimate reason for all movement not be a kind of *cause*? Why must it be a *telos*? Because, Aristotle reasons, a push or a pull itself involves movement. So we cannot explain the motion of the universe by saying that something got the ball rolling by pushing it. The push itself would remain to be explained (just as the Big Bang either "just happened," in which case there is no ultimate reason for any of the movement in the world, or else it was caused by something else, in which case it was not the true beginning of the universe). So, it seems, either we cannot ultimately explain why anything moves (we could only give local explanations like "Domino 13,766,684 moved because it was pushed by domino 13,766,683") or else the ultimate cause of movement must be a reason rather than a cause. It must be, in Aristotle's terminology, a final cause rather than an efficient cause. The ultimate or prime mover must not itself be a thing that moves. Instead, it must be more like a goal toward which other things strive. It must be an ultimate goal, the goaliest of goals, one that draws all things to it (or to wherever they are meant to go) with its goalitude. Somewhat as a desirable person turns heads without pushing or pulling them, so god, the most desirable, the best thing there could ever be, moves the universe.

In what direction does he move things? The heavenly bodies move around in circles (or so Aristotle thought), and we do not live good lives simply by moving toward some particular point of the compass. Rather, we should move in the direction of what is right and good. We should follow the path that nature has set for us, which is not a literal road but a way of living. We should seek our proper goal. According to the *Nicomachean Ethics*, this goal is happiness.

Happiness

The Greek word that Aristotle uses for this goal is **eudaimonia**, which means having a good life rather than feeling any particular way. Of course, many people now and in Aristotle's day have believed that a good life just is one in which feelings of pleasure predominate. But this is merely one particular view of the good life. It is not simply true by definition. As Aristotle says, people might generally agree that a good life, or happiness, is our proper goal, but they do not agree on what this means. Some wise people think of having a good life as something very different from what most people think of as happiness. Ordinary people typically identify happiness with pleasure or having lots of money or being famous. They disagree with each other about what it is and change their minds depending on their own fortunes. For instance, a sick person might feel that health is the most important thing one can have but then value money more when times are hard, and so on. Other possibilities that Aristotle thinks worth considering are that the good life is the life of doing good, the virtuous life of public service (with heartening innocence he calls this the life of politics), and that the good life is the life of the contemplative sage. There are no other serious candidates for the best kind of life a human being can live.

Why think that our natural goal is a good life? Well, what else could it possibly be? A bad life? Aristotle is much too practical and down to earth to consider every conceivable possibility. He wants to know what most people think and what the supposed experts think. Other views are not worth thinking about. After all, if nature has given us this goal, shouldn't we have at least an inkling as to what it is? And since (virtually) everyone agrees that the goal is a good life, a good life it must be.

But what constitutes a good life? Aristotle considers the three main ideas of which he is aware concerning the main ingredient in a good life. The first and most obvious is pleasure, especially physical (i.e., sensory) pleasure. The second is moral virtue. The third is using the mind, which we might call thinking or contemplating or just being conscious (in the fullest possible sense). An obvious possible life-goal that Aristotle spends little time considering is that of amassing as much money as possible. The reason for this neglect is that money is a means to an end, not an end in itself, except for the pathologically miserly. The reason people want money is, mostly, for the things that money can buy. And they mostly want these for the pleasure they bring. So let's consider the life devoted to pleasure (and not money itself) first.

Aristotle does not at all deny that sensory pleasure, the kind of pleasure we get from drinking, eating, and having sex, is part of any truly good human life. But he does deny that this is in itself what life is all about.

> The many, the most vulgar, would seem to conceive the good and happiness as pleasure, and hence they also like the life of gratification. In this they appear completely slavish, since the life they decide on is a life for grazing animals.[5]

It is not incomprehensible that people should be attracted to a life of pleasure, as Aristotle quite rightly points out. We all like pleasure and can see the appeal of having more of it. But there is something vulgar, slavish, and bestial about such a life. Aristotle might well have some of Plato's objections to the life of the lusty monster in mind here. He also has arguments of his own however.

After all, he says, not all pleasure is good. We might consider the pleasure provided by some drugs or kinds of sexual acts to be bad. Or, of course, we might not. But most people will accept that *some* pleasure is intrinsically bad. Think of a neo-Nazi smirking to himself at the thought of the Holocaust or anti-Americans jubilantly celebrating a terrorist attack that left thousands of civilians dead. If you are an anti-American neo-Nazi unmoved by these examples, think of the pleasure of any sadistic torturer or child molester. Or, if that does not appall you, of rich Americans decadently enjoying their prosperity. Surely, we can agree with Aristotle that pleasure itself is not the ultimate good in life. We must take into account what kind of pleasure it is, what causes it, or who feels it.

Aristotle also has some back-up arguments to strengthen his case. For one thing, not all good things always bring pleasure. Think of someone who fights doggedly, perhaps even unsuccessfully, for a good cause. This could be literal fighting in a just war or working for some good political cause or fighting against fire in order to rescue people from a burning building. There might be some grim satisfaction in such work, but there might not be. Certainly, there need be no *pleasure* involved, especially if the fight has a cost in human lives and if the fight is not wholly successful (not all the people are saved from the fire, e.g.). Surgery and burial rites are further examples of good things that often bring no pleasure. So the good is not identical with the pleasant.

Aristotle's final argument, not against pleasure but against the idea that pleasure is the only good, is that human beings are better than that. Perhaps physical pleasure is all that a dog might hope for from life (if a dog could hope), but a life devoid of, for instance, moral virtue, meaningful work, more than subnormal intelligence, or religious faith (feel free to add to or delete from this list, depending on what you value) would surely not be the best of all possible human lives just because it was a 70-year rollercoaster of orgiastic bliss. Consider the famous anecdote about George Best (the world's greatest ever soccer player, at least according to himself), who, when brought champagne in a bed containing Miss World and covered with cash, was asked "George, where did it all go wrong?" If only pleasure matters, then it might all seem to have gone wonderfully right for George Best. But the man bringing him the champagne thought that Best was wasting his talent. You might envy George Best (if not his liver) or Miss World, but imagine them without athletic skill, without much of a brain, with no moral character whatsoever. This kind of life would certainly not be the *worst* we can imagine, but few of us would really accept that it is the best we should hope for.

Firstly, a champagne lifestyle is in fact more, in some ways, than most of us can reasonably hope for. If you want a good life, it is not wise to set your sights on more money or sex or whatever than you are ever likely to be able to get. That is dreaming rather than planning. Goals might be best set high, but they should be somewhat realistic. Secondly, it seems that you would be missing something very important if your life's goal was to be a porn star high on cocaine or Ecstasy. Life is not one long wild Saturday night. This is true even leaving aside for a moment the obvious threats to your physical and financial health that such a lifestyle brings with it.

Now, some people will respond to this by claiming that it is simply a value judgment, a matter of opinion. Aristotle disagrees. He believes that we can discover a scientific basis for ideas about what we might call the meaning of life. Each kind of living thing, according to Aristotle, has a natural goal or function. It is the destiny of a puppy to become a dog, that of an acorn to become an oak, and so on. An acorn that fails to become a mighty oak has gone wrong somehow, whether by dying or by living in some stunted or sickly state. And just as dogs and plants can be judged by experts to be good specimens of their kind or not, so too we human beings have a natural purpose that we can fulfill or not in various ways and to various degrees. We can discover this purpose partly by observing what human beings (naturally) seek and what they (naturally) seek to avoid. We do seek good times, in the hedonistic sense, but we also seek other things; and some people strive to avoid hedonism. So there is at least some reason to believe that pleasure is not all that life is about.[6]

This brings us to the second kind of good life that Aristotle discusses, the life of moral virtue. This, of course, might well include a lot of pleasure, but that is not its main focus. (A virtuous person who successfully does a lot of good will take pleasure in doing so but will be motivated by a concern for justice, honesty, and other virtues rather than the mere desire for pleasure.) The life that Aristotle has in mind here is a life of public service, of helping others, especially those of one's own community. He calls it the life of politics, but the political system in Aristotle's Athens was quite different from those we know today, despite the fact that it was a democracy. It was more exclusive (e.g., women had no vote) and more direct (e.g., no house of elected representatives, just citizens voting). Athens was also much smaller than most countries, or even large cities, today. We might therefore expand Aristotle's political life to a life of public or community service. There is no reason a person who lives this kind of life (a good politician, say, or wealthy philanthropist) should not enjoy at least as much physical pleasure as most other people have in their lives. Aristotle is not a puritan. Public servants will also enjoy a different kind of pleasure, one not available to our imaginary, mentally and morally crippled version of George Best. This is the pleasure of doing good.

According to Aristotle, we acquire moral virtues mostly through a process of training. If we are raised well, then we will be led, by a familiar pattern of reward and punishment, to refrain from bad acts and to keep to good behavior. This training will no doubt involve explanations of what is good, bad, kind, brave, selfish, mean, and so on. But it will not be very philosophical, and saying "That was brave, well done!" to a little girl is not necessarily doing much more than saying "Good dog!" to my dog Bucky. Through such training, though, we lay the foundation for some later, more rational understanding of the nature of good and evil or right and wrong. In this way, we develop character traits both good (virtues) and bad (vices). One's virtue can be improved by going through a course in moral philosophy, to think through some hard cases; but the primary thing in being good is the development of a virtuous disposition.

These character traits are habits of acting and reacting in certain ways. A person with the virtue of honesty, for instance, will react negatively to lying and positively to telling the truth. Virtue and vice, in other words, are largely matters of how one feels in certain circumstances. A virtuous person (but not a vicious one) will take pleasure in doing good. There might be exceptions of the kind described above (e.g., fighting in a war is often not pleasurable even for brave people), but usually a good person will be pained by evil and take pleasure in good. A successful public servant, then, will probably experience quite a large amount of this moral pleasure.

There is what we might call yet another kind of pleasure, perhaps "species pleasure," that such public servants will also feel if Aristotle is right. Human beings are by their very nature, he says, political animals. That is, we naturally live in political communities or societies. Outside such a community, we are likely to suffer at the hands of the elements, wild beasts, bandits, and so on. But even if we survive, we will have no culture, no education, no civilization, no language, and no fellowship. We will, one way or another, have no real humanity. Such a life, Aristotle says, could be led only by an animal or a god. Being neither, we need to live in a society of some kind. Only then can we or nature be satisfied. And living successfully in society, getting along with others rather than simply being adjacent to them, requires moral virtue. Murderers and thieves are not likely to be tolerated. Nor is murdering one's neighbors really living with them in Aristotle's sense, so getting away with it is not enough.

A fully social, and therefore fully human, life is one in which the individual is fully integrated into the community, identifying his or her interests with those of his or her friends and neighbors (the state that Aristotle has in mind, remember, would be fairly small by modern standards). Ideally, selfishness and patriotism would then merge, as they perhaps do in great political leaders. For them, the distinction between asking "What can my country do for me?" and asking "What can I do for my country?" might be scarcely intelligible. As far as I am an Athenian, what I do for Athens *is* done for myself (along with my fellow Athenians, of course). And a true patriot might think of him- or herself first and foremost as an Athenian (or an American or a Korean or whatever). It follows that we cannot criticize this kind of life, the life of devoted public service, on the basis that it is insufficiently egoistic. It is completely egoistic, but the ego in question sees itself in a thoroughly social, allegedly natural, way.

Still, this life is open to criticism of a different kind. Aristotle himself seems to consider it to be only the second best of all possible lives. Why is that? Part of the problem is that not everyone can be a wealthy philanthropist. Much the same financial considerations also mean that not everyone can run for the office of president of the United States of America. Doing something useful for the community is not an option for everybody since it requires certain resources, if only of bodily strength (not being paralyzed, e.g.). A person might have great moral character (understood as a tendency to behave and feel in certain ways in certain circumstances) yet never really do anything of great significance. This could be because of physical infirmity or simply an accident of history. Disasters, for instance, throw up various heroes. Who knows how many people remain only potential heroes just because they live in nondisastrous times? A humble, unspectacular, but thoroughly moral life is not bad; but it is not the best we can imagine either. This is not a major problem, but it detracts from the ideal perfection of a way of life that Aristotle thinks we should be looking for. And morality on its own does not guarantee a good life because a moral person might be plagued by painful illness or some other kind of bad luck.

The life of public service is also less than ideal because it might be pursued from the wrong motive. Even Aristotle, who somewhat idealized politics, recognized that most visible "public servants" are not motivated by altruism so much as a desire for fame, prestige, and wealth. Needless to say, this kind of superficial concern with the adulation of the fickle public is not the best of all possible lives, precisely because it is so superficial and dependent on the undependable public.

Finally, public service is less good than using one's mind, in Aristotle's opinion. Using the mind, after all, is what Aristotle's god does, and god-like activity must surely be the best kind there is. Mental activity, then, is the kind of thing most in accordance with the greatest of virtues.

And, just as we are naturally social beings, so too we are by nature rational. Indeed, we have sociality in common with such animals as bees and ants, whereas reason is what distinguishes human beings from all lower life forms. It is this, therefore, that makes us most truly human. The ideal human being would have moral virtues, of course, but would live a life dominated not by public service but by the use of the mind (i.e., thinking or studying). And we should think well and about good things, such as ethics and politics. It is for this reason that the political life, good as it is, is only second best. The life of public service, of moral virtue, is then typically human and befits our nature as human beings; but it is only second best because to be god-like is even better than to be human. If we reject Aristotle's ideas about god, though, as most modern people, whether atheistic, agnostic, or religious, are inclined to do, then we have more reason to prefer what he calls the human kind of life.

Why Be Good?

Aristotle believes that the meaning of being good depends on the function of the thing in question. What it takes for an orange tree to be a good orange tree is not going to be the same as what is required to be a good human being. Orange trees should grow healthy, green leaves and juicy fruit. We should be healthy and grow too, but we are not plants; thus, there is more to a good human life than this. Specifically, we are rational and social beings. In order to live happily in society we need to be able to get along with others, so we need certain social virtues. In order to be godlike and to achieve our highest potential, we need to develop our intellectual virtues and to live a life of intellectual contemplation. This is what it means for us to be good, and we should be so because that is the way we are meant to be. It is our natural function and therefore likely, unless we are psychologically unnatural, badly raised, or just unlucky, to make us feel happier than any other kind of life will.

This, at least, is what Aristotle argues in the concluding chapter of his *Nicomachean Ethics*. The life he recommends there as the best for us is an almost otherworldly one of what he conceives as god-like contemplation. We will consider some objections to this idea below. Elsewhere, in other parts of the *Nicomachean Ethics* and in his *Eudemian Ethics*, however, Aristotle recommends a different kind of life, one that combines philosophical activity with engagement in social, political, and family life.[7] This is a more appealing ideal for many people, but the idea that there is any one life that can be proved best for everyone is doubtful, as we shall see in the next section. In what follows, I will bear both ideals in mind—both the mixed life of various goods and the pure life of godlike study—but I will concentrate on the more intellectualist one, which seems to be Aristotle's ultimate idea about what living a good life really means.

Now, why should we want to be the kind of rational, virtuous person he describes? How would Aristotle answer the likes of Thrasymachus and Glaucon? His answer is partly prudential. Virtues are qualities of character that it is useful to have. Courage helps one to achieve whatever it is that one wants. So does the intellectual virtue of intelligence, if there is such a thing. Honesty might not do this, but it does help to be *believed to be* honest if one wants to live socially, that is, in harmony with others. And one way, perhaps the best way, to make others believe that you are honest is really to be honest. Thrasymachus, of course, knows this but argues that the ideal is not honesty but skillful *dishonesty* combined with a reputation for honesty and other such moral virtues. Aristotle's answer to this, very roughly, is "Grow up!"

What I mean by this is not that Aristotle is impatient and insulting but that moral philosophy, thinking carefully about how we should live, is not suitable for those who have not been raised well. A dishonest person will not see the point of honesty and cannot be made to see it merely through reasoning. She needs to be trained in the practice of honesty, and then she not only will behave as honesty requires but will want to do so. Thrasymachus might try to argue that these acquired wants are somehow not genuine since they are artificially produced. He might claim that true self-interest requires seeking not what one has come to value as a result of training by others but what one naturally wants prior to any such training. But (1) why should I care only about my "genuine" desires and not simply the ones that I actually have (however they were produced), and (2) why should only the vague impulses of the baby count as genuine desires? Apart perhaps from an instinct to suckle, all our desires arise in the process of socialization. This is not to say that they are all *caused* by socialization, but it does mean that it is hard to answer questions about what is natural and what is a product of nurturing. Nurturing itself is a natural process after all, and any natural function will of course be influenced by the environment. For instance, eating is a natural process, but how we eat, what we eat, and whether we eat, depend on the food available to us. The same kind of consideration applies to natural processes in the brain. Thrasymachus almost seems to have in mind a highly unnatural human being who exists in an adult state without having been nurtured or socialized at all, without having grown up. An unsocialized person would lack morals and language, the very things (arguably) that make us truly human.

Still, Thrasymachus might wonder what benefit there is in being raised one particular way rather than another. Why is it better to be raised in a community of honest, rather than dishonest, people? Or why is it not best of all to be raised by cynical and brilliant criminals in a society of trusting and honest people?

We can see why life among honest people would be better than life among dishonest people. We do not want to be treated dishonestly by others. But why not be a thief or liar among honest dupes? Aristotle seems to believe two things about this. The first is that to be a truly successful fraud you would have to know how to behave honestly, and *that* knowledge only comes through the kind of training that will in fact cause you to value honesty. This is an empirical claim for which there is no evidence, that I know of; but it sounds somewhat plausible. Learning to act as if one were honest is like learning to play jazz as if one liked it. It is very hard to imagine a true hater of jazz ever pulling this off with complete success so that even the experts were fooled. Playing jazz really well involves liking it, or even loving it. Playing the part of the honest person likewise might well involve liking or even loving honesty or truth. Plato, who thought the theater should be censored, was especially wary of drama involving immoral characters. Even playing at evil has its dangers. Good artists identify with their roles, at least to some extent.

Plato partly anticipated this line of objection to Thrasymachus. In the *Gorgias*, he argued that advancing one's self-interest is not just a matter of getting whatever it is that one happens to want. The example he uses there is of a young male prostitute (a catamite) who seeks clients for gay sex.[8] Imagine that he is inundated with clients. Imagine also that he really likes his work (unlikely for a prostitute, but not utterly impossible). Does this mean that he is doing well, having a good life? Many people would say that it obviously does not. Plato is one of them. Less conservative people will not be so sure, but the example can be changed to make the point to almost anyone. Is the drug addict who finds a warehouse full of crack really lucky? Or the Nazi who has a "good" day rounding up victims? Or the anti-American terrorist who successfully kills hundreds of sleeping GIs? These people are all getting what they want, but they do not seem to be doing well. They seem seriously misguided, and what they might perceive as good fortune is in fact only likely to make their reform less probable. What looks like good luck to some people might really be bad luck, in other words. Thrasymachus has ignored or denied the possibility of bad desires. Plato has reminded us of it. Aristotle has helped to explain it and to fill in some of the details.

Not all the details though. Part of Aristotle's "vagueness" is quite deliberate. He does not believe that ethics can be an exact science, even if a perfect person could tell exactly what to do in any given situation. Such a person sees what is called for but cannot provide a formula or set of rules that will allow others to see what to do in other cases. Similarly, wise people know what character traits are virtues, while the unwise (e.g., Thrasymachus perhaps) do not. There is clearly much for Thrasymachus to dispute here. Is there really an ability to perceive what is noble or fine? And how can we determine who has it? On paper these objections look strong, but in practice we do tend to agree on who is wise and that some things really are noble and others not. Few people, for instance, despise Mother Theresa or Martin Luther King, Jr. Those who do typically do so for reasons other than the actions that are generally associated with their names. So Thrasymachus, or any skeptic about Aristotle's thoughts on practical wisdom, could be right; but agreeing with him involves going some way against common sense.

Common sense and Aristotle, though, are still somewhat vague on this issue. Although we might agree about Martin Luther King, there are not *many* people whom we would *all* agree are wise, and we will likely disagree about just how wise each of them is. Accepting the wisdom of past saints, heroes, and heroines could lead to moral conservatism on issues such as homosexuality, which not ev-eryone will accept as a good thing. Is the catamite's pleasure really shameful? It is easy to see how there could be disagreement about this and very hard to see how it might be settled satisfactorily. Certainly, Aristotle offers little by way of a solu-tion. The best life will tend to be more pleasant than other lives, he believes, but not all pleasure is good and not all good things are pleasant. Only the intuitively commonsensical, but on reflection rather mysterious, person of practical wisdom can really tell what is good and what is bad.

It does not follow, of course, that all our desires are *bad*, that we should go completely against our own will. Aristotle does not believe in denying the will, unless the will is bad in some way. In that case, we need **continence**, the ability to control our bad urges and stop ourselves from acting on them. An incontinent person is like someone who is drunk, who makes bad decisions out of a kind of ignorance.[9] Bad, that is, by the person's own standards, as when someone wants to quit smoking but smokes anyway. The ignorance here is of a special kind be-cause if you want to quit smoking you surely know that you want to quit. You cannot be completely ignorant of this. It is possible, though, to fail to understand or fully acknowledge such knowledge, a little like someone reciting words from memory without understanding or thinking about what they mean. The virtue of continence or strong will can help in such situations, to get you to sober up and think about what you are doing.

Aristotle thinks, though, that the ideal person, the truly virtuous person, will not need continence. Instead, his or her desires will be for what is good. The kind of strength of will we are talking about might help someone who loves telling lies or driving dangerously on public roads to give up his or her bad habits. But the best people will not even be tempted to do such things in the first place. They want only what is good. This good is what is good for the individual, so in that sense it is selfish or at least egoistic; but as we are social beings, what is good for the community or state is also good for the individual (and vice versa), so in this sense it is altruistic. The will is not to be denied but directed accurately toward the good, which is what it would want anyway if it knew what was good for it.

Objections

There are many objections that can be raised in response to Aristotle's theory, but I will concentrate on the following: his ideas about God, his ideas about nature, and his ideas about the relative value of thinking and public service.

First, God. Just as Aristotle's assumption that life must have some ultimate point can be questioned, so too can his assumption that movement must have some ultimate explanation. Why must it? Perhaps some things just exist and just exist in a certain way. Movement or energy might be one of these things. In fact, it seems as though something must "just be," whether this be God, energy, the Big Bang, or some other first being, cause, or mover. The religiously inclined will tend to think that God is the best candidate for this unique role in the scheme of things, but if God does not even exist, then of course he will not be the winning candidate. And the first mover need not be God in any meaningfully religious sense. Aristotle's god is not the God of the Bible, as we have seen; but Aristotle does hold him up as a moral paradigm. The real first mover, if there is one, could be morally indifferent or even evil. So Aristotle has by no means proved that there is a god or that he is good, or that, even if he is good, we should try to emulate him. After all, what is good for a god might not be good for us. Aristotle himself stresses the relativity of goodness to function. That is to say, a good lettuce might be one that is green, fresh, and crisp. But these are not absolutely good attributes that we should strive to have. Indeed, it would be mad to do so. No matter how good a lettuce might be, we should not try to be like it. Perhaps the same is true of trying to be like God. According to Aristotle, how we should be depends on what he calls our "function."

What is the human function? Aristotle says that it is to be rational and social. This seems reasonable. The problem is that, of the two, Aristotle and many others have agreed that being rational is more distinctively human than being social. Rats and wolves, after all, are social beings too. And the life of reason is not necessarily a very noble one since the intellectual virtues (which presumably a rational person would have) are not the same as the moral virtues. Aristotle is perhaps best read as holding that the best kind of person is one who has all the virtues to the greatest possible degree.

As I mentioned above, Aristotle's contribution to ethics can be regarded in large part as a kind of filling in of gaps left in Plato's work.[10] Assessing it is then a matter of assessing this filling in. Aristotle's full picture of the best possible human life is based on a certain view of nature, the teleological idea that we have a certain natural purpose and will be happiest if we live in accordance with it. Contemporary biologists, of course, tend not to think in such terms. Species do not exist for a purpose; they just exist as a result of random mutations and natural selection. Natural selection is not really selection at all. There is no Nature that does the picking.[11] Instead, individuals unsuited to their environment tend to die out. It is a process of natural attrition, not "selection" in the obvious sense.

Does this instantly invalidate Aristotle's ethics? I do not think so. For one thing, science is incapable of proving that there is not a god behind all things, who might indeed give us some special purpose, individually or by species. For another, Aristotle's idea is really just that what is best for us is a life most suited to our nature. This is likely to be the most pleasurable life (since all-out hedonism has a tendency to lead to poverty, disease, and death), and even if it is not, it is likely to be the most satisfying (since meaningless pleasure tends not to be satisfying). He values also the most noble, least slavish life, as we have seen; and this is not a biological idea at all.

Realistically speaking, then, Aristotle's description of a thoughtful, well-socialized member of a just society does seem to be pretty ideal. Glaucon, though, has already accepted that conventional goodness is a good thing in practice, given the nature of the real world. His problem arose, or became most clear, when we considered the *unrealistic* case of Gyges' magic ring. What if one lived in a community full of good people that was run in a good way and one was believed to be good *but one was in fact thoroughly bad?* Imagine that you had been raised by very cunning parents in such a way as to cultivate your vices and your fake virtues so that you take pleasure in these things and exercise them constantly. Imagine that you have all the other benefits that Aristotle describes as making up the perfect life: wealth, health, good looks, and so on. We must imagine (for the example to work at all) such a person to feel completely happy. What can Aristotle say now against such a life?

All he can say, it seems, is that you are not in fact happy if you live like this, any more than the successful Nazi has a genuinely good life. Why not? Because you lack qualities that we recognize as being desirable (the moral virtues). But, you might respond, who cares what "we" value? Then Aristotle can add that your life is not in fact good, is not in accordance with your nature as a human being. But is there such a nature? Do all human beings have it or only some (perhaps most)? And why is it good to be in accordance with nature, whatever that might mean exactly?

Here, I think, we see the biggest problem for Aristotle's ethics. The real problem is with his one-size-fits-all approach. It seems impossible to deny that we each have some sort of nature, albeit a changeable one that is hard to define or discover. We do have character or personality. But do all members of the species *Homo sapiens* share essential characteristics so that what satisfies one will satisfy all others? Before answering this question, we should be careful. Aristotle does not deny that individual differences exist. Nor does he claim that he can set out in full detail the precise life that will satisfy each of us. Near the beginning of his book, Aristotle famously advises us that he will be satisfied if he can "indicate the truth roughly and in outline" since in ethics we are talking more about rules of thumb than things that are *always* true. It is not a subject that allows us to be more exact than this.[12]

So we should not quickly dismiss his theory on the basis that it claims more precision than is reasonable. It does not. But we might still wonder what guarantee there is that there is any such thing as human nature that is common, deep, and exhaustive of all that is most important about each of us. Perhaps I will only be satisfied by a life with other people, sharing values with them and valuing character traits that allow us to achieve what we want, both collectively and as individuals. But what if you are different? What if you have a nature that is satisfied more by being a parasite, pretending to virtue while secretly reveling in vice and the material advantages it can bring? Why is that not possible? How can we be sure that human nature exists at all or that it is roughly the same for all people?

It is also relevant to ask here just what this nature, if it exists at all, is. Plato and Aristotle emphasize the rational nature of human beings. By this they do not mean that all people are very rational in everything they do. Obviously, that is not true. What they mean is closer to the idea that human beings can be evaluated with regard to their rationality so that all actions fall *somewhere* on a scale from rational to irrational. This is not true of inanimate objects or of animals if we think of them as acting primarily on instinct. It is not rational or irrational to kick your leg when a doctor hits your knee with a hammer. This is simply a reflexive reaction. But much of our behavior, at least so we like to think, is not like this. Even when someone behaves irrationally, in self-destructive ways, we are likely to try to reason with them. We would not do this with a rabid dog or runaway train. It is in this sense that human beings are said to be rational animals. And it is because we are open to reason that action in accordance with reason is especially suitable for us, or so some people think.

However, there are several problems with this line of thinking: (1) from our being open to reason, or capable of rational behavior, it does not follow that we ought to behave rationally, any more than our being capable of swimming or undergoing surgery means that we ought to swim or have surgery; (2) even if there is some connection between characteristics of human nature and how we ought to live, it seems that reason is not the only distinctive feature of human beings—we are also featherless bipeds with opposable thumbs who use language and sophisticated technology, so should we devote our concentration to one or more of these features more than to reason itself?—and (3) if we do emphasize reason, where does this leave morality or ethics? Indeed, where does it leave us? Aristotle argues that we ought to be like god as much as possible. His god, though, *is* intuitive reason and needs no research or proof to know what is true. His characteristic activity is the active consideration of ultimate truth.[13] We are not like this and are much more ignorant than god, so we can "do what god does" only to a very limited degree. The moral life has some appeal. A doomed attempt at being godlike has little.[14]

Conclusion

Thrasymachus argues, in effect, that we should not be good because it is not rational to be so. He has no problem with reason as he understands it. It is worrying to find Aristotle ranking the life of the mind, the life of reason, above the life of moral virtue. He is no Thrasymachus, but he still might be too close to him for our comfort. What we still seem to need if we are to follow the trail blazed by Plato and Aristotle away from Thrasymachus is some reason to believe that there is a common human nature *and* that moral goodness suits this nature more than any other way of life. But what could possibly guarantee that the world has been so kind as to make that true? One possible such guarantee might come from God, and it is to this idea that we turn in the next chapter.

Before that, let me emphasize some last points. Unlike Plato, Aristotle is not out to answer the question "why be good?" He explicitly says that there is no point addressing a book like his to people who are not already good, who have not had a good upbringing.[15] Instead, his goal is to help those who already believe in the value of goodness to see as precisely as possible what this involves. So it would be unfair to judge Aristotle's ethical theory negatively for failing to supply a very good answer to our question. And it does fail to do so, partly because Aristotle's ideal goal is not a *feeling* of happiness but true happiness or having a good life. A feeling of happiness might be caused by mental illness or drugs. What we want, he believes, is not this but something more like a life that ought to make us happy, that would make a normal person happy, we might say. But in referring to things like *normality* or what we *ought* to feel or having a *good* life, Aristotle is taking it for granted that goodness in this sense (i.e., normality, or what ought to be done, etc.) is good. So in a way he provides no answer at all to our question.

On the other hand, his work does provide at least a partial answer to it. In response to the question "Why should I (try to) be good?" Plato raised the counterquestion "which (part of) you?" He argued that the best you, or the best version of you, will have its soul in order, its parts operating harmoniously, and that this you will want to be good. Aristotle adds to this more emphasis on education and upbringing. A childish or badly brought-up you might well see no point in being good and might get little from it that you can appreciate as having value. But the well-raised you will, as Plato said, want to be good and take at least a certain amount of pleasure in doing good (and feel a kind of pain when you do bad things). If we are being realistic and you have been well-raised, then this is the only you we need to think about. There is, though, the further question of whether it is best to raise our own children (and we can include in this all children, our own and others', who receive an education provided by our community) to have the virtues that Aristotle describes. And that is quite doubtful, partly because some of his virtues seem out-of-date, if not ridiculous. Aristotle valued pride and something close to self-importance or pomposity. Christians, on the other hand, regard pride as a sin. In the eighteenth century, David Hume famously derided in turn the "monkish virtues" of Christianity (e.g., chastity and humility). So what it means to be good, what characteristics really are virtues and which are vices, is an open question. To answer it we need to consider the alternative views, and we shall do that starting with Christianity.

Questions for Further Thought

1. Can we understand the natural world without thinking in terms of purposes?
2. How should we rank moral goodness and intellectual or spiritual contemplation? Can we compare them?
3. Is it either legitimate or necessary to assume that life has a meaning?
4. Is there such a thing as human nature?
5. Does how we should live depend on how we do live so that biology or anthropology might be relevant to ethics?

Notes

1. Aristotle, *Nicomachean Ethics*, 1094a 1–3, trans. Terence Irwin (Indianapolis: Hackett Publishing Company, 1999).
2. Ibid., 1094a, 18–22.
3. In Greek myth, Endymion was a shepherd boy whom Zeus put to eternal sleep. He was loved by the moon goddess Selene.
4. Aristotle, *Nicomachean Ethics*, 1178b, 9–24.
5. Ibid., 1095b, 18–21.
6. Aristotle has been criticized for this idea. Some claim that he commits what G. E. Moore called the naturalistic fallacy, reasoning that if something is natural, then it is what *ought* to be done. See G. E. Moore, *Principia Ethica* (Cambridge: Cambridge University Press, 1903). Whether it is a fallacy to derive an "ought" from an "is" in this way is a question to which we will return in this chapter and, especially, in Chapters 4 and 6.
7. For more on this, see John M. Cooper, *Reason and Human Good in Aristotle* (Indianapolis: Hackett Publishing Company, 1986), especially 144–145.
8. See *Gorgias*, 494c–495a. Actually, a catamite is not necessarily a prostitute, but it is hard to translate Greek sexual ethics into modern terms. Sex between men and boys was generally considered all right, but homosexuality between equals was not. It was considered shameful to be the more passive partner, which is what a catamite was. For more details, see John Addington Symonds, *A Problem in Greek Ethics: Studies in Sexual Inversion* (Honolulu, HI: University Press of Hawaii, 2002).
9. See Aristotle, *Nicomachean Ethics*, 1147a, 17–18.
10. Although it is important to note his rejection of Plato's theory of forms too. See ibid., Book I Chapter 6.
11. Unless "intelligent design theory" is true, but this is not the view of most biologists. If there is such a thing as *the* theory of evolution, then it does not make any reference to God since it does not have to in order to explain what it seeks to explain. Of course, not everyone accepts this theory, but they, like Aristotle, tend to think teleologically. I am not here saying who is right, merely putting the case against Aristotle's way of thinking. It should be noted, though, that it is a strong case.
12. See Aristotle, *Nicomachean Ethics*, 1094b, 20–25.
13. See Gerold J. Hughes, *Aristotle on Ethics* (New York: Routledge, 2001), 46.
14. See J. O. Urmson, *Aristotle's Ethics* (Oxford: Blackwell), 123–124 and Hughes, *Aristotle on Ethics*, 47–48 for more criticism along these lines.
15. See Aristotle, *Nicomachean Ethics*, 1095b, 5–8.

Suggestions for Further Reading

Aristotle's key work on ethics is his *Nicomachean Ethics*. I have quoted from the translation by Terence Irwin (Indianapolis: Hackett Publishing Company, 1999). Another excellent translation with a detailed commentary is available in the edition by Sarah Broadie and Christopher Rowe (Oxford: Oxford University Press, 2002).

There are many commentaries on Aristotle's ethics. Some of the best are David Bostock, *Aristotle's Ethics* (Oxford: Oxford University Press, 2006); John M. Cooper, *Reason and Human Good in Aristotle* (Indianapolis: Hackett Publishing Company, 1986); Gerard J. Hughes, *Aristotle on Ethics* (New York: Routledge, 2001); and J. O. Urmson, *Aristotle's Ethics* (Oxford: Blackwell, 1988).

For a general introduction to Aristotle's work (i.e., not just on ethics), you should read Jonathan Barnes, *Aristotle: A Very Short Introduction* (Oxford: Oxford University Press, 2001). This is a wonderful book despite being, as the title says, very short.

CHAPTER 3

~~~~~~~

Christianity

To many people, it will seem obvious that questions about ethics should be related to ones about religion. This is not obvious to many philosophers, though, since they are concerned with what can be proved and religion is so often regarded as a matter of faith, not reason. Still, I think it is worth seeing whether religion can provide an answer to our question about moral goodness without simply assuming that it will turn out to have nothing more helpful to say than simply "Have faith." This raises another question, however—namely, which religion we should consider. We cannot possibly look at all of them. In this chapter, then, I will focus on the major Western religions and, in particular, on Christianity. This is partly because Christianity is the dominant religion in the English-speaking world and partly for reasons that I will explain below. It is not because I believe that Christianity is somehow philosophically better than other religions.

Perhaps the most popular and visible form of virtue ethics today is the "What Would Jesus Do?" (WWJD) campaign. This slogan can be seen on T-shirts, sweatbands, and bumper stickers. The idea is that rather than considering whether a given act is against the Ten Commandments or some other set of rules, we should instead take Jesus as our role model and consider the general kind of act in question. Indeed, we might not even break our behavior up into discrete units and consider each one separately (or each of the ones that seem particularly dodgy at least) but instead try to live in the spirit of Jesus. The emphasis is not on rules or principles, although of course Christians can have principles, but on being a certain kind of person, one like Jesus.

This is a particularly Christian idea, of course. Jewish ethics makes room for the virtues with the concept, for instance, of being a *mensch* (literally a man but really a kind of ideal of the virtuous person; a woman can be a *mensch* too). There is also the injunction in Leviticus 19:18 that "thou shalt love thy neighbour as thyself."[1] Only someone with the appropriate virtue of neighborliness or love might be able to follow this commandment perfectly. But Judaism also has a wealth of codes and rules that are more clear-cut, which individual Jews follow more or less strictly.

These include the Ten Commandments but also non-Christian rules, such as not eating cheeseburgers. These rules can seem hard to understand to people outside the Jewish tradition or at best might be thought of as primitive health regulations. In fact, however, they are based on the Bible. Some rules come directly from the Old Testament, some come from an oral tradition of commentary on the Old Testament, and some are principles derived from what the Bible says. For instance, Genesis 9:4 forbids the eating of blood, so Jews do not eat blood. Exodus 23:19 forbids the cooking of a young goat in its mother's milk, so Jews do not mix dairy products with meat. This goes beyond the letter of the biblical command, but in the spirit of tradition and a preference for personal inconvenience rather than disobedience to God, observant Jews tend to err on the safe side. This should not seem silly to any Christian, even those who disagree about what God requires of us.

The most famous such requirements are the Ten Commandments, which are important enough to be worth quoting in full here. Exodus 20 says

1 And God spake all these words, saying,

2 I am the Lord thy God, which have brought thee out of the land of Egypt, out of the house of bondage.

3 Thou shalt have no other gods before me.

4 Thou shalt not make unto thee any graven image, or any likeness of any thing that is in heaven above, or that is in the earth beneath, or that is in the water under the earth.

5 Thou shalt not bow down thyself to them, nor serve them: for I the Lord thy God am a jealous God, visiting the iniquity of the fathers upon the children unto the third and fourth generation of them that hate me;

6 And shewing mercy unto thousands of them that love me, and keep my commandments.

7 Thou shalt not take the name of the Lord thy God in vain; for the Lord will not hold him guiltless that taketh his name in vain.

8 Remember the sabbath day, to keep it holy.

9 Six days shalt thou labour, and do all thy work:

10 But the seventh day is the sabbath of the Lord thy God: in it thou shalt not do any work, thou, nor thy son, nor thy daughter, thy manservant, nor thy maidservant, nor thy cattle, nor thy stranger that is within thy gates:

11 For in six days the Lord made heaven and earth, the sea, and all that in them is, and rested the seventh day: wherefore the Lord blessed the sabbath day, and hallowed it.

12 Honour thy father and thy mother: that thy days may be long upon the land which the Lord thy God giveth thee.

13 Thou shalt not kill.

14 Thou shalt not commit adultery.

15 Thou shalt not steal.

16 Thou shalt not bear false witness against thy neighbour.

17 Thou shalt not covet thy neighbour's house, thou shalt not covet thy neighbour's wife, nor his manservant, nor his maidservant, nor his ox, nor his ass, nor any thing that is thy neighbour's.

Like traditional Judaism, Islam is very rule-focused and includes the Ten Commandments (which are also, of course, recognized by Christians). Muslims believe that the Ten Commandments are God's basic rules, that the Golden Rule taught by Jesus is a sort of clarification or update of these rules, and that the Koran contains all the details we need for right living. Again, there is nothing inherently wrong (from a religious point of view) about the idea of God's making certain rules and revealing them to us. Religious believers might agree that it is not ours to question these rules; we must merely follow them. It can seem presumptuous to question the rules or to try to pick and choose which ones make sense or appeal to us. Such picking and choosing is often derided as "cafeteria religion." It is certainly not popular among Muslims.

Christianity, though, is somewhat different. In the New Testament, Jesus often seems to be saying that we should not worry too much about sticking to the letter of God's law but should instead focus on the spirit of the law. That spirit, in a word, is love. Christians disagree among themselves about how far this is what Jesus is saying and how far it is only what he *seems* to be saying on a superficial reading. Traditional Catholics tend to believe that there are rules that should be followed strictly. No abortion, for instance. (Like some of the Jewish laws, this one is based on a certain interpretation of the Bible. Nowhere in the Bible is abortion explicitly forbidden.) More liberal Christians tend to think more readily about changing the rules traditionally thought to have come straight from God. And then there are some Protestants who believe in strict rules but reject the traditional ideas about what exactly these rules are, how worship should be conducted, and so on. Belief in tradition and belief in strictness are not the same thing, although the two often appeal to the same people.

Otherwise unchecked, the tendency to challenge tradition and question everything can lead to both wild progress and a kind of moral annihilation. Asking questions has brought huge advances in science and in politics. The tendency to accept what God gives unquestioningly surely helped support the idea that kings have a divine right to rule. After all, if God did not want them to rule, why would he not remove them from power? Start questioning this right, and revolution is not far behind and democracy not too far behind that (if you are lucky). Then, the world's political order is no longer seen as part of God's order or God's gift. In William Shakespeare's play *Macbeth* (written around 1606), the entire order of all things has a religious flavor to it so that Macbeth's sinful ambition to change the political order disturbs the very atmosphere itself. By the time of John Milton's *Paradise Lost* (written around 1650–1660), this kind of political conservatism is reserved for heaven. For Milton, God's authority is not to be questioned but the king's certainly can be. The social order is no longer thought of as something created by God, and in this sense God's place or role in the world is diminished. Coincidence or not, the rise of political freedom and the demands for individual rights and privileges have gone hand in hand with the rise of science, technology, and material comfort and the decline of religion and, some would say, a strong sense of values.

What does this have to do with virtue ethics? Well, one thing it does is point out that asking "What would Jesus do?" does not guarantee any one answer or set of answers. This is one reason that many people prefer rules to role models. If we see Jesus as essentially a person who asks questions of the old traditions, then living by the WWJD rule would lead in one way, whereas if we think of Jesus as a strict upholder of rules (turning over the tables of the moneylenders in the temple, e.g.), then trying to follow his example will lead in quite a different direction.

Another connection between the history of Christianity and virtue ethics, which emphasizes moral character more than rules of conduct, is that Jesus' example can be regarded by Christians as more important than any specific rules he might have taught. Trying to follow a set of rules brings problems of interpretation. The rules set out in the Bible are followed to the letter by some, ignored in accordance with "common sense" by others, and made into broader, more restrictive principles by others. For instance, as we have seen, the Bible's explicitly forbidding cooking a baby goat in its mother's milk has been taken by Jewish rabbis implicitly to forbid mixing *any* meat and dairy products together.

The literal interpreters of the Bible might sound the most right from a Jewish or Christian point of view, but it is the smallest group by far in practice. Almost every text is open to some amount of reasonable interpretation. For example, Joshua 10:13 says that the sun stopped in the sky, which was taken by some of Galileo's opponents to mean that the sun goes around the earth, rather than vice versa, as he claimed. Most people, though, would today read this text as meaning simply that the sun *appeared* to stop in the sky, perhaps because the earth stopped moving. Christians have an additional reason not to read the entire Bible literally. A notable feature of Jesus' teaching is the use of parables, which obviously *need* to be interpreted. When Jesus tells the story of the Good Samaritan and tells us to do as the Good Samaritan does, he does not mean that if you are a Samaritan and you find a Levite bleeding by the road, then you should do exactly what the Samaritan in his story did. At least it seems obvious that some broader message is intended, one that applies to people other than Samaritans and Levites. But we can then disagree about how broad this message is. Rather than try to develop some questionable and possibly very large set of rules, we might well prefer to say something like "Be like the Samaritan, develop a similar character, behave in the kind of way that he behaved." There are Christian reasons, in other words, for preferring virtue ethics (of a particular, Christian kind) to rule-based ethical theories (although there might be Christian reasons for the opposite preference too).

What would these Christian virtues be? A list can be derived from the Sermon on the Mount. Matthew 5 says

   3 Blessed *are* the poor in spirit: for theirs is the kingdom of heaven.
   4 Blessed *are* they that mourn: for they shall be comforted.
   5 Blessed *are* the meek: for they shall inherit the earth.
   6 Blessed *are* they which do hunger and thirst after righteousness: for they shall be filled.
   7 Blessed *are* the merciful: for they shall obtain mercy.
   8 Blessed *are* the pure in heart: for they shall see God.
   9 Blessed *are* the peacemakers: for they shall be called the children of God.
   10 Blessed *are* they which are persecuted for righteousness' sake: for theirs is the kingdom of heaven.
   11 Blessed are ye, when *men* shall revile you, and persecute *you*, and shall say all manner of evil against you falsely, for my sake.
   12 Rejoice, and be exceeding glad: for great *is* your reward in heaven: for so persecuted they the prophets which were before you.

Christians are also commanded to love God and their neighbors, just as Jews are, and to treat such love as more important than anything else. Thus, "You shall love the Lord God with all your heart, and with all your soul, and with all your mind. This is the first and great commandment" (Matthew 22:37–38) and "So whatever you wish that people would do to you, do so to them" (Matthew 7:12, Luke 6:31). There are very important similarities between these Christian teachings and those of Jews and Muslims. But Christians generally emphasize their differences from Jews, who came before them; and the main difference in ethics is the teaching of Jesus, which seems to put special emphasis on questions of virtue. Such questions are by no means absent from the Jewish tradition, as we have seen; but if Christian ethics are to be at all different from Jewish ethics (and if they are not, then Christians might wonder why Jesus preached at all), then this emphasis is the most obvious difference. Muslims also respect Jesus and his teachings but put more emphasis on the Koran, which contains quite specific rules for behavior, unlike Jesus' more ambiguous sayings and parables.

So, what did Jesus teach? A Christian should, arguably, be meek, hungry for righteousness, merciful, pure in heart, peacemaking, prepared to suffer for his or her faith. Jesus says that those who are thus are blessed. It is also possible, though, that he means that, while such people are blessed, we need not try to emulate them, any more than we would try to become poor in spirit or be persecuted just so that we will be blessed too. Jesus says that he has not come to change the law in any way. What he proceeds to do, therefore, is presumably a matter of correcting common misunderstandings of the law. These corrections themselves could be misunderstood too though, which is another reason for the Christian emphasis on acting in the right spirit, with the right kind of character.

This is not to say, therefore, that true Christians must believe in virtue ethics. It is, rather, an attempt to explain why virtue ethics might appeal to people living in the tradition of Christianity and that virtue ethics is by no means incompatible with Christian teaching. The virtuous can have principles, after all, and respect the law, whether it be handed down by governments or by God.

I have mentioned that Christianity is a tradition. Within it there are many different kinds of thought. It might help us, therefore, to look at some of these different ideas and the thinkers associated with them.

Simone Weil

One of the most interesting of these thinkers is Simone Weil (1909–1943). Some Christian ideas about ethics would be extremely uncongenial to Thrasymachus. Simone Weil, for instance, the great French thinker and ascetic, believed that it made no difference whether God existed or not. Being a Christian is not at all, for her, a matter of seeking or even desiring any reward for oneself. On the contrary, one should desire to have no self at all. Weil believes in putting God and God's creation so much before oneself that one's own will is, as near as possible, extinguished. Jesus taught that a man could have no greater love than to lay down his life for his friends. Weil seems to go even further and to advocate a destruction of the self. By this I do not mean literal suicide but a death of the individual will. This idea is reminiscent of the anti-Christian Arthur Schopenhauer's (1788–1860) beliefs that individual life is either boring or lonely or painful or some combination of the three and utterly meaningless. Schopenhauer believes that the great or only good thing is to become, as we inevitably will, simply part of the living cosmos.[2]

Thrasymachus asks "What's in it for me?" Weil replies that you are nothing and should want to be nothing, a mere object at the mercy of God's magnificent (but not necessarily very nice) will. "The self," she writes in *Gravity and Grace*, "is only the shadow which sin and error cast by stopping the light of God, and I take this shadow for a being."[3] All forms and degrees of egoism are mistaken or even sinful. Taking as far as possible the idea of wanting God's will, not one's own, to be done, Weil comes to reject her own will and in that sense her own self and even to deny its reality. We take the self to be a being, but it is really only a shadow.

Schopenhauer, in emphasizing the horrors of life and the consolation of a fairly nihilistic philosophy, might encourage Thrasymachus to think along similar lines. He too regards the egoistic will as a kind of illusion so that it is not only contrary to right ethics but also unreal. It is not that Weil offers Thrasymachus what he wants—quite the contrary. But Schopenhauer argues that Thrasymachus will best get what he wants—will minimize his suffering, that is to say—if he thinks roughly the way that Weil thinks. The selfishly grasping will is bound to find life unsatisfactory. If it does not get what it wants, then it is unhappy. If it does, then it is either bored, like a spoiled child, or disappointed to find that what it wanted does not, in fact, satisfy. And illness, injury, and death can never be fully avoided. The egoistic self loses everything it values when it dies, so death is an especially terrifying prospect for it. If you love the world, though, while you will not want to leave it, you might at least take comfort in the knowledge that it will continue after your death. The same goes for those who love other people or anything other than themselves. Schopenhauer's ideal person, like Weil's, cares only for things other than him- or herself. In this way, rather like the Stoics (see Chapter 4), they can escape the evils of this world and so, if not acquire great joy, at least minimize their suffering. So there could be, ironically enough, self-interested reasons for rejecting the interests of the self. Whether one can transform one's mind-set or values to this extent just as a result of wanting to do so is a question that remains unanswered, however. But someone desiring conversion, even if for bad reasons, might seek and find it. It does not follow that they *should* do so, but Christianity can have a kind of answer, albeit an indirect one, to the challenge of Thrasymachus.

It is significant that this answer should be indirect. For one thing, it means that Thrasymachus might well reject it since it does not immediately offer him what he wants. This can be regarded as a criticism of Christianity. On the other hand, Christians would be likely to see it as a strength. Thrasymachus, they would say, is wrong, his whole outlook is wrong, so of course the teachings of Jesus will not appeal to such a person. But he could be brought around to a better way of looking at things. Schopenhauer's philosophy might be a suitable halfway house between Thrasymachean cynical egoism and Christian selflessness. Buddhism, which teaches that the root of individual suffering is selfish desire, might also be useful. If Thrasymachus could be brought to something approaching despair, then he might be ripe for Christianity.

Søren Kierkegaard

The Danish philosopher Søren Kierkegaard (1813–1855) might agree with this idea. Kierkegaard presented this world as offering a choice between three kinds of life: the aesthetic life of trying to feel good, the ethical life of trying to do one's moral duty, and the religious life of trying to serve God. Since these aims are not the same, they are potentially incompatible, and this has implications for our evaluation of any kind of life. Thrasymachus will not value the religious life because he seems interested only in an aesthetic life (the opposite of life under anesthetic). He is therefore blind to the value of a religious, or an ethical, life. Similarly, though, the ethical or religious person will be incapable of making any but subjective criticisms of the aesthetic life. If it is ungodly or immoral, the aesthete will say "So what?"—just as the religious person will not be moved by arguments that the religious life is boring or difficult. If it is, so what?

Kierkegaard therefore regarded objective, rational argument about the best way to live to be impossible. We can only evaluate in terms of some goal or goals, and whatever evaluative framework we start from will inevitably bias our judgment one way or another. Thrasymachus cannot be persuaded rationally to be ethical or religious. But he might be persuaded subjectively, as it were, to make a leap into another sphere of value. If his egoistic approach to life fails to satisfy him again and again, then he might give up on it and try something else. He might choose the leap of faith into the religious life, although this life cannot be proved to be correct. Kierkegaard himself seems to have believed that the aesthetic and the ethical lives were recipes for despair; however, there is no proof that this is so, and one can imagine a person dying before ever becoming conscious of a feeling of despair (e.g., a hedonistic aesthete dying young, before the pointless monotony of his rock star lifestyle hits home). The religious life itself might be a waste of time, as far as Kierkegaard claims to know, because we cannot prove that God exists at all, never mind proving that serving God is the best way to live.

So some sort of crisis of confidence might lead Thrasymachus to opt for Christianity, but it is otherwise unlikely to appeal to him at all. Christianity calls for selfless devotion to God and to others, a rejection of egoistic desires. In some Christian thinkers, such as Weil, this is treated as a love of nothingness, a desire to be annihilated. Needless to say, this will not appeal to those who ask "What's in it for me?" They might, of course, be led to ask a different kind of question, especially if they could be persuaded that they are in fact nothing, that they are mere dust or earth. But such persuasion can never be guaranteed to work, even if it is considered desirable.

G. K. Chesterton

Why else might someone become a Christian? There are many reasons, but one more worth looking at here comes from G. K. Chesterton (1874–1936). Chesterton became convinced that there was a God by considering the amazing and very handy reliability of the world. Why, he wondered, should the world exist at all? No reason. Why should it operate according to unchanging laws? No reason. On this, he agrees with Sartre.[4] But whereas Sartre is nauseated by the pointlessness and apparent unreliability of the world, Chesterton is delighted by it all and cannot help believing that some benevolent force is at work behind the scenes, so to speak, making the world run smoothly. After all, as Sartre argues, without God there is no reason at all why the world should be reliable, but it proves itself to be so day after day. Chesterton rejoices and wants to give something back to God in gratitude. Perhaps Thrasymachus could be brought to share this desire, although of course this might not work out and Chesterton has not strictly proved that God must exist. We might just be very lucky (or unlucky, if you take Schopenhauer's view of life).

Alternatively, you might think, luck has nothing to do with it. The world is reliable because of the laws of nature. The sun rises every morning not because of some miracle or dumb luck but because of well-known principles of physics. The problem with this line of argument, though, is that it does not explain why these principles are true in the first place and why they do not change. If you think about it, it seems that laws of physics describe how the world works. They do not tell us *why* it works like that. Even if one law or posited force does tell us this, we can always still ask why that law is true or why that force happens to exist. And for this it seems that there must either be no reason or a reason from outside nature, a supernatural reason or cause. This is where Sartre and Chesterton part company. Sartre believes in no reason and Chesterton, in God.

There is more to Chesterton's philosophy than this. He also argues that Christianity in particular fits life as he has found it to be. It commands what strikes him as right and forbids what strikes him as wrong. Where Chesterton feels torn on an issue, Christianity gives reasons for feeling each of the ways in question (although it will tend ultimately to favor one over the other). It tells us, for instance, to hate the sin but love the sinner. Chesterton feels that this, like all Christian teachings, is right; and he hopes that his readers will feel the same way. This is an entirely subjective valuation of Christianity, however; and you can only judge for yourself whether this argument has any weight for you.

Finally, Chesterton also argues that Christian ethics involves a proper appreciation of the worth of things. Life is something that he regards as immeasurably valuable. Those who commit what he thinks of as the sin of suicide have failed to appreciate this. Thus, he writes as follows:

> Not only is suicide a sin, it is the sin. It is the ultimate and absolute evil, the refusal to take an interest in existence; the refusal to take the oath of loyalty to life. The man who kills a man, kills a man. The man who kills himself, kills all men; as far as he is concerned he wipes out the world. His act is worse (symbolically considered) than any rape or dynamite outrage. For it destroys all buildings: it insults all women. The thief is satisfied with diamonds; but the suicide is not: that is his crime. He cannot be bribed, even by the blazing stones of the Celestial City. The thief compliments the things he steals, if not the owner of them. But the suicide insults everything on earth by not stealing it. He defiles every flower by refusing to live for its sake. There is not a tiny creature in the cosmos at whom his death is not a sneer.[5]

It is important to note that Chesterton is not saying that suicide is actually, all things considered, worse than rape or terrorism. He is speaking of the symbolic aspect of suicide. Nevertheless, he does call it not just a sin but *the* sin. It is, or represents, the ultimate failure to appreciate the great gift of life.

Something similar can be said about sexual promiscuity. Those who truly appreciate the wonders of sex will be quite happy limiting themselves to one partner in life, Chesterton says. Those who are not satisfied lack a mature appreciation of sex. They are like kids in a candy store rather than connoisseurs who never tire of their beloved Michelangelo sculpture or Picasso painting. It might seem that not every person is the equivalent of a Michelangelo, but to think this way, Chesterton believes, is to show a lack of appreciation for the wonders of each human being. Again, you must judge for yourself; but if Chesterton is right, then there might be something objectively wrong with Thrasymachus' skepticism. He might be missing out on a full enjoyment of life's pleasures by refusing the focused, limited gratification that Christian ethics commends.

But all this is very subjective, as I have emphasized and as Chesterton and Kierkegaard would freely admit. Schopenhauer and Weil have in common a kind of radical altruism. Egoism is rejected utterly by them, and a desire for the nullification of the individual will is embraced. For Christians of this kind, what is instead elevated and longed for is the will of God, or indeed of almost any other (one's neighbor, say, or the world in general). How possible this view is, either logically or psychologically, is an interesting question. It can seem that it must be possible to will the good, as we will see in more detail in Chapter 7. And if the good must be willable, then it is doubtful whether it even makes sense to define or identify the good as the utter denial of one's own will. God's will, or what God wills, can be willed, of course (assuming that God exists). But if what I call good must be something that I can will, then can my own destruction, or my own will's annihilation, be good? It is reasonable to wonder whether it makes sense to say that I could will the destruction of my will. Certainly, it would be psychologically difficult to achieve such a state.

Chesterton is more positive. He celebrates not the individual will but the will of the universe and specifically the will of all humankind, past and present. This is similar to Aristotle's identification of the virtuous individual will with the will of that individual's city-state, but Chesterton expands the scope of the relevant community about as generously as is possible. Perhaps this is not so different from Weil's view, but it has a different flavor to it; also, Chesterton's optimism is the very opposite of Schopenhauer's pessimism (although the latter is fueled with such relish that it almost seems to undercut or contradict itself).

Miracles

One way to make religious belief a less subjective affair, less dependent on what flavor we prefer, might be to prove that God exists. If we could do that, then God's existence would not be a matter of faith but of knowledge. (That in itself is a reason not to look for, or to expect to find, such a proof, according to some believers. Religion must be subjective, must require faith and personal commitment, if it is to retain its unique character. Or so people like Kierkegaard think.) Nevertheless, the faithful often do try to prove that God exists. One popular way is by appealing to miracles. If miracles occur, then surely there must be a God behind them? The most famous argument against this idea comes from David Hume (1711–1776).

Hume defines a miracle as an event caused by God or some other supernatural agent that breaks a law of nature. He does not, therefore, count the birth of a child as a miracle or the rising of the sun or the creation of the universe. His definition might be questioned by believers because of this, but he has in mind such well-known alleged miracles as Jesus' turning water into wine and Moses' parting of the Red Sea. Hume does not deny that such events might have occurred.

What he denies is that we should believe that they did. After all, he says, we ought to base our beliefs on the balance of the evidence.

What evidence is there that the Red Sea ever parted so that people could walk across the sea bed without getting wet? A story in a book, written long ago. In other words, we have the testimony of witnesses but not witnesses we know personally to be reliable people and not witnesses who are around now to be interrogated about the incident. It is possible that whoever wrote this part of the Bible made a mistake, exaggerated, made the whole thing up, or sincerely believed the testimony of someone else who was exaggerating, making it up, or honestly mistaken. In other words, from the point of view of a neutral reader of the Bible, there is a distinct possibility that any given story in the book is not in fact true.

What evidence do we have that the Red Sea did not part like this? Well, look at the Red Sea now. It is not parted and is not seemingly capable of being parted. For that matter, look at any other body of water, large or small, that you care to examine. It will not part. Countless human experiences of water have shown that it does not part like that. There are very well-established laws describing the behavior of water, and spontaneous, large-scale parting is not remotely consistent with these laws. So there is massive evidence against any claim that the Red Sea once parted.

This is a slightly odd argument coming from Hume though. He is famous for arguing that there is no reason to expect nature to behave in a uniform manner. Sure enough, it does. The sun did rise this morning, as it does every day, and no sea parted today, just as no sea parted yesterday. But there is no contradiction in the idea of a sea parting. No contradiction, that is, of anything but a law of nature. But these laws, according to Hume, are really only descriptions of observed regularities. Observed cases tell us nothing about unobserved ones. And we were not there to observe whether the Red Sea parted on that fateful day or not. Hume's argument about laws of nature is that it is an interesting feature of human psychology that when we observe a certain phenomenon happening time and again we naturally expect it to be that way every time. In fact, we feel that it *must* happen that way every time. But since logic does not say that it must be that way (there is no *logical* impossibility in water turning to wine, no contradiction in the very idea of this happening) and since experience cannot tell us anything about events that we do not experience and since logic and experience are our only guides to the truth, whatever we might *feel*, it is not strictly rational for us to believe in laws of nature, or the necessity of their being universal in time and space. So, according to Hume's psychology, a normal person who knows a little about science *will not* believe the biblical story about the parting of the Red Sea (without some other influence, such as an experience or cultural climate that inclines him or her to believe the Bible, of course). But it does not follow from this part of his theory that people *should not* believe this story. And, of course, many people do believe it.

Now, Hume might point out that there is something strange about believing that there are laws of nature (as there must be if God is going to break them) and that these are broken from time to time. Why believe in them in the first place except on the basis of experience? And if we do go by experience, then why believe stories of miracles? And, he might go on, who is supposed by these stories to have broken the laws of nature? Why, their allegedly perfect creator! How perfect is that? If the laws were perfect, they surely would not need to be broken. This makes either God's original creation of the laws of nature or else his later violation of them seem to be imperfect. So there is something strange about belief in miracles; however, Hume does not claim to have proved that they never occur, and he accepts that belief in them is a matter of faith. What he does not accept is that it can ever be wise to believe in a *particular* miracle. It is always more likely, he says, that the witnesses are deceived or are deceiving you than that their testimony is 100% correct. This is true, he thinks, even if the witness is you yourself. The odds against a miracle are as great as they can be. The odds against your making a mistake or hallucinating or whatever are always going to be less than that. Hence, if you are rational, you will believe in no miracles.

There are a few more points worth making about miracles. One is that even if the Red Sea did part, this proves nothing about what caused it to part. The cause might have been something entirely natural: a tsunami, a natural phenomenon unknown to us, alien beings with advanced technology, or what have you. Even if it was supernatural, it might have been good, evil, or morally indifferent. And even if it was good, there would still be the question of whether it would be good for us to obey that being and, if so, what that would entail and why. That is, even if we somehow knew that a good, supernatural being caused a miracle to happen, could we also be sure that we ought to do whatever it told us to do? If so, how would we know what it commanded? Should we read the Koran or the Talmud or the Bible or something else? Whether we should believe in miracles or not really seems to tell us very little about how we should live our lives.

The Problem of Evil

The main way that people try to disprove God's existence, apart from shooting down alleged proofs of his existence and claiming that one should never believe without proof, is to point to the bad things that happen in the world. If God is all-knowing, all-powerful, and all-good, they say, then why do bad things happen to good people? Why doesn't God intervene? This question becomes especially pressing whenever a natural disaster occurs, such as the tsunami that hit parts of Asia on December 26, 2004.

Various responses were made to that horrific event. Most common were feelings of sympathy and the desire to help somehow, but others were less charitable. Some people said that the victims were not good people after all but, rather, sinners who deserved what happened to them. This kind of claim can be made in two ways. The first is to claim that the victims were unusually bad people. This is not plausible when we think of the children who died and compare them with the worst people we can think of who were not affected at all. God should surely have better aim than this. The other claim of this kind is that all people are sinful and so deserve death. This makes one wonder, though, why God spares some and not others. How could the selection not be arbitrary and, hence, unfair?

Another kind of answer is that bad things do not happen at all, only seemingly bad things. The innocent victims of the tsunami, we might say, are in heaven now (or will be eventually), and the tragedy brought out a lot of good in other people. The world will be a better place in the long run because of this apparent disaster. So some people argue.

But this kind of argument can seem horribly insensitive to the suffering of the victims. In his novel *The Brothers Karamazov,* in the chapter called "Rebellion," Fyodor Dostoevsky brings out how terrible it is to say that the painful and terrifying death of a small child could be justified by *any* greater good that it helps to bring about. Think of a small child dying cold, alone, and frightened, and think of this as *intended* by God. Perhaps in some way that we cannot understand this kind of suffering will be made good eventually, but surely nobody with a heart would ever think so. Or so the character Ivan Karamazov argues, quite plausibly. What kind of divine plan could require such cruelty? There is also the problem of how we could ever measure good and evil in order to reach a conclusion about whether the total amount of good produced outweighed the total amount of evil. Who has such scales?

We might also consider two references to the damage that the sea can do, written by religious authors long before this particular event. The English poet Sir John Betjeman (1906–1984) wrote of the sea as "consolingly disastrous" in his poem "By the Seaside." How could disaster be consoling? Weil might have the answer. In *Waiting for God,* she wrote as follows:

> The mechanism of necessity can be transposed to any level while still remaining true to itself. It is the same in the world of pure matter, in the animal world, among nations, and in souls. Seen from our present standpoint, and in human perspective, it is quite blind. If, however, we transport our hearts beyond ourselves, beyond the universe, beyond space and time to where our Father dwells, and if from there we behold this mechanism, it appears quite different. What seemed to be necessity becomes obedience. Matter is entirely passive and in consequence entirely obedient to God's will. It is a perfect model for us. . . . The beauty of the world gives us an intimation of its claim to a place in our heart. In the beauty of the world brute necessity becomes an object of love. What is more beautiful than the action of gravity on the fugitive folds of the sea waves, or on the almost eternal folds of the mountains?
>
> The sea is not less beautiful in our eyes because we know that sometimes ships are wrecked by it. On the contrary, this adds to its beauty. If it altered the movement of its waves to spare a boat, it would be a creature gifted with discernment and choice and not this fluid, perfectly obedient to every external pressure. It is this perfect obedience that constitutes the sea's beauty. . . . All the horrors produced in this world are like the folds imposed upon the waves by gravity. That is why they contain an element of beauty.[6]

The idea that Weil and Betjeman seem to share is that not human will but God's will should be done. It is good, beautiful, and consoling when this is what happens. And it is what we see when we look at nature, even including natural disasters. If nature were one big disaster, we might not be able to feel this way; but it is not. Tragedy is not the whole of life; but it is part of it, and life is richer for it. We might be blind to this fact if we take a narrowly selfish, or human-centered, view of things; but if we take a more God's-eye point of view, then we will see that it is true. I will leave you to decide whether it is possible for us to have this kind of perspective on things and whether doing so involves the kind of heartlessness that concerned Dostoevsky.

Finally, it is worth noting that not all believers claim to be able to explain suffering away. The archbishop of Canterbury, Rowan Williams, said that the tsunami shook his faith and that he could not explain why God would allow such a thing. But his faith was not destroyed by this shaking because it was, he said, based on a different source. If you believe in God just because you think nothing very bad ever happens, then a terrible event like the tsunami or the Holocaust might undermine your faith completely; but if you believe for other reasons, then those reasons might continue to outweigh the reasons that make you doubt. Williams seemed to say that his faith came from a particular kind of experience of the world, that his life convinced him that God is real. If your life convinces you of this, then no philosophical argument is likely to change your mind. But, of course, your life might not have this character, especially if you have been directly affected by a natural disaster.

It is very hard, if not impossible, in other words, to talk generally about the character of life or the nature of the world. Some things are good and some things are bad. Every word in the dictionary has a use. And new words are invented all the time. There is no limit to what we might want to say about life or the world. If you are inclined to say good things, then perhaps you are more likely to believe in God. If not, you are more likely to find it impossible to believe that everything is ruled by a benevolent parent. (Of course, you could still be religious. Buddhists, for instance, do not believe in a personal God like the one described in the Bible and the Koran.)

Another alternative is that you might be impressed by the very richness, the variety of life. The combination of good and bad, comic and tragic, might impress you as it did Weil and Betjeman. You might find yourself in awe of the world or of life and unable to pick any particular word or set of words from the dictionary to describe your view because it is precisely the fact that they can all apply that impresses you. Clichés about life's rich pageant don't capture what you want to say. But if words cannot express what you mean, then you will not be able to say anything about it. In the end, you will have to judge for yourself whether life is good, bad, inexpressibly wonderful, unspeakably awful, or somewhere in between. You might also want to decide whether you think the most relevant virtue in making a judgment like this is honesty or something else, such as avoiding cynicism or simply the prudential consideration of what will most help you get through life happily.

The *Euthyphro* Problem

In the next chapter, we will look at a Christian thinker who is especially popular with Catholics, St. Thomas Aquinas. In doing so, I will assume that we have not so far proved that there is any reason to be Christian or religious or good. Before that, however, let us ask one more important question about the relation between ethics and religion. Assuming for the moment that God exists, we can still ask why we should obey God (or the gods)? This is a question as old as Plato's dialogue the *Euthyphro*. In this dialogue, the question is raised whether good things are good because the gods say so or for some other reason. If the former, then we might well wonder why the gods say that these things are good and those are bad. If murder, for instance, is only bad because God says so, then what reason can he possibly have had for saying it is bad? God's commandments look arbitrary rather than good. We might still obey God prudentially, out of fear perhaps, but not because his commandments are wise.

On the other hand, if good things are good and evil things are evil for some reason other than God's say-so, then the fact that God has made certain commandments would actually be irrelevant to the ethical question of what we should do. It might be wise to do as God says not just out of fear of hell or desire for heavenly reward but also because God is thought to know best. But his knowledge or teaching of good and evil would not itself be what made anything good or evil. Even if he did not exist, those things would still, presumably, be good and evil. So the problem is this: if "good" means something like "commanded by God" and "evil" means something like "forbidden by God," then God's commandments look arbitrary and it is hard to see what *ethical* reason we could have for doing good and shunning evil. If, on the other hand, "good" and "evil" mean something else, then whether God exists at all seems to be irrelevant to what is good and evil and we are left with the unanswered question "What, if anything, is the meaning of 'good' and 'evil'?" God might then reveal knowledge about ethics to us, but he would be little more than a messenger.

For believers in God, this appears to be quite a problem. If God's commandments are arbitrary, then we cannot really call them good in any meaningful way. We can choose to define the word "good" as whatever God commands or whatever is godly, but if we define it this way, then it makes little sense to admire or praise God for being good. He is simply good by definition. If good acts are simply those that God commands, then his commandments can, it seems, have no basis in what really is good or bad since until he makes these commandments, the things he commands are not good or bad at all. This arbitrariness hardly seems wise, rational, or, to some people, god-like.

The alternative is that God's commandments are not arbitrary and are indeed wise. But this depends on the idea that God knows what is good and what is evil, or what is right and what is wrong, and commands accordingly. His commandments, that is to say, do not create right and wrong but instead reflect a preexisting moral order that must therefore be independent of those commandments themselves. God is not then the creator of the moral law, in the way that a king might make a law, but more like a good lawyer who gives reliable advice as to what is legal and what is not. This does not seem very god-like either, and it means that God's existence is unnecessary for the existence of a moral law and possibly for the successful following of such a law. One can have the sense that God is pushed out of the center of the picture, and maybe even all the way out of the picture, by this alternative.

One kind of belief involved in what is sometimes called the "*Euthyphro* problem" is the divine command theory. This theory ignores, or even embraces, the apparent arbitrariness of God's commandments and insists that, indeed, good is what God tells us to do and evil is what he tells us not to do. This might seem to make God arbitrary and to make an empty tautology out of the claim that God is good, but so be it. It is not for us to judge God, and we cannot hope to understand why he does what he does; thus it hardly matters that his commandments *seem* arbitrary to us. Some would say that we should have faith and do as we are told.

Why Be Good?

Now, what would Thrasymachus make of all this? He certainly would not accept that we should unquestioningly obey a seemingly arbitrary God. What other reason does Jesus give for being good? The primary reason is out of respect for God. God is presented in the Bible as a loving creator, a sort of father figure, who both deserves and is likely to get our affection as a consequence. He is also presented as a lord or master, a being superior to us not in this way or that but just in general and one that must be served and obeyed accordingly. The idea seems at times to be that God is much more powerful than we are and should be obeyed merely prudentially or else we will end up in a fiery pit or something of the sort. Thrasymachus might respond positively to such a line of reasoning, which is perhaps why it is there, if only he could be convinced that God, heaven, and hell are real.

But at times the idea can also, or instead, seem to be that it is part of the natural order that some beings are above others, as a monarch was once believed to be above the peasantry or as human beings are usually thought to be above worms, and that we should recognize this superiority of God's over us and act accordingly. It is not so much, in other words, that we should obey God out of fear or the desire for a reward in heaven, although the fear of God might be the *beginning* of wisdom, but that obedience to God is simply right. This is a similar idea to the one we find in Aristotle, that certain things are right because they are natural in a sense that is meant to be both descriptive (describing the nature of reality) and prescriptive (recommending a certain course of action). Thrasymachus would have none of this, of course.

One popular but not very sophisticated understanding of the ethics of all three major Western religions (Judaism, Christianity, and Islam) is that God is an enormously powerful being who can, and will, reward us greatly if we do as he says and torture us horribly if we do not. So we had better do as he says. Unfortunately, heaven is quite hard to imagine, except as a rather dull place in which people sit around on clouds listening to harp music. Listening to harps is not a popular pastime on earth, so it has little appeal. On the other hand, we know all too well about being burned, stabbed, and so on, so the usual portrayals of hell are easy to relate to. The fear of hell is doubtless a powerful motivator for many who believe in it and even for those who believe it is merely a possibility, perhaps even quite a remote one. When the cost of losing is as bad as eternal torture, there is a strong incentive to play safe and obey God's rules as best you can.

Objections

Thrasymachus might be moved by the threat of hell and the promise of heavenly rewards, especially if he could be convinced that he does not actually have to do any good deeds but must simply accept Jesus Christ as his personal savior. This, though, is not how the main Christian churches officially view the matter. Most Muslims and Jews would agree with the Christians on this too. If we only obey the rules because we have been coerced by threats, then do we deserve any credit for doing so? A concern with one's own skin is not properly religious. Instead, one is supposed to love God and one's neighbor. So perhaps acting out of a fear of hell might be one way to ensure that your soul ends up just there. One needs to do things for others and to deny the self in accordance with God's laws (though not necessarily any more than this—self-denial is not usually considered good in itself) in order to do the right thing. This alone, however, might not be enough. There is still the question of why you are doing these things, of where your heart lies. Are you motivated by love of others or of God or by a desire to obey God regardless of what might be in it for yourself? That is the question. So the key is to have the right kind of motivation.

Some people believe that you can influence this yourself. For instance, you might decide to work for Habitat for Humanity, building houses for people who cannot afford to buy one through the usual channels. At first, this work might be unpleasant to you, and your motivation might be solely the terrifying thought of a possible waking nightmare at the hands of scaly demons after you die. But after a while, perhaps, you start to get good at building, you take pride in and gain satisfaction from your work. You might, more to the point, also come to know the people who will be living in the house. You might start to like them, or at least the idea of their having a home of their own. You might start to feel good about what you are doing and thus come to do it for its own sake or for the sake of others. You have now, some people think, become a better person and made progress on the way to heaven. Of course, there are no guarantees, but something like this might happen.

So one way to get to heaven, or to put yourself on the road to it at least, might be to put yourself in the kind of situation that might lead to a change in your heart. You might also work on your attitude yourself. It is possible to try to see the good side of someone and to make an effort to be friendlier toward him or her. So it seems that it ought to be possible to do this generally, looking for the best in everyone, attributing good motives to their actions, smiling at them, and so on. Of course, this might be nothing more than an act that you cannot sustain with any sincerity. But it might work, especially if the interpretation of others as good is at least as successful at predicting or explaining their actions as are more cynical interpretations. It might help also to pay attention to your own faults so that when other people go wrong you realize that this does not make them all that different from you.

However, as I have noted, all this depends partly on luck. You just might be incurably cynical, or the people around you might really have very little good in them to be found, their good sides might be negligible, and you might just not like helping other people at all. If Aristotle is right, then whether you do will depend largely on how you were raised and on what the people around you are like. These things are really beyond your control. We might wonder, then, whether some people are just stuck on the highway to hell with no possible way of getting off it.

But that would be to forget about God's power. If there is a hell at all, then presumably there is a God too who created it and decides who winds up there. (There is no logical reason why this must be. There could, perhaps, be a life after death that was absolutely hellish without there being any lord or father that created it and that might save us from it, a hell unlinked to any question of justice or desert. But nobody believes that this is the case, and all we can do is hope that it is not.) So God might get us on the right road.

Indeed, many Christians believe that *only* God can do this. Divine justice, they argue, is not a system that we can manipulate or a game that we can play. It is all in God's hands. So I cannot save my soul by doing good deeds or thinking good thoughts. Only God, so the argument goes, can save it or damn it. Indeed, many Christians believe that God makes these decisions in advance since he does not need to wait and see how we behave before deciding what we deserve. What we all deserve is death because we all sin. But in his goodness, God decides to spare some undeserving souls and give them the joys of heaven instead.

Those who believe this cite such biblical passages as Romans 8:29–30, in which St. Paul writes as follows:

> For those God foreknew he also predestined to be conformed to the likeness of his Son. . . . And those he predestined, he also called; those he called, he also justified; those he justified, he also glorified.

Now, the Bible is notoriously open to interpretation, as we have mentioned; but this passage seems to be saying that God knows in advance who will have the faith that makes us right with God despite our sins and who will not. Those on the "not" list are presumably bound for hell. This might not seem very fair, but it is how God operates, or so Paul seems to believe.

He is not alone. St. Augustine (354–430) believes that virtue is the perfect love of God and that having such love is not completely within our control. We need, he thinks, some help from God in order to rise above our sinful nature. Similarly, the former Augustinian monk who founded Protestantism, Martin Luther, described faith as "God's work within us" and hence as something beyond our control.[7] Those who have this faith "cannot help doing good works constantly"[8] (so there is an important connection between faith and works—it is not as if unreformed rapists and murderers are going to go to heaven). If this is true, then Thrasymachus' question seems to be irrelevant. We cannot really choose what we do or whether we are good or bad. Others believe that we do have the freedom or power to accept or reject God's gift of grace. If an eternity in either heaven or hell is what faces your immortal soul, then it is pretty obvious what you should choose to do if offered such a gift. But again, we seem to be back to the kind of self-interested reasoning that many religious believers want to get away from.

Conclusion

It is hard to know whether God exists at all, let alone which religion has the truth about God's nature and commandments. Even if we are sure that God does exist, though, it does not follow that this makes a big difference as far as ethics goes. Perhaps God is only necessary for ethics as a source of knowledge about what is right and wrong. If so, we still have the problem of which alleged revelations to believe. Thrasymachus is not going to believe any particular such claim. To answer him, then, we need to move on. In the next chapter, we will consider another kind of response to the *Euthyphro* and some of the best-known attempts to prove that there really is a God.

Questions for Further Thought

1. If religious believers must love God more than they love themselves, can heaven and hell motivate them at all? If not, what purpose might heaven and hell serve?

2. Is religion more about love (of God or one's neighbor) or about doing certain deeds? Or something else?

3. Does evil disprove God's existence?

4. Does evil make it indecent or disrespectful of its victims to believe in God?

5. Can the *Euthyphro* problem be solved?

Notes

1. All biblical quotes are taken from the King James version.
2. Indeed, it might be the influence of Schopenhauer on the philosopher Ludwig Wittgenstein that has led some commentators to read Weil as a kindred spirit of Wittgenstein's.

3. Simone Weil, *Gravity and Grace*, trans. Emma Crawford and Mario von der Ruhr (London: Routledge, 2002), 40.

4. See Chapter 2.

5. G. K. Chesterton, *Orthodoxy* (San Francisco: Ignatius Press, 1995), 78.

6. Simone Weil, *Waiting for God* (New York: Perennial Classics, 2001), 76.

7. "An Introduction to St. Paul's Letter to the Romans," Luther's German Bible of 1522 by Martin Luther, 1483–1546, trans. Rev. Robert E. Smith from Johann K. Irmischer, ed. *Dr. Martin Luther's Vermischte Deutsche Schriften*, Vol. 63 (Erlangen: Heyder and Zimmer, 1854), 124.

8. Ibid.

Suggestions for Further Reading

A good place to learn more about Jewish ethics is Louis E. Newman, *An Introduction to Jewish Ethics*, (Englewood Cliffs, NJ: Prentice Hall, 2004). For Islamic ethics, try starting with Jonathan E. Brockopp, ed., *Islamic Ethics of Life: Abortion, War, and Euthanasia* (Columbia: University of South Carolina Press, 2003). This book focuses on the specific issues listed in the subtitle, but the first chapter gives a more general introduction to ethics from a Muslim point of view. For more on Christian ethics, I recommend Robin Gills, ed., *The Cambridge Companion to Christian Ethics* (Cambridge: Cambridge University Press, 2005.)

If you want to read more of Simone Weil's thoughts, I suggest her books *Gravity and Grace*, translated by Emma Crawford and Mario von der Ruhr, (London: Routledge, 2002), and *Waiting for God*, (New York: Harper Perennial Modern Classics, 2001). A nice introduction to Schopenhauer's philosophy is Christopher Janaway, *Schopenhauer: A Very Short Introduction* (Oxford: Oxford University Press, 2002).

An anthology of Kierkegaard's writings that emphasizes his Christianity is W. H. Auden, ed., *The Living Thoughts of Kierkegaard* (New York: New York Review Books, 1999). Beware, though, of any anthology of works by Kierkegaard since he is known for his irony and selections taken out of context can be extremely misleading. Another good way into his thought is *The Present Age*, introduced by Walter Kaufmann (New York: Harper Torchbooks, 1962).

Chesterton's classic is *Orthodoxy* (San Francisco: Ignatius Press, 1995).

Two books worth reading on Hume's argument against belief in miracles are John Earman, *Hume's Abject Failure: The Argument against Miracles* (Oxford: Oxford University Press, 2006), and Robert J. Fogelin, *A Defense of Hume on Miracles* (Princeton: Princeton University Press, 2005).

On the problem of evil, see Mark J. Larrimore, ed., *The Problem of Evil: A Reader* (Oxford: Blackwell, 2000).

Finally, it seems relevant to mention Michael Martin, ed., *The Cambridge Companion to Atheism* (Cambridge: Cambridge University Press, 2006).

CHAPTER 4

Aquinas

One of the problems faced by virtue theorists such as Plato and Aristotle is explaining exactly which traits are virtues, which are vices, and which are neither. Aristotle's aristocratic, pagan ideals were not those taught by the Bible. Later Christian thinkers, such as St. Thomas Aquinas (1225–1274), were bound to disagree with at least some elements of Aristotle's theory. Aquinas was a great admirer of Aristotle's work, but it was inevitable that the ethical theory of Aquinas—a Christian so devout that even being kidnapped, imprisoned, and faced with extreme sexual temptation could not keep him from joining the monastic order of his choice—would deviate somewhat from Aristotle's theory.[1]

For instance, Aristotle considered magnanimity to be a virtue. Today, "magnanimity" means being generous or big-hearted, so this does indeed sound like a virtue. But to Aristotle, being magnanimous meant bearing oneself in a god-like or kingly way. The magnanimous person will "have slow movements, a deep voice, and calm speech," rather like the actor James Earl Jones.[2] He (surely Aristotle has only men in mind when he thinks of this virtue) will seem arrogant to others, has fine possessions, and will seek to impress people of reputation but not others (because that would be too easy for him). Aristotelian magnanimity is the virtue, roughly speaking, of being truly impressive. We can, I think, see what Aristotle is getting at. He lived in an aristocratic society and shared most of the values of his culture. We might understand what it means to value kingly behavior, but bearing oneself in this kind of impressive way is not a characteristic that many modern people would immediately think of when asked to list the virtues. For one thing, it sounds a little too close to pomposity to be an undeniably good trait. For another, it seems more like a collection of different traits that might or might not be found together than a single characteristic. So we have to ask ourselves what characteristics are to count as virtues and how we can tell. Christian virtues, for instance, which include humility, are not the same as pagan virtues, which include pride, and modern virtues are not necessarily the same as those in ancient or medieval times.

Stoicism and Christianity

Part of the reason for the difference between Christian conceptions of virtue and Aristotle's conception is the influence of what Friedrich Nietzsche (see Chapter 9) called "slave moralities." Stoic philosophers, such as Epictetus, who was literally a slave, argued that Aristotle's ideal person was too rounded, valuing too many diverse things. Aristotle valued not only moral virtues such as courage and justice but also "intellectual virtues" such as the ability to understand, "goods of the body" such as health and good looks, and "external goods" such as friends and money. To Stoics, only moral virtue mattered. They agreed with Aristotle that it was important to live in harmony with nature and that developing a good character was essential to this project. But they thought that he was wrong to see any value at all in pleasure, in close relationships with others, or in mere contemplation. Aristotle's ideal was a life of pleasant philosophizing and noble public service. The Stoic ideal was a life of endurance in which one grins (but does not really laugh) and bears what life dumps on one's plate. Thus, Epictetus writes in his *Enchiridion*, "Do not seek to have events happen as you want them to, but instead want them to happen as they do happen, and your life will go well."[3]

This is an understandable view for a slave like Epictetus, whose owner was a sadist who tortured him for fun, or a troubled emperor like Marcus Aurelius, whose empire was under threat (see the opening scenes of *Gladiator*) and whose wife was reported to be unfaithful to him while he was off battling the barbarians. But it has little real appeal for most of us today, except as how we often like our movie heroes to be (see *Gladiator* again or almost any movie starring Clint Eastwood). The ultimate Stoic would seem to be a kind of cheerful (but not too cheerful) victim and probably would not be truly magnanimous in Aristotle's sense.

The most important "slave morality" of all, though, at least for Nietzsche, is that of Christianity. Christians believe that it is virtuous to be humble and meek. Judging by Jesus' Sermon on the Mount, it seems that it is good ("blessed") to be poor in spirit, mourning, meek, and persecuted for the sake of righteousness. Even deserved self-esteem is no part of the traditional Christian ideal. God alone is worthy of our esteem. The self is as nothing.

In the thirteenth century, St. Thomas Aquinas produced a kind of Christianized version of Aristotle's ethics. The basic structure of Aristotle's theory remained, but the list of virtues changed. Aquinas can be regarded as improving on Aristotle's ethics by showing that a good life consists of more than just philosophical contemplation, or any single thing for that matter. Instead, he recognizes as basic goods such things as existence, having children, the education of these children, knowledge, sociable living, reasonableness in one's choices and actions, and so on.[4] Another important change was that God was made even more important than he had been in Aristotle's version of the theory. According to Aristotle, God exists and should be imitated as far as possible, but nature is also important. Moreover, as he sees it, nature was not created by God because not even God can create something from nothing, so nature must always have existed. According to Aquinas, God created nature and this is the reason we should try to live in accordance with it. Saying that we should obey the "law of nature" is just another way of saying that we should obey God. Or, more precisely, natural law is not identical with, but depends on, a more fundamental eternal law, which is the same thing as divine providence. God is behind or beneath it all.

Natural Law Theory

Aquinas' natural law theory is generally considered to be an improvement on the divine command theory's recommendation that we follow apparently arbitrary rules of conduct. After all, if you are going just to have faith and follow a seemingly random code, why put your faith in God and his (alleged) code and not, say, Hitler and his or Lenin and his or any arbitrarily chosen cult leader? Aquinas suggests that only one kind of life is best for human beings and that this kind of life accords not with some otherwise unjustified set of commands but with nature itself, including our own human nature. Most important of all, for Aquinas, is God's nature. Since God is perfect, Aquinas argues, his nature is perfect. And so, of course, his moral commands are perfect too. They are not arbitrary, that is to say. Instead, they flow from God's perfect nature. They are exactly the kind of commands that you would expect to come from such a being. They are good commands.

This argument depends on there being two senses of the word "good." The problem of arbitrariness arises if we think only of moral goodness, or goodness in the moral sense, and then claim that good is whatever God commands. Aquinas, though, believes that there is another kind of goodness or sense of the word "good." We might call this "metaphysical goodness" as it is a kind of goodness that pertains to one's nature as a being, rather than having to do with obedience to the moral law. The idea, then, is that moral goodness is obedience to God's law, whatever it might be, but that this law is not therefore neither good nor bad since it is the product of a perfectly good being (in the metaphysical sense). God will not command just any old thing because he is not only non-arbitrary but rational and wise, perfectly so in fact.

The problem now is what to make of this new idea of metaphysical goodness. It sounds at least somewhat plausible, and, as we shall see, it offers a way out of the *Euthyphro* dilemma (does God *make* good things good simply by commanding them, or are they *already* good, independent of his commands?). But will it hold up to criticism? One appealing thing about the idea is that it does match other ideas that we have. For instance, God is generally thought of as an all-perfect being (regardless of whether you think such a being exists), and this is not usually taken to mean only that he is morally perfect. He is also, in the traditional conception, in possession of all qualities that it is good to have and to the utmost possible degree. This is what the French philosopher René Descartes (1596–1650) had in mind when he defined God as an all-perfect being, a being that possesses all perfections. God is therefore, by this definition, not only all good but also all-knowing and all-powerful. It is, Descartes assumes, good to be knowledgeable and powerful, even though we do not usually think of these as moral qualities. So the idea of a nonmoral sense of goodness does seem to make sense. This might not be enough though.

If God is good in nonmoral ways, does it follow that his commandments will be morally good? Apparently not. A powerful being will not necessarily make good laws, for instance. Being all-knowing might seem to be advantageous in this connection but only if there can be knowledge of or pertaining to right and wrong or good and evil prior to God's making his commandments. In other words, God's omniscience will only help him make a wise moral law if what is morally good is not completely determined by what God commands. If *whatever* God commands is going to be good, just by *definition*, then he does not need to be omniscient to make good commands. In fact, his omniscience would be irrelevant to the goodness of his commands. It would only be relevant if there were some goodness independent of his commands that he could know about, in which case we are back to pushing God out of the picture and into the role of legal adviser. If nonmoral goodness really can be distinguished from moral goodness, as Aquinas' position requires, then it seems that it cannot really help us out of the *Euthyphro* dilemma.

An alternative view would be that senses of goodness cannot be distinguished in this kind of way, that power and knowledge are good for precisely the same reason that, say, honesty is good—namely, that they help us to live good lives, happy lives, fulfilled lives. But this kind of Aristotelian idea leaves little room for God's commandments having a central place. Aristotle's ethics are based on a certain understanding of nature, and of human nature in particular. Whether God exists at all is almost irrelevant from his point of view. We certainly do not need God's word to know what is natural or fulfilling for human beings. Or so Aristotle thought, and so seems to be the case. We might, of course, need God's revelation to know what is good or right but only if this is something other than what is most natural or fulfilling for us, in which case the whole question of what it means to say that something is good comes up again and with it the *Euthyphro* dilemma.

We should not simply abandon Aquinas' ethical theory at this point however. Natural law theory does not have to refer to God at all. Indeed, a leading contemporary natural law theorist, John Finnis, used this aspect of the theory to argue in court that laws opposing homosexuality need not have a religious basis and so do not violate the separation of church and state.[5] So we should now consider what it might mean to say that the virtues are determined by nature.

What Is Natural?

What does basing ethics on nature mean in practice? Well, for one thing, it means that life itself, or human life at least, is taken to be valuable. All things in nature strive to stay alive, and we are no different. It is therefore unnatural to choose death for oneself or for others. Suicide, assisted suicide, euthanasia, abortion, and murder are all therefore wrong. Not all killing of other human beings is necessarily wrong though. Self-defense is natural and good and might require the use of force. If this force is so great that one's attacker dies as a result, this is morally acceptable as long as his or her death was not your goal (but the byproduct of an act of self-preservation), the force you used was no more than was necessary to secure this end, and the result produced more good than bad (e.g., you did not destroy a whole building full of people just to stop the one person who was trying to kill you). Similarly, Aquinas would hold that abortion (the deliberate killing of a fetus) is wrong but that it could be all right to save a pregnant woman's life by removing her diseased womb, thereby causing the death of her unborn child. It is important in such cases, though, that the deaths of innocent individuals, born or unborn, should not be intended either as a means or as an end. So abortion itself is not justified, even if the pregnant woman will die without it, according to Aquinas' argument. This line of reasoning can also be used to justify some wars (in defense of innocent nations under attack) and some collateral damage in war. It is known as the "doctrine of double effect" because the good, intended effect (saving one's life, say) is distinguished from the bad, unintended effect (e.g., the death of one's assailant).[6]

Aquinas' ideas about what is natural with regard to matters of life and death should be quite familiar. They have become fairly standard among Christians, especially Catholics. Perhaps equally familiar are natural law teachings on sexual ethics. The orthodox view here is that sex is a gift from God for the purpose of reproduction. It does not follow that all sex for any other reason is wrong however. It is only wrong if it goes against God's will. The Catholic view of sex is that it is all right as long as it is carried out in a way that could—not in your particular case, necessarily, but generally—lead to reproduction. In other words, sex for fun is acceptable, within marriage, as long as nothing is done to prevent pregnancy and as long as it is of the kind that could lead to pregnancy.

What is not acceptable then? Masturbation, contraception, anal sex, and oral sex. If you happen to know that pregnancy cannot occur because of the time of the month or a narrow urethra or any other natural reason, then you are free, with your consenting spouse, to engage in vaginal sex. You do not, that is to say, have to be trying to make a baby in order to have the kind of sex that is acceptable to the Catholic Church. What you do have to be doing is having the kind of sex that could make a baby and in the context of a marriage so that if a baby should result, it will have two parents to look after it and each other. Nor should one's partner be treated as a mere object. The moral point of sex for fun in this sense is to bring a couple together in mutual appreciation and pleasure.

Why is marriage so important? Because of the natural link between sex and having children. Natural law theorists argue, as did Aristotle, that the family is the natural and best place for children to be raised. So sex should be limited to people who have the necessary family structure already in place. This will also make it less likely that the sex will be exploitative or excessively casual, treating one or both parties (and, of course, more than two would be an immoral crowd) as simply a warm body or sex toy. Thus, while Catholics and other natural law theorists want to avoid sin, they are not against sex or the body or pleasure as such. Remember, they believe that all things are created by God, so all things are good. As Chesterton puts it, "Any extreme of Catholic asceticism is a wise, or unwise, precaution against the evil of the Fall; it is *never* a doubt about the good of the Creation."[7]

Obviously, there are a number of objections that can be raised against this view, most of which could also be raised against Aristotle's original idea that it is somehow good to live in accordance with nature. What makes nature so great? Aquinas would say that it is God. He created nature, and it expresses his divine nature. But then, how do we know that Catholics have interpreted nature correctly? If it is OK for Hank Hill to have sex just for fun because he knows that he has a urethra too narrow to get his wife Peggy pregnant, why can't Adam and Steve have gay sex just for fun because they know that Steve has no womb or ovaries?[8] Peggy, a natural law theorist might argue, is the kind of being that can get pregnant, whereas Steve is not. But what about Hank's urethra? If it really is too narrow for him to father a child, then in what sense is he the kind of being who could impregnate a woman?

Aquinas might appeal to the doctrine of essential and accidental properties here. As a human male, Hank belongs to the group of creatures that can naturally impregnate human females. It is part of his essence that he is a man, and men naturally can impregnate women. A narrow urethra is an abnormality, a defect of nature, an accidental feature of Hank's anatomy. It is, we might say, a quirk of fate that Hank cannot impregnate Peggy. But, this line of reasoning would continue, it is no accident that Adam and Steve cannot conceive a baby together. It does not just so happen that Steve has no womb. He is a man!

This is a very familiar line of thought, but it has been challenged. Can we say what Steve's essence is so easily? What if he disagrees? What if, for example, he says that he is a woman who happens to have been born in the body of a man? It is by no means easy to see how a claim like this could be either proved or disproved. If it is true, however, then being a man seems more of an accident than an essential feature of who Steve is.

And, of course, it is not as if all gay men feel that they are really, essentially women. Some feel essentially male, while others will question the whole idea of essential identity, especially if it is supposed to be conferred by biology. It should be obvious that the same goes for nongay men and women too. We might feel that we have no defining essence or that we choose our essences for ourselves or that one's essence is a matter of religious faith, political commitment, or any number of things other than the particular kind of reproductive organs that we happen to have or to lack. The very idea of natural essences seems to go hand in hand with the idea that there is a certain way that nature intends us to be. So the metaphysics of essence seems more to be part of the theory of natural law than an independent fact that can be used to support that theory.

Returning to the question of sexual ethics, we might further ask what exactly counts as sex? Is kissing outside marriage wrong? After all, it cannot lead to pregnancy and is a source of erotic pleasure. Perhaps sex would have to be defined as directly involving reproductive organs, and immoral sex would be any sex that, by the very nature of the act in question, cannot result in pregnancy, despite the fact that reproductive organs are involved. This still leaves room for people of the same sex to kiss each other and for anyone to engage in various acts that would normally be considered sexual but that fall short of the definition given here. Topless dancing, for instance, is considered immoral by many people but does not directly involve reproductive organs. So we might want to redefine sex in terms of certain types of arousal or desire—except that just about any act has the potential to arouse someone.

Part of the point of natural law theory is that, like laws passed by governments, it tells us what acts are acceptable and what are not. Like Aristotle, Aquinas believes that we need virtues to see what exactly we should do in any situation but the natural law, as far as reason reveals it to us, is at least meant to be a useful guide. Prudence and conscience can guide the virtuous person, but there are general principles that we can teach our children and that should guide us all through life. For instance, any human law that violates the natural law is invalid, says Aquinas, and may justly be disregarded. Martin Luther King, Jr., appealed to this principle in order to justify civil disobedience of segregationist laws. So natural law is held up as a practical guide, and so far as it fails to offer practical guidance, it fails to do its job.

Besides this problem, we might well ask whether anything we want to do can really be unnatural. If so, why did God or nature give us the desire and the ability to do it? Masturbation and homosexual sex certainly occur in the other species, as do a variety of acts that in humans would be considered good (e.g., nurturing and protecting the young) or bad (e.g., rape and other forms of unprovoked violence against members of one's own species). If natural law is the law of nature properly understood and if we cannot reach agreement on how properly to understand nature, then the theory seems to be in trouble.

Perhaps, therefore, we should not take nature as our guide. At times, after all, nature is red in tooth and claw, as the poet Alfred, Lord Tennyson wrote. Surely, we should not go around with blood dripping from our hands and teeth. Of course, this is not what natural law theorists mean by living in accordance with nature. But what exactly do they mean? That is the question. They mean that a man should do, in Macbeth's words, "all that may become a man" and that, "Who dares do more is none."[9] In other words, human beings should act humanely, not inhumanely. Rational animals should behave rationally. Social beings should be sociable, not antisocial. Living beings should be on the side of life, not death. The natural law is not the law of the jungle because human beings do not naturally live in jungles. That is to say, the true environment for natural human life is the human community. Even if this community is located within a jungle (or rain forest), it is a community of people, not of wild beasts, and the natural values of human beings should prevail.

Is Belief in God Rational?

Natural law ethics seems to many people really to depend on belief in God. Only if nature is God's creation is there any obvious reason to think that it is good—that is, not just containing more good things than bad but so good that we can safely let ourselves be guided by it when it comes to controversial ethical matters. So it is reasonable to ask here why we should believe in God. We have considered already the problem of evil and reasons for thinking that we should not believe in God. In this chapter, I want to look at the famous "five ways" that Aquinas offered for believing in God. These are short and, so, easily quotable. Since in my discussion I will paraphrase them significantly, I will quote most of them at length so that you can judge for yourself whether my paraphrases are reasonable. First comes the argument from motion:

> It is certain, and evident . . . that in the world some things are in motion. . . . If that by which it is moved must itself be moved, then this also needs to be moved by another. . . . But this cannot go on to infinity, because then there would be no first mover, and consequently, no other mover, seeing as subsequent movers move only inasmuch as they are moved by the first mover; as the staff moves only because it is moved by the hand. Therefore it is necessary to arrive at the first mover, moved by no other; and this everyone understands to be God.[10]

This first way is a variation of an argument offered by Aristotle, which we might update and paraphrase as follows: there is energy in the world; there must be an explanation for this fact; the fact cannot be explained by reference to anything in the world (since that would then need to be explained, and so on); so the energy in the world must be explained by reference to something beyond or outside the world. This supernatural energy source is God.

Aquinas' second argument, called the "cosmological argument" because it starts from the existence of the world or cosmos, is very similar. It is based on the idea that everything in nature would not exist if not for some cause. The argument can be rendered as follows: there is matter in the world; there must be an explanation for this fact; the fact cannot be explained by reference to anything in the world (since that would then need to be explained, and so on); so the matter in the world must be explained by reference to something beyond or outside the world. This supernatural creator is God.

These arguments are quite nice and seem to express in logical form the common feeling that there has to be a creator God. If it all started with the Big Bang, then what caused that? Where did everything come from? The only appealing answers are (1) nowhere (which might not seem like an answer at all) and (2) God. "Coming from nowhere" and "caused by nothing" can seem like pure nonsense, so God might appear to be the only possible answer to these questions, which are as old as the child's question "Why?"

However, there are a couple of problems with these first two arguments. One is with the assumption that there has to be an explanation for every fact,

whether or not this explanation is known or knowable to us. This can seem like
the only rational thing to believe, but it can also seem like naïve optimism in
the face of an irrational world. Who says everything must make sense? We have
encountered this line of thought before (see Chapter 2). The other objection
is to the idea that God is an answer to the question posed. If God exists, after
all, doesn't that fact need to be explained? And how can it be? If God needs
no creator, then (1) why not? and (2) why does the cosmos need one? It looks
as though we should investigate the remaining three ways to see if they offer
anything more.

The third way addresses the question of why God exists:

> We find in nature things that are possible to be and not to be, since they are found to
> be generated, and to be corrupted. . . . But it is impossible for these always to exist,
> for that which can not-be at some time is not. Therefore, if everything can not-be,
> then at one time there was nothing in existence. Now if this were true, even now
> there would be nothing in existence, because that which does not exist begins to
> exist only through something already existing. . . . Therefore, we cannot but admit
> the existence of some being having of itself its own necessity. . . . This all men speak
> of as God.[11]

Perhaps the first thing to note about this argument is that it relies on a claim
that is not necessarily true—namely, "that which can not-be at some time is not."
A being that is capable of nonexistence might nevertheless be lucky enough to
exist at all times. Nobody does everything he or she can. So just because a being
can not-be, it does not follow that it ever *will* not-be. When Aquinas says "Therefore, if everything *can* not-be, then at one time there was nothing in existence,"
he is making a mistake. Even if no single thing capable of nonexistence happened
to last forever, each might survive long enough to create or give birth to another
so that there was never a time when nothing existed. We can reject the argument
right here, therefore; but perhaps Aquinas is onto something that we will miss if
we do not look further.

Everything that exists, Aquinas says, is either necessary (it could not fail to
exist) or contingent (it might not have existed but does). For every contingent
thing there has to be an explanation as to why it happens to exist since it did not
have to. It is quite capable of not existing. We can explain one contingent thing
(e.g., me) in terms of another (my mother), but this will only get us so far. Why do
any people at all exist, after all? Ultimately, it seems, there has to be a necessary
being in order to explain all the contingent beings. This argument is related to the
so-called ontological argument—from **ontology**, the study of being—since it has
to do with the nature of God's being. That argument says that it is God's nature
or essence to contain all perfect qualities. Since existence is a perfect quality (i.e.,
a quality, property, or characteristic that a truly perfect being would have), God
must have the quality of existence. That is, God must exist.

The third way assumes that every fact must have an explanation, so we might
reject it just for that reason; but this is not such a bad thing to believe. We might

prefer to reject the argument, if we must reject it at all, therefore, on the grounds that it treats the existence of a necessary being as an explanation rather than a mystery. Being just sounds to some people like a contingent thing, so that "necessary being" makes no sense. If God could not possibly not exist, any more than a triangle could have four sides, then it seems that it can make no sense to talk about God's non-existence. Indeed, some versions of the ontological argument insist that atheism is self-contradictory, and hence false, because what it says, in effect, is that a being that is all-good, all-knowing, and-all perfect and exists does not exist. To see what is wrong with this, just abbreviate that sentence as follows: A being that . . . exists does not exist. This is just blatantly self-contradictory, but that, the argument goes, is what "God does not exist" means. If so, however, then some philosophers would argue that "God exists" cannot make sense either since self-contradictory statements make no sense and the negation of nonsense is not sense but more nonsense. For instance, if you say "Finedexter razbollo," it will not make sense for me to assert that it is not the case that finedexter razbollo. Other philosophers will want to distinguish, though, between sheer nonsense like this and intelligible self-contradiction. "Finedexter razbollo is not true," might make no sense, but "Onions are not onions" is perfectly intelligible. We know what it means; it is just obviously false. If the people who think this way are right, then theism is supported, not undermined, by the ontological argument. (If it works, that is.)

There are still two important objections to make to the ontological argument though. The first comes from the medieval monk Gaunilo. He pointed out that if the argument works, it proves the existence of a being that is perfect in every way. If this is the case, then why couldn't someone use parallel logic to prove the existence of an island that is perfect in every way or a car that is perfect in every way or a perfect sandwich, monkey, or laundromat? That is to say, if the logic of the ontological argument is right, then it follows that we can prove the existence of anything we like, so long as it is perfect. And that seems absurd. So there must be something wrong with the logic of the ontological argument. Now, according to that argument, perfection belongs to the essence of God. It might not follow that there is any sandwich or monkey to whose essence perfection belongs. Even if Gaunilo's objection does work, though, he has not shown *what* is wrong with the argument's logic. At most he has shown that *something* must be wrong with it.

The best answer to the question of what might be wrong with it was developed by Immanuel Kant (1724–1804). He said that existence is not a quality or property. It cannot be part of the essence of anything. Rather, existence is a prerequisite for having properties. This is reflected in modern logic, which solves various problems by expressing statements about existence in the form "There exists an x such that x has the properties a, b, and c," rather than treating existence itself as a property. Whether this proves that existence is not in fact a property is another matter, but it is generally felt that the ontological argument *must* be wrong, and this is the most promising objection yet made to it.

So we move on to the fourth and fifth ways. The fourth way is reminiscent of one of Plato's arguments for the forms (see Chapter 1).

> Among beings there are some more and some less good, true, noble, and the like. But more and less are predicated of different things according as they resemble in their different ways something which is the maximum. . . . Now the maximum in any genus is the cause of all in that genus, as fire, which is the maximum of heat, is the cause of all hot things. . . . Therefore, there must also be something which is to all beings the cause of their being, goodness, and every other perfection; and this we call God.[12]

Things exist that possess varying degrees of goodness or perfection. If it is an objective fact that some things are better than others—that children's lives are more valuable than worms', say—then there must be an objective standard of goodness or value. When we rightly call something slightly good or very good indeed, we must be measuring it against some standard of goodness whose scale (presumably) goes even higher than very good indeed. Now, we might not be able to measure things like this exactly, and we might even have to guess; but if there is a true and a false of the matter, then there must be some paradigm of goodness, some perfectly good thing. Or so it seems. And this thing is God.

This argument is questionable. Plato used something like it to argue that tallness must exist as a form, but few people today would accept that there is any such object as tallness. We might deny that there is any objective standard of goodness and insist instead that goodness is only ever relative, whether to a species or an individual or a purpose. Money is good if you want to buy things, manure is good for roses, donkeys are good for calming horses, courage is useful and admirable in human beings, and so on. One might want to insist that there is such a thing as absolute goodness, but it is not clear exactly what this means. In the absence of clear proof that absolute goodness exists, it is not the kind of undeniable fact on which one could prove beyond a doubt that God must exist. Rather, it is more a matter of something like faith, just as belief in God appears to be.

Finally, the fifth way argues that there is clear evidence of intelligent design in nature.

> We see that things which lack knowledge, such as natural bodies, act for an end, and this is evident from their acting always, or nearly always, in the same way, so as to obtain the best result. Hence it is plain that they achieve their end, not fortuitously, but designedly. Now whatever lacks knowledge cannot move towards an end, unless it be directed by some being endowed with . . . intelligence; as the arrow is directed by the archer. Therefore, some intelligent being exists by whom all natural things are directed to their end; and this being we call God.[13]

Nature does not work randomly, Aquinas says, and its regularity is good. For instance, it is entirely predictable what kind of fruit will come from a banana tree, and it is good for bananas (or banana trees) that this is so. They would die out if they did not regularly reproduce themselves. It is also good for people who like to eat bananas. Not all banana trees bear healthy fruit all the time, but the tendency is in that direction. Such benign order in the world, which is by no means a feature of bananas only, cannot plausibly be the result of chance. Clearly, a benign intelligence is at work, bringing order to the world. This is God.

This argument is extremely controversial today, of course. It is contradicted by the theory of evolution, which says that living things produce not exact replicas of themselves but variations. These variations are somewhat random. They are not entirely random: people do not give birth to goats or footballs. But plenty of mutations and deformities are possible and do occur naturally. Some of these variations are useful in a given environment, while others are useless or positively harmful. Beings with useful traits will tend to survive and reproduce more, while those with harmful traits will tend to die out. Hence, over time, species change as individuals and whole species die out. Those most fitted to their environment survive (until that environment changes or some other disaster occurs). So, of course, bananas have evolved to produce healthy fruit reliably. Plants that do not reproduce healthily die out. It is not a miracle. The "selection" of adapted beings is entirely natural. Whether this theory is true or false (and the evidence that it is true is overwhelming[14]), its very existence is enough to show that the fifth way does not *prove* that God exists. There is an alternative explanation for the phenomenon it seeks to explain. So, alas, it looks as though belief in God really is a matter of faith.

Is Nonrational Belief Justifiable?

It is worth considering whether it is right or good to believe in God on the basis of faith alone. One famous argument says that it is dishonest to believe in anything without sufficient proof so that faith is really just a form of credulity or childish naiveté. Some people argue that it is a form of naiveté that leads to conflict, oppression, terrorism, war, and genocide. Certainly, religion is involved in political conflicts around the globe and many people have killed others in the name of their religion. That is, they have claimed that they were killing for religious reasons, even if others deny that God wants anybody to act this way. If beliefs that are regarded by their holders as religious can lead to such extreme acts, then it seems that we ought to be especially sure of ourselves before we allow beliefs that we regard as religious into our hearts or minds. Yet, what evidence can there be that any religious belief is true?

The American philosopher and psychologist William James (1842–1910) argued in an essay called "The Will to Believe" that we have a right to believe things that cannot be proved, in certain circumstances.[15] If God's existence can be neither proved nor disproved by science or logic and it remains something that we can seriously consider believing in, then we must allow our passions or feelings, our hopes and fears, to decide whether we are to believe or not. This is so because the question of God's existence is too momentous for us to ignore it, and whatever we believe about it will be an intellectually unjustified belief. That is to say, in James' view, science and logic do not prove either atheism or belief in God to be true. Nor do they prove one to be more probable than the other. And agnosticism, keeping an open mind because of a supposed lack of evidence for or against God's existence, is not really better from an intellectual point of view because it has consequences that are equally significant for life and that are no more justified intellectually than those of atheism or theism. A theist might have more hope than others, more of an inclination to behave ethically, more friends perhaps, and so on. Why should agnostics and atheists deny themselves these benefits if they do not have any more intellectual justification for their position than the believer? James does not insist that it really is better to be religious, but in the absence of other kinds of reason to adopt atheism, agnosticism, or theism, he thinks that we really have no option but to be swayed by our feelings. At least, he says, we can have the *right* to believe in God despite a lack of proof that God exists.

This is not to defend just any belief that we happen to like or to say that James would have supported religiously motivated acts of violence. Indeed, that kind of extremism is not what he calls a "live option" for most of us, not something that we can really imagine ourselves believing. So it is not the kind of belief that James is talking about. He is talking about choices between beliefs that are "live, momentous, and forced." He is only concerned, in other words, with beliefs that we really might hold, that involve very important things (so we cannot simply ignore the decision to be made), and that *have* to be decided on, one way or another, about things that the facts do not decide for us. On the other hand, some people obviously do believe in violent forms of religious extremism. For them the option is very much live and momentous. It might even be forced, that is, something that they must decide on. The planned attack on the infidel is about to start, are you coming or not? Science and reason do not tell you that the people to be bombed are "the infidel," but they do not tell you otherwise either. You must, and may, let your passions decide. What do you choose? If James would defend the right to believe in this kind of case, then surely that counts against his argument.

Bertrand Russell (1872–1970) argued on grounds like these against religious belief. Certainty that one is right, even in the face of a complete lack of evidence, leads to terrible harm. Here he saw parallels between the histories of the communist Soviet Union and Christianity. The latter has seen alleged witches burned at the stake, heretics tortured, and people of other faiths, notably Jews, persecuted. The former, similarly, was marked by torture, murder, and persecution. These become a danger especially when the belief in question, be it communism or Christianity, is held to be essential to morality or some form of salvation. In an essay called "Can Religion Cure Our Troubles?" Russell writes as follows:

> As soon as it is held that any belief, no matter what, is important for some other reason than that it is true, a whole host of evils is ready to spring up. Discouragement

of inquiry . . . is the first of these, but others are pretty sure to follow. Positions of authority will be open [only] to the orthodox. Historical records must be falsified if they throw doubt on received opinions. Sooner or later unorthodoxy will come to be considered a crime to be dealt with by the stake, the purge, or the concentration camp.[16]

This might seem to be an exaggeration, especially since Christians mostly gave up such measures a long time ago (although some people still advocate violent measures in the name of Christianity). According to Russell, though, this is only because belief in Christianity has waned. Where belief is still alive and strong, in the Soviet Union in his day and perhaps under the Taliban in ours, we do see violent persecution of unbelievers. What we need, in Russell's view, is less faith and more open-mindedness. We should seek the truth and believe only what we know. On other matters, we should suspend judgment. Certainly, we should tolerate differences of opinion on these matters and never defend a belief on grounds other than its truth. Now, where does this leave belief in God? Russell was a self-confessed agnostic, but he expressed some admiration for Aquinas' defense of his belief in God. After all, Aquinas did not rely on appeals to morals or the authority of the Church. He tried to prove that God must exist, using reason. That is, he used reason to support his ethics, not ethics to support beliefs that cannot be justified rationally. The problem is that it seems reason really cannot support ethics in that way.

Why Be Good?

Aquinas tries to take a very rational view of ethics, which ought to please Thrasymachus. His view is that reason proves that God exists and that God's moral law can be discovered by a rational study of nature. The reasons he can bring forward for being good, then, amount largely to those brought forth by Aristotle (it is required by nature, including our own human nature) and those put forward by religious believers (e.g., that God will reward the good and punish the bad). The objections to these views have already been covered in the previous two chapters.

What is new is Aquinas' extended and multifaceted attempt to prove that God exists and the level of detail that can be found in work by him and those who have followed in his footsteps about such questions as what kinds of sexual activity are permissible. If reason really can prove that God exists, then this is surely significant. Even if it cannot do that, it is also significant if reason can lead us to very specific conclusions about what we may and may not do. Thrasymachus believes in reason, after all, and would not want to do anything irrational. What he does not believe in is God, or any other basis for the belief that we ought to do what is natural. Thrasymachus will have no objection to doing unnatural things unless they truly are irrational in a sense of that word that he would accept. We need now to consider whether it is really rational to believe in the natural law as Aquinas describes it or whether this is actually more a matter of faith.

Objections

Natural law ethics faces two main problems. The first is that it is all so vague. Is abortion inhumane? Is it irrational to take drugs? Is it antisocial to play loud music in one's own home after nine o'clock? And what if it is? Would we therefore be justified in executing those found guilty of such antisocial behavior? Or locking them in prison? Or fining them? Or scowling at them? Or tutting a bit when we think of them and their wild ways? There might be some such thing as human nature, and it might be that we should live in accordance with it; but figuring out exactly what this does and does not allow seems to be an impossible task—impossible not because it would take a long time to do the reckoning but because there is no apparent method for doing any such reckoning. A natural set of vague hints or gestures seems more credible than the idea of a natural *law*, with all the detail and precision that word implies.

The second big problem with natural law theory is just why we should obey any such law. Why should rational beings be rational, for instance? Why should anything be what it is? Of course, there is no such thing as not being what one is, but that is a point of logic, not ethics. If it is true that being rational is what distinguishes human beings from other species, then we are all rational in that sense (roughly, we are all at least related to beings that are capable of reason). From this it does not follow logically that we *ought* to behave rationally. Some mentally handicapped or mentally ill people might be incapable of rational behavior, despite being related to fully rational people. Are they therefore morally in the wrong? Surely not. If all my relatives have tattoos saying "Girl Power" in Chinese, it in no way follows that I should get myself similarly tattooed. And if I *am* tattooed, it does not follow that I *should* be tattooed, so why would anyone think it follows from my *being* rational that I *ought to be* rational?

The answer has to do with the idea we discussed above that some properties are essential and others are accidental. Essential properties are those without which one would not be who (or what) one is. Accidental properties are those that can change without any loss of identity. With or without my tattoo, I am still me. So any tattoo I might have is an accidental property, even if I had it done quite deliberately. But if I become vapor, then I am probably no longer me. The same might be true if I undergo a major personality switch or religious conversion. There is disagreement about which properties are essential and which are accidental. There is also disagreement about whether any property is ever really essential, but before we come to any conclusions about this, we ought to look more at what essences are supposed to be.

Aquinas believes in essences. Accidental properties are not essential (by definition), so they are not really important. What is essential is important. Why?

Because that is what God made you. He did not give you your tattoos or piercings or hair plugs. He gave you your life, your rationality, your humanity. It is these things that must be preserved as they are gifts from God. Anything else is a kind of blasphemy, a rejection of God. Or so Aquinas would argue. Those who do not believe in God or who do not believe in essences, will disagree, of course. They might, however, have a strong sense of who they are and a strong belief that they do not want to be anyone, or anything, else. You do not have to believe in God in order to value what you take to be your essence.

This second reason for preserving one's essence has to do with integrity or authenticity. There is a kind of contradiction or dishonesty involved in a dog acting like a cat or a rational being disowning its own rationality. Behaving in a manner unbefitting what one is, is a kind of denial of one's reality, a pretense. Think of a gay man living as if he were straight. Such a life is likely to be hard work for him and to make him miserable. But regardless of the effect on his emotions, it is also likely to strike him and others as living a lie, as being wrong because it is dishonest, not just imprudent from a hedonistic point of view. There are two problems with this idea though.

One is, what is living a lie and what is not? Is a gay man trying to be straight really living a lie, or is homosexual life rather, as some people claim, a lie? Is homosexuality, or heterosexuality, natural or not? The answer one gives will depend on how one defines "nature." One could beg the question (i.e., simply assume the truth of the point in question) and define "nature" as being intrinsically moral. Then, whether homosexuality is *good* will determine whether it is natural, rather than the other way around. Or else we could define "nature" as being whatever occurs without artifice or outside interference. In this case, homosexual acts would appear to be natural, but there will always be room for argument about what constitutes outside interference. When penguins are observed to have gay sex, is this the result of human observation (unlikely, but could you prove it?)? Or are they simply making an honest mistake each time? Apparently, gay penguin couples are quite loyal to each other, so it is not a mistake of identity that they are making.[17] But it could, I suppose, be argued that there is some moral error in such cases.

The second problem is why such "dishonesty" is wrong. Natural law theory is supposed to explain not only which acts or character traits are bad but also why they are bad. It would be circular, though, to say that dishonesty is bad because it is unnatural and that being unnatural is bad because it is dishonest. Ultimately, both are thought to be bad because they are against God, and we know or believe that they are bad because (or rather if) we have faith in certain revelations. Really, we are back to a form of divine command theory here: good is what God says it is.

Aquinas' version of virtue theory brings out some of the problems faced by any virtue theorist. It offers, unwittingly, a way out via divine command theory; but this sort of "God-says-so" approach will not impress the likes of Thrasymachus, should we still care about him and his challenge. If the moral skeptic is to be moved by natural law theory, it will be through a consideration of nature, not the supernatural, and of what reason there is to think of nature as good—unless, that is, we can really prove that God exists. Aquinas thinks he can, and many people still believe that this is possible; but every proposed proof appears to be flawed.

Conclusion

One of the best books ever written on Aquinas says that

> [N]obody will begin to understand the Thomist philosophy, or indeed the Catholic philosophy, who does not realise that the primary and fundamental part of it is entirely the praise of Life, the praise of Being, the praise of God as the Creator of the World.[18]

St. Augustine is famous for having argued that evil has no positive existence, that it is not some thing or entity that God created. "For, evil has no positive nature; what we call evil is merely the lack of something that is good," he writes in *The City of God*.[19] After all, why would God create such a thing as evil? Evil is not an object or force in the world but a kind of act—namely, the act of turning the will away from God in the direction of something else. This something else will itself be good since it is part of the world that God created, but it will be less good than God. Evil is a matter of directing the will toward a lesser good or using a good thing in an evil, unnatural way, one unintended by God. So evil is all about the will. But goodness is not about denying the individual will, only of pointing it in the right direction. Aquinas would regard this as being the natural direction, the one that will most satisfy the will. So there is no conflict between rational self-interest and doing or being good from his point of view.

Nevertheless, it seems that natural law theory does depend on belief in God. That is no bad thing in itself necessarily, but it seems to be bad news for natural law theory, if it really is to be a theory and not simply an article of faith. Faith will never appeal to Thrasymachus after all, which is not to say that the rest of us should reject it too. What it does mean is that we need to look elsewhere if we are to find a really convincing answer to his skepticism. As with Aristotle's theory, Thrasymachus might agree that one must seek one's own happiness and do what is good. He might also agree with Aquinas that it is good for him to keep himself alive, take care of his children, and seek to know the truth. What he will probably not accept is that the highest good available to him lies in God or that charity, the care of others, is a genuine good for him to attain. Aquinas believes that it takes God to infuse this virtue properly into us, acknowledging that it is impossible for us to persuade each other fully of its value. As far as Thrasymachus, or any of us, lacks this virtue, there is reason to believe that God has not infused us with it and, hence, a (rather weak) kind of evidence that God does not exist at all.

In the next chapter, we will look at the views of Thomas Hobbes and see whether his much more secular reasoning can counter the doubts we have been trying to battle.

Questions for Further Thought

1. Can God's existence be proved at all? Does it matter?
2. Is there an essential human nature? Should ethics be based on it?
3. Does religion, even false religion, tend to promote ethical behavior? Can this justify religious belief?
4. If we only believe what we can prove, what other kinds of belief might we have to give up?
5. Are there any unnatural acts? Does it matter?

Notes

1. See G. K. Chesterton, *Saint Thomas Aquinas* (New York: Image Books, 1956), 39–44, for the full story.
2. Aristotle, *Nicomachean Ethics,* trans. Terence Irwin (Indianapolis: Hackett, 1999), Book IV, Chapter 3, §34, 1125a.
3. Epictetus, *The Handbook (The Enchiridion),* trans. Nicholas P. White (Indianapolis: Hackett, 1992), 13, §8.
4. For more details, see John Finnis, *Fundamentals of Ethics* (Washington DC: Georgetown University Press, 1983), 68–69.
5. See John Finnis, "'Shameless Acts' in Colorado: Abuse of Scholarship in Constitutional Cases," *Academic Questions* Volume 7. no 4 (1994): 10–41, and Martha Nussbaum, "Platonic Love and Colorado Love," in *The Greeks and Us: Essays in Honor of A. W. H. Adkins,* ed. R. B. Louden and P. Schollmeier (Chicago: Univesity of Chicago Press, 1996), 168–218.
6. Perhaps a better name would be the "doctrine of two kinds of effect," but "double effect" is how the principle has been labeled.
7. Chesterton, Saint Thomas Aquinas, 82.
8. Hank and Peggy Hill are characters from the television show *King of the Hill*. They have one son, Bobby, but supposedly cannot have any more because of Hank's narrow urethra. Adam and Steve are not characters from this show, but fictional gay characters who are often contrasted with nongay Adam and Eve whom God is said to have created.
9. William Shakespeare *Macbeth* eds. Barbara A. Mowat and Paul Werstine (New York: Washington Square Press, 1992), act I, scene vii.
10. St. Thomas Aquinas, *Summa Theologica*, 1, 2, 3, from Peter Kreeft, ed. *A Summa of the Summa* (San Francisco: Ignatius Press, 1990), 65.
11. Ibid., 67–68.

12. Ibid., 68–69.
13. Ibid., 69.
14. See www.talkorigins.org, especially the FAQ section, for more.
15. William James, *The Will to Believe and Other Essays in Popular Philosophy* (New York: Cosimo Classics, 2006).
16. Bertrand Russell, "Can Religion Cure Our Troubles?" in *The Basic Writings of Bertrand Russell,* eds. Robert E. Egner and Lester E. Denonn (New York: Simon and Schuster, 1961), 600.
17. See, for instance, the story "Zoo Tempts Gay Penguins To Go Straight," at www.ananova.com, January 8, 2005, for details.
18. Chesterton, *Saint Thomas Aquinas,* 81.
19. Augustine, *City of God* (New York: Image Books, 1958), 217.

Suggestions for Further Reading

The best introduction to the life and thought of Aquinas is probably G. K. Chesterton, *Saint Thomas Aquinas* (New York: Image Books, 1956). Some of Aquinas' main ideas are included, with excellent commentary, in Christopher Martin, ed., *The Philosophy of Thomas Aquinas: Introductory Readings* (London: Routledge, 1988).

If you want to learn more specifically about Aquinas' thought on ethics, see the selections and interpretive essays in Paul E. Sigmund, ed., *St. Thomas Aquinas on Politics and Ethics* (New York: W. W. Norton & Company, 1988).

John Finnis, *Fundamentals of Ethics* (Washington DC: Georgetown University Press, 1983), is a readable introduction to the thought of one of the most prominent contemporary natural law theorists.

CHAPTER 5

Hobbes

Thomas Hobbes (1588–1679) could almost be said to have lived in a different world from that of Thomas Aquinas. Aquinas was probably the greatest philosopher of the Middle Ages, an age of faith. Hobbes was one of the pioneers of modern philosophy, of the age of reason. Of course, as we have seen, Aquinas might dispute the contrast between faith and reason implied by these labels; but there is no doubt that the age of modern science was different from the medieval period. Science in Hobbes' day was materialistic and did not leave much room for anything supernatural. Hobbes' contemporary René Descartes (1596–1650) developed a theory of metaphysical dualism, according to which there are ultimately two kinds of reality: the mental or spiritual, on the one hand, and the material, on the other. The physical universe is material, but God is spiritual; thus, science can tell us all about physics, chemistry, and the material aspects of biology, for example, but nothing at all about God and our immaterial souls or minds. This would suggest that there could never be a science of psychology since the mind belongs to the realm of the invisible. Indeed, not being physical or material, it cannot be sensed in any way at all, according to Descartes. No telescope or microscope can ever reveal anything about the mind to us.

Hobbes disagreed. He was a materialist, not a dualist, about human beings. As he saw it, we are basically machines of flesh and blood, operating according to physical laws. In Hobbes' view, the relevant laws governing human behavior involve pushing and pulling. The world we live in is made of small, material atoms, and these operate in much the same way as larger material objects, like rocks or billiard balls. Every human movement must be the result of a chain of other movements, with atoms or things made of atoms pushing or pulling each other to produce the final result. If I move toward a bowl of blueberry cobbler, this movement must be started by some pushing or pulling, presumably in my brain. If we think in purely physical terms, then what causes my movement is a physical event in my brain, a movement of atoms. But in psychological language, what would we say causes me to move toward the cobbler? Well, it might be almost anything. Perhaps my mother used to give me cobbler when I was good as a child. If we keep things simple, though, perhaps we might just say that it is my desire for cobbler that causes me to move toward it. Continuing to keep things simple, it is tempting to think that there can only be one real cause of any action. If my movement is caused by both a movement in my brain and my desire for cobbler, then this desire must *be* that movement. (If not, then there would be two causes of the action, which we just ruled out as a possibility.) Similarly, if I move away from the cobbler, my aversion to it (the opposite of desire for it) will be some other movement in my brain. So desire and aversion, far from being mysterious, scientifically unknowable "things" in the Cartesian (as in Des*Cartes*) soul, are in fact material events in the brain. They could, at least in theory, be observed just like any other moving body in the universe, be it a massive planet or a tiny blood vessel.

Now, what does all this have to do with ethics? Hobbes' view is that every action, including good and bad ones, is motivated by either desire or aversion. Like Plato, he thought that if I desire cobbler, then I must, in some sense, think that cobbler is good. If I am averse to it, then I think it is bad. Similarly, if I vote for increased spending on the military, say, then I must think that is good, I must desire it. My belief that it is good is the same kind of movement that causes me to reach for the cobbler. Not exactly the same movement, of course, since the end result is different but something similar. What people call "good" is what they like, and what they call "bad" is what they dislike. What else could "good" and "bad" mean? As Hobbes puts it: "whatsoever is the object of any man's appetite or desire, that is it which he for his part calleth *good* . . . these words of good, evil . . . are ever used with relation to the person that useth them: there being nothing simply and absolutely so . . . ."[1] Good and evil are not entities themselves or properties of objects or actions. Different people call different things "good" and "bad," with equal meaning, even though we will inevitably think that some of them speak truly and that others have it all wrong. So "good" and "bad" cannot mean something objective, in the way that "dog" and "red" have objective meanings. It is a matter of objective scientific fact what things are dogs and what things are red. There is no real room for disagreement. Ethics is not like this. Our judgments reflect our preferences or tastes or whatever else you want to call them (our values, perhaps). And they move us to do certain actions and to refrain from others, just as my love of cobbler moves me to eat it and my detestation of raisins moves me to avoid them.

Now, since what we like and dislike, or value and disvalue, varies from person to person, it is quite subjective. There is nothing that in its nature is good or bad. Some things are naturally good for you (such as eating celery) and others are bad for you (such as jumping into a volcano), but it does not follow that these things are good or bad as such, even from your subjective point of view. You might not like eating celery, and you might want to die in a volcano. So good and bad would seem to depend entirely on what we happen to want. But life is not simply a matter of individuals living in nature. There is society to take into consideration.

Imagine no society, just individuals in nature. They all have different tastes and values, but they also have common needs. They all need to eat, and everybody's digestive system is basically the same; thus, there will be competition for the same food supplies. In theory, there might be no such competition since there could be unlimited supplies of fruit, vegetables, and whatever meat people wanted to eat. But in reality that is not likely. There will be competition for food and water and other resources such as firewood, and this is likely to lead to conflict. If you and I are both hoping to spear the same opossum for dinner, then we become rivals. This rivalry might be quite friendly and even lead to cooperation, but it could also lead to a desperate struggle with clubs and spears flying (while the opossum sneaks away).

Conflict can also arise out of anticipation. Remembering the last whack I got on the head when I went opossum hunting, I might be on the lookout for potential rivals. When I see one, I might lie low and hope she goes away or propose a truce, but I might also throw my spear first and ask questions later.

Also, conflict could arise not from competition or anticipation but from ambition. Perhaps you fight me for the opossum not because you are so hungry but simply because you love to win and hate to lose. Perhaps you enjoy the fear in people's eyes when they see you coming and the reputation of being the baddest opossum clubber in the woods. Just for this reason you might attack or intimidate your neighbors, and they in turn might either attack you or go to great lengths to defend themselves.

For three reasons, then, people in what Hobbes calls a "state of nature" would be likely to find themselves on a war footing. They will not be fighting night and day, but they will be wary of each other. They might form family or tribal groups, but each group will need to spend time working on defending itself and is likely to avoid other groups, except, on occasion, to attack them. Ambition too could be a problem, and it only takes one Genghis Khan or Julius Caesar or Adolf Hitler to make life miserable for many, many people. Anticipation is more likely to lead to defense than offense, but that still takes up resources and affects the nature of one's relations with others. And competition seems quite likely to lead to actual violence and death. Life in such a world, Hobbes famously predicted, would be short.

He also said that it would be solitary, poor, nasty, and brutish (animal-like). Let me explain why. It would be solitary because people would tend to keep to themselves. I can suggest that we form an alliance to go and kill the scary guy who lives over the hill or to watch each other's children while one of us goes picking carrots, but how can you trust me? In this world there is no sheriff or king you can go to if I turn out to be in league with the scary guy or if I take your children to be my slaves while you innocently pick carrots for the two of us. Without laws and law enforcement, people will be wary of each other and tend to keep to themselves. Because of this, there will be little trade or cooperative agriculture or industry. Each person will pretty much live on what he or she can gather or grow on his or her own. So people will tend to be poor. This lonely, poor, dangerous life will, of course, be quite nasty. And it will be brutish because life will be all about survival. There will be no culture, no society, no education, precious little communication, and not much opportunity to travel or to find your soulmate. Our life, in short, will lack most of the things that give it value and make it distinctively human.

Sooner or later, therefore, someone is likely to make a change. Sick of the scary guy over the hill, the valley people will band together to fight him off. Sooner or later, too, the scary guy will team up with other scary guys to keep the little valley people down, perhaps enslaving them or taking their crops. It will take a big organization to protect the harmless little people from the big, aggressive ones. An organization like that will need rules, and these rules will need to be enforced. In short, as Hobbes sees it, it will need a king or someone like a king:

> The only way to erect such a common power, as may be able to defend them from the invasion of foreigners, and the injuries of one another, and thereby to secure them in such sort, as that by their own industry, and by the fruits of the earth, they may nourish themselves and live contentedly; is to confer all their power and strength upon one man, or upon one assembly of men, that may reduce all their wills, by plurality of voices, unto one will. . . .[2]

Perhaps there will be more than one ruler, like the seven samurai or the dirty dozen; but there will have to be some head to this body. The situation is this: in nature there is no good or bad, and each person is free to do just whatever he or she pleases, limited only by his or her physical ability. Everybody is equal too, in the sense that all have roughly the same power. There is no one so strong that he or she cannot be killed while sleeping, and no one is so weak that he or she cannot kill at least a sleeping enemy. All this freedom and equality might sound almost too good to be true, but in fact, if Hobbes is right, it would be a nightmare. The only way out is to give up this freedom, to agree to obey someone else, in return for law and order. This agreement is not with the ruler: the weak who need him, her, or them are in no position to bargain. It is an agreement among the people to obey the ruler: "I authorize and give up my right of governing myself to this man, or to this assembly of men, on this condition, that thou give up thy right to him, and authorize all his actions in like manner."[3] In return, that is, not only for protection but for all the good things that civilized living among people who know they can trust one another can bring.

Among the things that this kind of life brings is morality. In the state of nature there are no rules, no good and bad. As Hobbes sees it, " . . . every man has a right to every thing; even to one another's body."[4] His view is basically that all is fair in war and that a state of nature is a state of war. It might be a cold war, more of a standoff than a battle most of the time, but it is still a state of war. In such a war there are no rules, so there can be no cheating or injustice.

But there is one kind of law in a state of nature: the law of nature.[5] This "is a precept, or general rule, found out by reason, by which a man is forbidden to do, that, which is destructive of his life, or taketh away the means of preserving the same; and to omit, that, by which he thinketh it may be best preserved."[6] In a purely material universe, we might wonder where such a law comes from, who or what is forbidding us from harming ourselves. Perhaps Hobbes believed in God; the evidence is not clear. It seems, though, that this so-called law is not really any more a law than the law of the jungle is. In fact, it pretty much is the law of the jungle. Our own reason tells us that we must not fail to do what we need to do to keep ourselves alive. Put positively, we have to do what we have to do in order to survive. And what is that, exactly? Well, it could be just about anything. Each person will have his or her own view of what he or she needs and how best to get it.

In a society, though, peace reigns. There are rules, and breaking them threatens to undermine the society, plunging its people back into the Neanderthal nightmare they thought they had escaped. Hobbes was influenced in his thinking here by his experience of civil war in England. Many people were unhappy with the way the king had been running things, but the violent chaos that ensued when they rebelled against him was worse, in many people's eyes, than the alleged tyranny they were trying to free themselves from. Moreover, the result was a puritanical military dictatorship that lasted for 11 years, so the rebellion was arguably not worthwhile at all—except for the winners, perhaps. As Hobbes sees things, the rules ought to be obeyed, no matter what they are. The risks of disobedience are simply too great to justify it.

The relevant point for ethical theory is that Hobbes sees society as introducing ethics into the world. In the state of nature, the question "Why be good?" does not arise because there really is no good or bad there. In a society, though, being good means following the rules of that society and being bad means breaking them. If you are not good, then the society itself will punish you. Going against society threatens to undermine it and throw you back into the dreaded state of nature. It is, roughly speaking, suicidal. These are the reasons to be good.

Being on your own, at war with everyone else, is no way to live. But perhaps people would not really live alone. Family groups seem quite likely to arise and perhaps are inevitable if the human race is not to die out completely. Friends might group together too, or gangs or tribes. But then these groups are likely to fight just as much as individuals would. They are likely also to be threatened by bigger groups. And really large groups will not be held together by family ties or the goodness in people's hearts. They need rules or laws backed up by the credible threat of force. So the choice is ultimately war or peace through mutual obedience of some authority. It should be obvious that peace is better than war, so the means to peace are desirable. If we all see the means to peace as good, then we should tend to seek them out. That means seeking an end to the state of nature, an end to lawlessness. And that means finding some authority that can make and, most importantly, enforce laws. Compared with the nightmares of the state of nature, it almost does not matter what these laws are. The priority is establishing an effective sovereign.

This can be done in two ways. We can simply agree to obey some individual or group and, thus, give up some of our freedom for the sake of security and all the benefits that go with it. Or we can be threatened by some conqueror and promise obedience to protect ourselves. Either way, a sovereign is established whose authority we have agreed to accept. Anyone who does not agree is an outlaw and has no protection. It does not matter how the sovereign came to power. What matters is that the people who gave up the complete freedom of living under no rules for the limited freedom of living under some rules should be protected from outside threats and from those who refuse to abide by the rules, whatever they may be.

Now, we might wonder how the agreement to obey a sovereign can come about. If civil order depends on the mutual agreement of lawless individuals, can it ever reasonably be expected to get off the ground? Will such people ever keep their agreements? We know that some people do not, that people break promises, break the law, refuse to give in to threats even when it is obvious that the threats are not idle. All we need, though, is for most people to obey, to keep the agreement. And Hobbes thinks that most people will keep agreements, even ones made within a state of nature, because people tend to be rational and it is rational to keep the agreements you have made.

To prove his point, he imagines an extreme case involving a kind of Thrasymachus figure that Hobbes calls "the fool." Imagine you are in a state of nature, where no law, moral or political, tells you that you have to keep your promises or stick to the terms of contracts you have signed. Imagine further that you have made an agreement with someone, perhaps to trade a herd of goats for some barrels of oil. Imagine further still that the other person either has already handed over the goats or else can be made to do so because you have a gang of armed men waiting to pounce with Kalashnikov rifles if she does not fulfill her side of the bargain. Now, should you hand over the promised oil? The fool says no, but Hobbes says yes.

It is true, he concedes, that you might make more profit from breaking your word. It might even seem quite certain that you will do so. But you cannot know the future. You cannot count on things going as you expect and on other people not coming to know that you are not to be trusted. If, like the fool, you see it as simply irrational to keep your word, then you are likely to make a habit of such behavior, which will make detection of your lying ways all the more likely. Even in just one instance, though, there is a chance that you will be found out. And who then will ever trade with you? Will your armed men even stick around, knowing that you are someone to whom honesty means nothing? If they are not morally repelled by this, they might simply calculate that you are likely to betray them sooner or later. If people even *suspect* that you might be untrustworthy, you will find it hard to make trades or find people who will help protect you from mutual threats. In a war of all against all, you need all the friends and allies you can get. Without their trust, your life is likely to be even more solitary and even more short. So it is rational to seek a reputation for honesty, and it is rational to behave honestly for this reason, even in cases where it looks safe to cheat. You cannot count on that safety, and there is too much at stake for the risk to be worth taking. Unless your life is directly threatened, you ought to keep your agreements. Thus Hobbes answers the fool. If it is rational to keep the agreements we make in the state of nature, then it is rational to keep the agreement that gets us out of a state of nature and into a political society. It is rational, in other words, to keep the social contract, to obey the rules.

So, we ought to give up some of our freedom to a government in return for protection, stability, and so on. This government, Hobbes says, must have absolute authority. Checks and balances, he thinks, can result in stalemate or division, putting the state on a slippery slope to civil war. There must be no question as to who is ultimately in control. It is possible that he does not mean that the king, if the sovereign takes the form of a monarch, must do everything that belongs to the function of government. Ministers could be appointed, for instance, to make laws. But the king must then have the power to hire and fire those ministers. This is what makes his political theory so unattractive. In return for law and order, Hobbes seems to grant the government almost absolute power. Is there no other way out of the state of nature? Hobbes' fellow countryman John Locke thought there was.

John Locke

John Locke (1632–1704) had a different conception of the state of nature, which helped lead him to different political conclusions. When Hobbes thought of the state of nature, he thought of civil war. When Locke thought of the state of nature, he thought of America; and when he thought of America, he thought of an open, fertile land waiting to be claimed and developed. (He did not, that is, think of it as a place already owned by Native Americans.) On the basis of this rosier conception of the natural state, he constructed a political philosophy that has had more appeal than Hobbes'. Locke's theory had significant consequences, for it more than any other influenced Thomas Jefferson's political philosophy and, thus, shaped the future of the most powerful country in the Americas, not to mention the world. One of the ideas that most attracted Jefferson to Locke's way of thinking was that citizens could have a moral right to revolt against the king or queen.

Unlike Hobbes, Locke believed that there is a moral law even in a state of nature. This law is given by God and can be discovered by us, somewhat like Hobbes' law of nature. It is not, however, a Hobbesian law sanctioning whatever seems necessary to survive but a more restrictive law that forbids people from harming the "Life, Health, Liberty, or Possessions" of others.[7] People have natural rights, in other words, and we may not violate these even if we think we must. An Englishman in America in the sixteenth century who was starving and who was still in a state of nature with regard to the native people of the land (i.e., he had not agreed to recognize anybody as sovereign over himself and the Native Americans) would be allowed by Hobbes' law of nature to steal whatever food he needed from them. Indeed, if necessary, he would be allowed to kidnap or kill them. In turn, they would be allowed to do whatever they perceived to be necessary for their survival, including killing the meddling Englishman.

For Locke the situation is not so simple or so amoral. If the Native Americans possess food, then they have a right not to have it stolen from them, even in a state of nature. So the Englishman may not do whatever he sees as necessary. He is bound by a moral law and must either break it (which is wrong) or else get his food honestly, by trading, begging, or going elsewhere to find it. It might seem strange, then, that Locke thought of America as a land of freely available resources. According to his theory of property, a person becomes the owner of, say, some land (that is not already owned) by mixing labor with it—for instance, by plowing the land and sowing seeds in it. If I do that to some untaken land, then that land becomes rightfully mine. Locke did not think that the land in America had been through this process of having labor mixed with it by the Native Americans. If Native Americans lived only by hunting and gathering, then this would not count, by his standards, as mixing their labor with the land. So any Englishmen (or Frenchmen or Spaniards, etc.) who moved in and farmed it would do so quite legitimately, as Locke saw it. If any of it was farmed, then presumably he would have conceded ownership of it to the people who farmed it. Any ignorance about Native American agriculture on his part would not invalidate his theory.

So there is room in Locke's theory for stealing being wrong even in a state of nature. In that sense, his theory is less amoral than Hobbes' or, rather, his state of nature is less amoral than Hobbes'. But it is also less simple because the question arises whether the supposed owner of whatever is alleged to be property really has the right of ownership. Has he or she mixed labor with the thing or with the land that produced the thing? Or has he or she traded legally for it with someone who mixed his or her labor in order to produce it? And so on. Even if we accept the mixing labor theory of property (and by no means everyone does), there is room for disagreement and doubt about borderline cases where relatively little labor seems to have been mixed with a relatively large quantity of natural resources. If I plow just enough land for my family's farm, then perhaps I have a right to that land. But how much land is enough, and how well must I plow it for my claim to be good? Moral rules or laws bring the possibility of disagreement, and disagreement brings the possibility of disputes and fights.

Like Hobbes, then, Locke foresees a state of nature being unstable and liable to devolve into a state of war. This could be a result of a dispute about who owns what or because someone has straightforwardly stolen from someone else or committed murder or any other crime against the natural law. Without a government to turn to for protection, individuals in a state of nature have little option but to resort to force if they are to defend themselves when their rights are threatened or violated. Thus, as Hobbes argued, individuals should contract together to form a civil government. The government is legitimate, according to Locke, as long as it protects the rights given to individuals by the law of nature. If it fails to protect these rights properly, then it is no longer a legitimate government and the people may rightfully overthrow it. Hobbes also allows for individuals to disobey the government, but the necessary circumstances are more extreme than those Locke envisions. Hobbes allows disobedience only when life or honor is at stake, whereas Locke counts property rights, for example, as natural also. And Hobbes allows disobedience, which must not overthrow the state or cause it to collapse, whereas Locke allows outright rebellion. This intolerance of tyranny makes Locke's political philosophy more popular today than Hobbes'.

Ethics by Agreement

You might be wondering what all this centuries-old political theory has to do with ethics. The answer, in part, is that Hobbes and Locke, who have many followers today, believe that ethics and politics are not easily separated. A state of nature is a nonpolitical state of affairs, and according to Hobbes, it is quite amoral, containing no more right and wrong than the law of nature, which, we saw, is not very different from the law of the jungle. Without a civil society, there is little room for ethics, as Hobbes sees things. Locke's view is different, but it still makes an important connection between ethics and politics. There is, as Locke sees it, a moral law that limits what governments may do. If they break this law, they lose their legitimacy and may be disobeyed quite ethically. This is the kind of reasoning used by Martin Luther King, Jr. to justify breaking segregation laws and by others after World War II to support the idea that there was no excuse for obeying Nazi laws. If a law is fundamentally immoral, if it violates the law of nature, then it is an illegitimate law, not really a law at all, and may be broken with impunity. It might even be one's moral duty to break it. Or so it has been argued.

There is another important link, though, between the kind of "social contract theory" that Hobbes and Locke propose in politics and thinking about ethics. Inspired by Hobbes, the Canadian philosopher David Gauthier has developed a carefully reasoned ethical theory, which he set out in his 1986 book *Morals by Agreement*.[8] Like Hobbes, Gauthier believes that people are mostly self-interested. Nevertheless, he believes that if they are rational, people will behave morally. In other words, he thinks that Thrasymachus can be answered and develops a basically Hobbesian theory in order to do so.

Hobbes' noncooperative state of nature is very unappealing. However egoistic we might be, there is much to be said for cooperation. Faced with an outside threat, for instance, we are much more likely to survive if we band together than if we each defend ourselves alone, thereby letting the enemy pick us off one by one. The same goes in times of peace. Economically we are generally much better off if we specialize and then trade with others, rather than each trying to do everything alone. We cannot all be good farmers and doctors and entertainers and engineers and teachers and so on. It makes sense to trade goods and services, but trade involves cooperation and works best when there is reason to trust each other. If Aristotle is right that we are naturally social beings, then a life of mutual assistance and cooperation will also be more satisfying in itself than a life of fierce independence. Cooperation, then, has multiple likely advantages, from a purely self-interested point of view. And cooperation requires accepting certain limits on what one does to others. It rules out killing them in their sleep, taking their stuff when their backs are turned, lying to them about your ability to pay back the money you want to borrow, and so on. In short, it rules out what Gauthier means by immorality.

Since a situation in which individuals cooperate is preferable to one in which they do not (from the self-interested point of view of each individual), it makes rational sense for individuals to agree to cooperate. It is one thing, though, to agree to cooperate, and another thing to actually cooperate after the agreement. Thrasymachus might gladly agree to a set of rules limiting what others can do to him and pretend to agree not to do those things to others. But would he actually keep to the agreement? Why should he? Well, imagine a whole bunch of Thrasymachuses. Each does just what he wants, making himself quite happy. But each gets done to him just whatever others want to do to him, making him quite miserable. Since he is not irrational, merely amoral, each realizes that he would be better off in a state of mutually agreed cooperation of the kind outlined above. But he also realizes that each has an incentive to break the agreement, so mere words will not be enough. The best possible situation will only be achieved if there is some way to make sure that the agreement is kept. For Hobbes, this meant the strong arm of the law. For Gauthier, talking about morality rather than legality, the enforcement can have a different source. It can come from within. That is to say, if each individual can get himself or herself to *want* to keep the agreement, to *value* its terms, the rules of morality, then the agreement will work. It is rational, therefore, for individuals to dispose themselves, as far as they can, to keep to the agreements they make with others. For only if they are so disposed will others trust them enough to bother making agreements with them. And such agreements are in one's own self-interest. Any individual who cannot be trusted will not be invited to join the club of those who behave morally. These people will be left out in the amoral cold, not a good place to be in any sense of the word "good."

John Rawls

John Rawls (1921–2002) developed another theory based on the idea of a social contract. This theory was published originally in 1971 as *A Theory of Justice* but then revised and reworked throughout the rest of Rawls' life.[9] While Gauthier's theory is designed to answer skepticism about ethics by starting from premises that even Thrasymachus would accept, Rawls starts with an openly ethical assumption, the assumption that we have a moral obligation to accept only principles that can be justified to each rational person. This obligation is required by our duty to respect persons, a duty that we will consider more in Chapter 7 when we look at Immanuel Kant, whose thinking influenced Rawls enormously. If we respect people, then we should not act toward them on the basis of principles that they could not possibly understand or accept, Rawls believes.

So, what kind of principles will be acceptable to rational people? We could try to look around the world and see what people believe, but people believe all kinds of things and are quite liable to have irrational beliefs, based on prejudice or personal bias. I might be prejudiced against people of a different race or sex from my own, for instance, or I might simply care more about my own interests and those of people like me than I care about others'. To get around this kind of difficulty, Rawls asks us to imagine people in what he calls the "original position." Being in the original position, a kind of abstract version of the state of nature, means being behind what he calls the veil of ignorance. Here, people do not know their position in the world. They do not know what race or sex they are (or will be, once they are out of the original position and in the real world). They do not know what talents they have or what disabilities. They do not know whether they are rich or poor, old or young. They do not know whether they are a member of a religious minority or not, whether they are liberal or conservative. Now, what kind of world or society would be acceptable to these people?

They will not, Rawls believes, support any kind of discrimination on racial, sexual, religious, or political grounds. A rational, self-interested person is hardly likely to support apartheid if he or she might turn out to be on the receiving end of it. So there will be no irrational bias or prejudice in a truly fair world, a truly just world, a truly rational world. Instead, everything else (the constitution, e.g., and the laws made within its constraints) will be limited by two guiding principles of justice:

1. Each individual is to have as much liberty as possible, compatible with equal liberty for all.

2. Social and economic advantages are to be equally open to everyone and may only exist when they are to the advantage of all.

Liberty must not be sacrificed for economic gain, Rawls says, so the first principle has priority over the second. No rational person would agree to being sold into slavery. Rawls' conception of justice places a premium on respect for individual freedom but also values socioeconomic equality. If my making myself fabulously rich really does benefit everyone else, then this is all right. For instance, perhaps I pay a lot of taxes that provide services for others, or I get rich by providing entertainment that everyone enjoys. On the other hand, if I make money from others (thereby making them poorer) without making them better off in any way, then maybe I should not be allowed to do so. Exactly how to balance the values of freedom and equality is a controversial issue, but Rawls' theory has found more followers than many others.

Why Be Good?

If Thrasymachus asked you in a state of nature why you should be good, then, according to Hobbes, this question would be quite meaningless. All you can do is what works for you. There are simply your own likes and needs and whatever ways you can find to satisfy these desires and meet those needs. Nobody has any rights that you could violate. In a society, things are different. The laws might confer property rights, for instance, on people and outlaw such acts as murder, which will be defined some particular way by the laws in that society (if only as "whatever the king says is murder"). So you now have reason to be good in the sense of obeying particular laws—if you do not, then you will be punished—and reason to obey the laws in general—if you do not, then society might collapse into anarchy and your life will be solitary, poor, nasty, brutish, and short.

So, how exactly would someone like Hobbes or Gauthier answer Thrasymachus? I will focus on what Gauthier says since it is fundamentally Hobbesian in spirit while being also more clear and precise about ethical questions than Hobbes ever was. Rather than getting into vexed and possibly unanswerable questions about what Hobbes really meant, I will look at what Gauthier means instead. He accepts Thrasymachus' belief that we are better off having others around us be good. Roughly, his idea is that if we are rational, we will want others to be good to us; and this is most likely if they believe us to be good. That in turn is most likely if we actually are good in reality. Therefore, we have reason to be good.

Objections

Let's start with the political aspect of the theories we have been looking at in this chapter. Few people today believe in absolute power for the government. We know that a system of checks and balances can survive, although in times of emergency there are often calls for the government to be given increased powers. We can see, too, that civil war could arise in an absolute monarchy, if ministers refused to go when fired or if the people refused to accept tyranny any longer. Indeed, Hobbes himself granted that individuals have the right to disobey the sovereign rather than sacrifice their life or honor, so long as the very existence of the commonwealth is not at stake. Even an absolute monarch cannot murder and rape at will. Still, this protection is probably not enough to convince us to accept rule by a monarch or group of people wielding the powers of a monarch collectively.

If we accept Locke's belief in natural rights, then we might well accept the rest of his theory, or much of it at least; but a real skeptic is unlikely to accept any theory based on belief in God-given rights or moral truths that are held to be self-evident. This is a problem for Locke's theory generally and a problem particularly for anyone who might want to use his theory for something that it was not intended to be used for—namely, combating moral skepticism. It would be unfair to condemn his theory for that reason, but the problem is worth noting. We have seen already some of the problems that arise when a view claims to tell us what God says is right or what nature reveals to be right. Similarly, Rawls' theory cannot really be used to answer the skeptic since certain ideas about fairness are fundamental to it and must be taken as given or else justified by reference to other arguments. We will see what some of these might be in Chapter 7.

Otherwise, there are two main ways that one might try to object to Rawls. The first would be to question the principles of justice that Rawls thinks people in the original position would agree on. You might argue that it is not rational to care so much about equality. What if someone were to gain an economic advantage without violating anyone's rights or liberties but in a way that harmed some people? Would that necessarily be unfair or unjust? Imagine, for example, people voluntarily acting to their own disadvantage, perhaps by gambling all their money away. Is it really irrational to allow them to do so? Or you might argue that it is not rational to value liberty more than economic goods. You might (like David Hume, whose ideas we will consider in the next chapter) think that no relative evaluation is more or less rational than any other. Second, you might question Rawls' procedure itself. The original position involves something like disembodied souls waiting to become embodied and reasoning among themselves about what kind of world they want to be placed into. This kind of rational heaven might be one picture of a fair-and-just-principle factory, but it might not be the only one possible. And perhaps a different way of arriving at principles of justice would bring us to different principles. It has been wondered why we should care what these hypothetical people would hypothetically agree to. Rawls' answer to that is basically that we do. In the 1999 edition of his book, he writes as follows:

> the hypothetical nature of the original position invites the question: why should we take any interest in it, moral or otherwise. Recall the answer: the conditions embodied in the description of this situation are ones that we do in fact accept.[10]

In other words, he does not claim to be able to prove that it is fair to support principles that would be accepted by imaginary people behind a veil of ignorance concerning precisely the things he includes and no others. But it does sound fair, it does sound reasonable, doesn't it? Thrasymachus might simply refuse to play the game, rejecting the very notion of fairness, but that does not mean that we should not play along and see what happens. Some who do play end up agreeing with Rawls; others do not. You can, of course, decide for yourself.

The main objection to Hobbes' political philosophy is that he goes too far in defending tyranny. Absolute authority in the hands of one sovereign is neither necessary nor sufficient to prevent civil war. Indeed, Hobbes himself allowed for limits to the authority of the sovereign, albeit perhaps not as many as we would like. The main objection to Hobbes' thinking on ethics is that it is so hard to make out what it is. He seems to say one thing at one time and then another at another. There are, consequently, many different interpretations of what his moral theory is. That is one good reason for looking more at Gauthier's theory instead of Hobbes'.

There are two main challenges to Gauthier's theory. The first involves the idea of disposing oneself to keep agreements and the second involves the question of whether morals by agreement are really morals at all. Some people would insist that there is more to morality than the golden rule, than treating others as you would have them treat you, which is the kind of morality that most concerns social contract theorists. For instance, Immanuel Kant believes that we have duties to ourselves. Hobbes might agree that we have a duty to refrain from suicide, but if this is based on self-interest alone, then there could be cases where suicide was justified—for instance, in cases in which death was certain and the person was in great pain. If you think that certain acts are wrong even when everyone involved is a consenting adult, then you are likely to think that Gauthier has not defended the whole of morality. You might also think that what he has defended is not morality itself but the pretence of morality. He has, that is to say, given reasons for *acting* like a good person but not for *being* a good person.

How strong these objections are depends on what really counts as morality. Some conceptions of morality see it as concerning one's actions with regard to God or oneself; others do not. Some see it as concerning actions alone, or at least primarily, while others emphasize attitudes, inner thoughts, and so on. With regard to the question of being good versus acting good, that is where disposing oneself to keep agreements comes in. If you successfully dispose yourself to keep an agreement to be moral, then it is hard to see what difference there would be between you and a genuinely moral person. We might well wonder how far it is possible to dispose ourselves to want or value things that we do not already want or value, but then that is a question about how far someone like Thrasymachus is *capable* of being good. If Gauthier is right, Thrasymachus has a good reason to want to be good. Whether he is capable of becoming so is another matter, but if he is not, this does not make Gauthier's theory false. And most of us, thankfully, are not like Thrasymachus. We do try to do the right thing most of the time and so do not need to work hard at disposing ourselves to do the right thing.

But is Gauthier right? Is it rational to agree to be moral as he understands what that involves? Imagine you are Thrasymachus in a moral state of nature surrounded by other Thrasymachuses. Where you are, point A, is a bad place to be. A world in which everyone is good, let us assume for the sake of argument, would be better for everybody. Call that point B. Does it follow that it is rational for you to do what it takes to get from A to B? Not necessarily. Maybe point C, where everyone is good but you only appear to be good, would be even better. In that case, the rational thing might be for you to dispose yourself to appear to be good, to do what it takes to get a good reputation as a keeper of agreements, without actually becoming such a person in fact. Then you would still be Thrasymachus and we would have made no advance on Plato.

Finally, it is worth looking at some objections that have been made to social contract theory quite generally. One important problem is that a contract only binds the parties to the contract. If the reasons for contracting in the first place are self-interested, then people will only contract with those who are likely to be able to benefit them in some way. If we derive our ethics from this kind of contract, then those who cannot benefit us will be left outside the sphere of morality. If rights, for instance, come not mysteriously from nature or God but explicitly from a contract made for mutual benefit, then those unable to offer such benefits will be left without rights. So will those who cannot enter into a meaningful contract, such as infants and some people with mental illnesses. This is another reason for thinking that we cannot derive or support the whole of morality by hypothetical agreement.

Another type of objection is to a kind of mythology that is thought by some people to go along with thinking in terms of a social contract. Prior to the social contract, the people who are to be bound by it are thought of as independent agents. In Rawls' version of social contract theory, they are independent even of their bodies. At least, they do not know their sex or their race. Of course, this in itself is not a criticism. It is not as if Rawls failed to realize that the original position is not realistic. It is not meant to be realistic. It is a kind of ideal, designed to help us think without prejudice or bias. In the end, though, what we are to think about or to apply our principles of justice to is ourselves in the real world. And in the real world we are not completely independent. We depend on our mothers to give birth to us and then on a host of caregivers (family members, teachers, neighbors, and so on) to protect and raise us until we are adults. Even then, we are members of a society that provides us with various goods (military protection, public highways, etc.) and expects certain things from us in return. We might be rational, but we are not completely independent. Social contract theory, in inviting us to identify with independent, amoral, self-interested agents at the bargaining table, might encourage a false view of who we are and where we have come from.

Historically, the people thought of as independent and rational have been white men, while women and African Americans have often been treated as irrational and dependent. The African American law professor Patricia J. Williams raises concerns about this in her paper "On Being the Object of Property."[11] It could be argued that thinking like Rawls' and Gauthier's shows how irrational racism and sexism are since it would hardly be prudent to deny yourself contracts with people who might benefit you just because you did not like their race or sex. To the extent that Rawls' and Gauthier's kind of thinking makes clear some of the disadvantages of racism and sexism, it is surely a good thing. But it does not follow that there are no dangers involved with it. Children and caregivers (who in reality are most often women) do not fit the traditional model of independent agents. Nor do many human relationships fit the model of voluntary associations entered into for mutual advantage.

Annette Baier has argued that thinking of human relations in terms of contracts distorts our understanding of those relations, encouraging us to ignore the importance of love and such necessary relations as those between mother and child.[12] The point is not that it is a woman's function to have children or that love between parents and children is inevitable. The point is, rather, that we do not come into the world as either independent or rational. We can only *become* independent and rational, and to do so we need help from others. This help should not be ignored if we are to understand ourselves and our relations to others. Excessive focus on hypothetical relations between idealized independent agents might do more harm than good. Charles W. Mills reminds us of the horrors of some real-world contracts (those involved in buying and selling Africans as slaves, e.g.) and argues that racial distinctions themselves are a product of a kind of social contract, a contract between whites at the expense of all nonwhites.[13] Carole Pateman makes a similar claim in relation to sexism and was an inspiration for Mills.[14]

On the other hand, Jean Hampton argues that theories like Hobbes' can actually be especially good for feminists.[15] As admirable as altruism might be, taken to an extreme it can amount to a denial of the self. This kind of denial has often been pushed on women as an ideal to which they, more than men, should aspire. A little Hobbesian egoism might be just what these women need to reclaim their lives. Perhaps an ideal moral theory would treat each person with equal respect, quite possibly advocating altruism but not exploiting virtues such as charity and devotion. Contract theories allow for this kind of equality. If it can be shown that it is rational for each of us to be good purely in terms of self-interest, then we can be confident that being good is not being exploited or taken for a ride.

Unfortunately, though, it looks as if the very self-interested individualism that holds out this promise also makes such theories incapable of supporting genuinely moral conclusions. It is dubious, Hampton says, that we can control or will into being the kind of dispositions that Gauthier's theory requires. We cannot, she suspects, simply dispose ourselves to be good, as Gauthier thinks we should. Even if this is possible, it might be more rational only to pretend to be so disposed and so to act otherwise when you can get away with it. Moreover, the nature of Hobbes' attempt to justify morality amorally means that it cannot reach the conclusion that any person has intrinsic value, that someone might have value except as a means to some end. That is to say, if we start by viewing people in a purely self-interested way, then they cannot end up having more than instrumental value for us. If we cannot benefit from trading with them, for instance, then they will have no value for us. And if we do value them, it will only be to get things we want, as means rather than as ends. A truly Hobbesian theory can never reach the conclusion that people should be respected as ends in themselves. Those who sympathize with Immanuel Kant's ethics (see Chapter 7) therefore think that Hobbesian theories can never justify *ethics* or being *good*. They can only, at best, justify acting *as if* you were good.

Conclusion

Hobbes develops a very interesting political theory out of a scientific and psychological theory that might now seem somewhat dated and simplistic. The science of his day was based on the idea of a mechanical universe of solid atoms. Today, we think of matter as a form of energy, and old-fashioned causal laws do not apply at the quantum level. Hobbes' ideas about how the brain works have little appeal. His political theory, though, is still regarded as important and useful for understanding human relations. Moreover, we can develop a moral theory on the basis of Hobbes' political theory, and this kind of theory is often thought to hold out hope of answering Thrasymachus and enabling us to work out what our ethical principles ought to be. We would thus kill two birds with one stone: answer the question why we should be moral or try to do the right thing and answer all the questions we have about just what the right thing is.

Unfortunately, this kind of contractarian theory has yet to satisfy everybody. It is not clear in what sense, if any, a moral equivalent of Hobbes' state of nature might ensue if I do not follow society's standards of ethical conduct. So if I am more liberal or conservative than everybody else on some issue, why should I conform? And what about those who could not possibly be involved in a moral agreement, such as infants and the mentally handicapped? If I agree to a rule against lying, then that gives me some reason not to lie. Breaking society's standard would mean breaking my own agreement (not that Thrasymachus would care about that). But what about a rule designed to protect the lives of newborn infants? That would only come into existence if non-newborns chose to implement it. Yet surely, you might think, baby murdering ought to be ruled out regardless of what nonbabies happen to accept? Social contract ethics do not seem to have the right foundation or priorities. Babies have rights, we might say, whether society accepts them or not. Similarly, I should not murder people, not simply because to do so would mean breaking my promise or going against my own self-interest but because it is *unjust*, regardless of whether I have agreed not to commit murder or would be rational to agree to such a policy. We might be able to work out good policies by thinking of what reasonable people would be likely to agree to, but there seems to be more to ethics than this.

Social contract theory is not one thing. It is political and it is moral. It has been used by thinkers with quite different politics to answer quite different questions, on the basis of a variety of assumptions. It is, or ought to be, hard to generalize about it. What is most interesting from our point of view is two things. One is that, in some of its forms, it tries to respond to Thrasymachus on his own terms. Whether it succeeds is open to doubt; but the attempt itself seems worthwhile, and Gauthier's work has earned itself many admirers. It cannot lightly be dismissed. The other most interesting thing from the perspective of someone trying to answer Thrasymachus is the challenge that trying to do so on his terms might seriously corrupt or distort our own thinking. If we try to see things from an amoral point of view, disregarding feelings of love, say, or commitment to human rights whether these can be explained or not, then perhaps we will find it hard to regain the things that made us unlike Thrasymachus, the things that made us human. The danger might not be great, but it is worth considering. Or perhaps the danger lies not so much in answering moral skepticism but in the particular way that social contract theories try to do so, by abstracting from the real, historical world into an idealized one. If social contract thinking is itself a moral danger, then it is just as well that this chapter is over.

Questions for Further Thought

1. Can political questions be distinguished from ethical ones?

2. How dangerous is philosophical abstraction?

3. Should we care about the hypothetical agreements of hypothetical people?

4. Is ethics all about how we treat other people?

5. Where might rights come from?

Notes

1. Thomas Hobbes, *Leviathan*, ed. J. C. A. Gaskin (Oxford: Oxford University Press, 1998), 35.
2. Ibid., 114.
3. Ibid.
4. Ibid., 87.
5. In fact, there are 19 Hobbesian laws of nature, but almost all are principles of rational prudence or self-interest. See Gregory S. Kavka, *Hobbesian Moral and Political Theory* (Princeton: Princeton University Press, 1986), 343, for the full list.
6. Hobbes, *Leviathan*, 86.
7. John Locke, *Second Treatise of Government*, in *Two Treatises of Government*, ed. Peter Laslett (Cambridge: Cambridge University Press, 1988), Chapter II, § 6.
8. David Gauthier, *Morals by Agreement* (Oxford: Oxford University Press, 1986).
9. John Rawls, *A Theory of Justice* (Cambridge, MA: Harvard University Press, 1971).
10. John Rawls, *A Theory of Justice* (Cambridge, MA: Belknap Press, 1999), 514.
11. In her book *The Alchemy of Race and Rights* (Cambridge, MA: Harvard University Press, 1992).
12. See Annette Baier, *Moral Prejudices* (Cambridge, MA: Harvard University Press, 1995), especially "What Do Women Want in an Ethical Theory?"
13. See Charles W. Mills, *The Racial Contract* (Ithaca, NY: Cornell University Press, 1999).
14. See Carole Pateman, *The Sexual Contract* (Palo Alto, CA: Stanford University Press, 1988).
15. See Jean Hampton, "Two Faces of Contractarian Thought," in Peter Vallentyne, ed., *Contractarianism and Rational Choice: Essays on David Gauthier's Morals by Agreement* (New York: Cambridge University Press, 1991), 31–55.

Suggestions for Further Reading

The main works referred to in this chapter are as follows: Thomas Hobbes, *Leviathan*, ed. J. C. A. Gaskin (Oxford: Oxford University Press, 1998); Gregory S. Kavka, *Hobbesian Moral and Political Theory* (Princeton: Princeton University Press, 1986); John Locke, *Two Treatises of Government*, ed. Peter Laslett, (Cambridge: Cambridge University Press, 1988); David Gauthier, *Morals by Agreement* (Oxford: Oxford University Press, 1986); John Rawls, *A Theory of Justice* (Cambridge, MA: Belknap Press, 1999); Charles W. Mills, *The Racial Contract* (Ithaca, NY: Cornell University Press, 1999); Carole Pateman, *The Sexual Contract* (Palo Alto Stanford University Press, 1988); and Peter Vallentyne, ed., *Contractarianism and Rational Choice: Essays on David Gauthier's Morals by Agreement*, (Cambridge: Cambridge University Press, 1991).

You might also want to explore readings in Stephen Darwall, ed., *Contractarianism/Contractualism* (Oxford: Blackwell, 2002), which includes key passages from Hobbes, Gauthier, and Rawls, among others. Also relevant are T. M. Scanlon, *What We Owe to Each Other* (Cambridge, MA: Belknap Press, 2000), and Philip Stratton-Lake, ed., *On What We Owe to Each Other* (Oxford: Blackwell, 2004), which is a collection of essays about Scanlon's book.

CHAPTER 6

Hume

The Scotsman David Hume (1711–1776) was influenced by Hobbes' interest in a scientific approach to moral psychology. Also like Hobbes, Hume's ethics were quite unlike those of Thomas Aquinas. Hume derided what he called the "monk-ish virtues" of chastity, silence, and other "slavish" (to use Friedrich Nietzsche's word) Christian values.[1] He also took on natural law theory in his defense of suicide. Traditional natural law theorists argue that suicide is wrong because it is against nature (and hence, most of them would add, against God). We know it is against nature because, in the words of a later philosopher,

> Surely one cannot will one's own destruction, and anybody who had visualized what is in practice involved in the act of suicide knows that suicide is always a *rushing of one's own defences.*[2]

These words seem to encapsulate the Thomistic idea that suicide is bad because it is a kind of crime against the self and because it is profoundly un-natural. One needs to rush one's own defenses in order to commit suicide be-cause it cannot be done with one's own complete, conscious consent. It just goes against the grain too much, and this grain is part of human nature. Aquinas would add, following Aristotle, that it is also culpably antisocial since suicide deprives the community of one of its members (think, e.g., of the effect on one's family).

Hume disagrees with much of this. The individual is in the best position to know what is good for him- or herself, he argues. So those who want to commit suicide might well know best what is in their own interests. The rest of us should not presume otherwise. As for the community, we do not condemn those who go off to live on their own. Suicide is merely a permanent withdrawal, different in degree but not in kind from being a hermit. So it cannot always be wrong on this score. Perhaps it is wrong for some people to become hermits—if they have children or patients who depend on them, say—but unless all hermits are con-sidered to be in the wrong, then not all suicides should be condemned on the grounds that they are too antisocial.

Most importantly, Hume attacks the idea that suicide (or really anything at all) might be wrong just because it goes against the natural course of events. Diverting a river, he points out, is an interference with nature; but no one usually deems it a crime. Why then is it wrong to divert the course of the blood in our veins? The physics is the same in each case. So how can one be against nature and the other not?

Perhaps, Hume concedes, the argument is that it is wrong to interfere in matters of life and death. There, we should let nature take its course. But what if someone would die if we did not interfere? Surely, we can agree that it is all right to go against nature in order to save a life? The issue is not, Hume thinks, whether nature is interfered with but whether the best interests of people are served. And in some cases the people in the best position to judge this determine that suicide is their best option. So what natural law objection remains to ending one's life? Hume's conclusion is not that we should all kill ourselves but that natural law theory gives no justification for moral opposition to all suicide. In at least some cases it might be quite natural to use our God-given power of self-destruction to end a painful life that it is natural to want to end.

The Subjective Basis of Ethics

If we do not base our ethics on nature, though, on what should we base them? Hume's answer is **utility**, understood as what is useful (and what therefore leads indirectly to pleasure or reduced displeasure) and what is agreeable (directly pleasurable). Ethics is all about character traits (i.e., virtues and vices). We never disapprove of an act itself, he argues, only the vice that we believe must have given rise to it. Which character traits are virtues and which are vices? Virtues are traits that are useful or agreeable either to the person who has them or to others. Vices are harmful or disagreeable to oneself or others. The virtuous person will be the kind of man one would want one's daughter to marry, says Hume, in his rather politically incorrect way. The ideal son-in-law will be fair and kind and, thus, useful to others; a good student likely to have a successful career and, therefore, useful to himself; witty, polite, gallant, and unpretentious and, therefore, agreeable to others; cheerful and able to overcome misfortune and thus, agreeable to himself.

It follows from this, Hume believes, that some traditional values, notably Christian ones, are in fact not virtues at all but vices:

> Celibacy, fasting, penance, mortification, self-denial, humility, silence, solitude, and the whole train of monkish virtues; for what reason are they every where rejected by men of sense, but because they serve to no manner of purpose . . . ? We observe, on the contrary, that they . . . stupify [sic] the understanding and harden the heart, obscure the fancy and sour the temper. We justly, therefore, transfer them to the opposite column, and place them in the catalogue of vices.[3]

While Hume's ideal person is recognizable as a good type, as a moral ideal it is a far cry from that of Jesus. Hume was especially opposed to puritanical forms of

Christianity, but his values seem hard to square with those of Christians in general or, indeed, of other religious believers who locate ultimate value beyond the human sphere. Jesus (like Moses and Muhammad) was a man of many qualities, but *useful and pleasant* is probably not the brief description of him that first springs to mind. Hume's view could be considered somewhat superficial. It might seem to be a reflection of his own society and its rather comfortable values. Before we even attempt to judge his ideal, though, we should consider what justification there is for it. The justification is meant to be empirical or scientific. Hume takes himself in his primary works to be not advocating a particular view about how we ought to behave but describing the workings of human psychology. As a matter of fact, he says, when we consider some immoral act (an instance of murder, say), we find nothing vicious or evil in the objective state of affairs. Death in itself is not immoral, however bad it might be. Nor is causing death, as we see if we think of a falling tree causing someone's death. This is a terrible thing, but we do not blame the tree for it.

The basis of ethics, Hume concludes, is subjective. We find no moral wrongness in our investigation until we look inside ourselves and explore our feelings. There, we will find feelings of approval or disapproval. And of what do we disapprove? Not death, not causing death, but the character of a person who would do such a thing as cause an innocent's death. Such a characteristic might be useful to the person who possesses it (as long as he or she does not get caught and punished), but it is hardly useful to others and is certainly not agreeable.

Hume wrote in a time when philosophers were arguing about whether ethics was a matter of reason (which would hold out considerable hope of the kind of justification of ethics that we want) or of sentiment or feeling (which would not necessarily be disastrous but would lend itself more to the skeptic's cause). He is associated with this latter school of thought, but in fact he says we should not try to settle the matter at this kind of abstract level. Instead, we should look at real-life examples of what we regard as good if we want a clear view of what ethics is all about.

Something like a scientific approach is relatively easy to adopt. Consider the case of a man lying dead on a road. As we have seen, there is something sad about this case but nothing especially moral about it. He might, after all, have died of natural causes. It is only when we think of a person having caused his death that we start to get moral feelings about it. The actual act of killing might be exactly the same whether committed by a falling branch or a swinging club, so evil and good lie not in the act but in the motive, the cause of the act—and then only if this cause is something within the character of a human being.

"Reason is and ought only to be the slave of the passions," Hume says.[4] In part, he seems to make this extreme statement to shock people out of the traditional, Platonic idea that reason and passion are in conflict and that reason always should win out. The implication is that there really is no alternative to reason's obeying the directions of passion but also that any such alternative should be rejected even if it did somehow arise. Reason can tell us what is the case, but it takes some emotion or passion, some motive, to get us to act on that information one way or another. An attempt to act on the basis of reason alone is bound to fail, leading either to inaction or to some self-deception about one's true motive. Some passions or wills are more normal than others, and some might be downright psychopathic; but these are judged as such by reference simply to the normal will, normal passions, not to any extrahuman or objective standard. A desire for cookies is normal, while a desire to inflict pain on others is not. If this sounds subjective to you, then you agree with Hume. Moral judgments are made from a standpoint that is as impartial as possible, but he still thinks they are subjective. What is good is what is useful or agreeable to oneself or others, and the reference to agreeableness here (implicit in the reference to usefulness) means that what is good can only be judged by us, by human beings, on the basis of what we find agreeable.

We react to the things that come into our minds through the senses with pleasure and displeasure, and reason cannot help this. It can only help us to find ways to maximize our chances of feeling pleasure rather than displeasure. For instance, if I find that putting green beans in my mouth causes me to feel great displeasure, reason might advise me to spit them out or at least not to eat them again. But no amount of rational thinking will make my tongue react differently to food I simply do not like. (This is not to say that tastes cannot change over time or even be "educated" by nonrational means. Adults tend to like candy less than children do, and one can train oneself not to crave cigarettes, for example, by a Pavlovian process of associating bad things with smoking.) So rational argument will not change our moral sentiments, but it might lead us to put ourselves in a position to perceive things differently, to train our bodies to react differently to things, and consequently to feel different sentiments. For instance, a sadist might take pleasure in witnessing a fire. Reason might then prompt him to take a closer look at the fire. This further investigation could reveal that his own friends are in danger, making him now feel not pleasure but anxious concern. He is no less a sadist than he was before, but his feelings about the fire have changed. Or the pleasure that a nonsadistic but not very imaginative person might take in the spectacle of a fire could be replaced by displeasure once that person's attention is drawn to the suffering of its victims. In the same kind of way, Hume believes, reason cannot change our natures but it can play a part in changing opinions about moral matters. We will return to this below. Before that, if we are to understand Hume's theory, then we need to look more at what he has to say about moral psychology.

Sympathy

Hume believes that all ideas come from experience, that they exist in the mind only after the senses have provided the necessary ingredients. Everything in the mind, then, is, or is composed of, either impressions ("live" sensations) or simple ideas (thoughts or copies of impressions). Simple ideas can then be combined to make new, complex ideas that correspond to nothing we have ever experienced. For instance, if I combine my idea of the color gold with my idea of a mountain, I can create the idea of a golden mountain, even though I have never witnessed such a thing. But all genuine ideas can in principle be traced back to the original impressions from which they are composed. Indeed, any "idea" that fails to meet this standard is merely an empty word and should be rejected, Hume says. Now, if all that is present to the mind is perceptions (i.e., impressions and ideas) and if the only ideas that have real meaning are those that can be traced back to some original impression, then the ideas of vice and virtue must, if they are to have meaning, come from something like sensory perception. Hence, Hume has to believe in something like a moral sense, a way of getting impressions from which moral ideas could be derived, if he is to avoid Thrasymachean skepticism. We will see how this works below.

The relatively abstract idea of someone else's passion or feelings, Hume says, can be turned into a much more lively feeling or impression by what he calls "sympathy." This is a natural, almost mechanical process that he observes in people and animals. "The howlings and lamentations of a dog produce a sensible concern in his fellows," he writes.[5] In the same way, we are made sad by the sight of someone crying, happy by the sight of someone smiling.

> In general we may remark, that the minds of men are mirrors to one another, not only because they reflect each others emotions, but also because those rays of passions, sentiments and opinions may be often reverberated, and may decay away by insensible degrees.[6]

So sympathy can die away over time, but before it does so even the *thought* of happy people might make us happy, while the thought of people suffering famine or natural disasters overseas can make us sad. Some people have more sympathy than others, but it does indeed appear to be a feature of the human mind that it sometimes operates in this way. What we perceive or imagine others to be feeling, we, sometimes, feel spontaneously ourselves.

But not always. Sometimes we feel glad that others are suffering, especially if they are our rivals in some way. Just as sympathy is natural, Hume argues, so too is comparison of our own lot with that of others. If someone else's success makes me feel relatively a failure, then I might not be sympathetic at all. Quite the reverse. This is Hume's explanation for such phenomena as envy, malice, and *Schadenfreude* (i.e., taking pleasure in someone else's misfortune).

On the other hand, sympathy can be increased by perceived similarities with the people in question. If I see people do well who speak my language or share my nationality or personality or who are members of my family, say, then I am likely to be pleased rather than envious—more pleased than I would be if someone completely foreign to me shared the same good fortune. This is why, Hume believes, we often care more about disasters that occur closer to home or that affect people who look like us. The largely white developed world certainly seemed to care more about genocide in the largely white former

Yugoslavia than it did about the appalling massacres that took place in Rwanda. Hume offers a plausible, if somewhat depressing, explanation of this.

It is not a feature of human nature that he endorses. In fact, this kind of bias is something that hinders our efforts to be moral and to make accurate moral judgments. In that sense, it is just as bad, just as much a problem, as comparison. Proper moral judgments, then, while subjective, require perception from a general point of view, not a narrowly selfish or biased one.

Virtue and Vice

We have seen that Hume has reason to believe in a kind of moral sense. He calls this the "moral sentiment." The moral sentiment, as Hume understands it, is a particular kind of pleasure that we take in character traits that are useful and agreeable when considered from a "general and steady" point of view. This feeling is what makes the traits in question virtues or vices.

> [W]hen you pronounce any action or character to be vicious, you mean nothing, but that from the constitution of your nature you have a feeling or sentiment of blame from the contemplation of it.[7]

> To have the sense of virtue, is nothing but to *feel* a satisfaction of a particular kind from the contemplation of a character. The very *feeling* constitutes our praise or admiration. We go no farther; nor do we enquire into the cause of the satisfaction. We do not infer a character to be virtuous, because it pleases: But in feeling that it pleases after such a particular manner, we in effect feel that it is virtuous.[8]

That is, "virtue" means a character trait that gives rise to this specific kind of pleasure. So not only is ethics subjective, in Hume's view, but it is defined in subjective terms, in relation to a feeling. It is *essentially* subjective. Not in an individual, relativist way, though. To judge that something is virtuous, say, we must adopt a general point of view, and we must judge that normally constituted, well-informed, impartial people would feel about it as we do. Nevertheless, ethical judgment is, for Hume, fundamentally a matter of feeling.

One good feature of Hume's theory is that it takes account of the fact that not everything disagreeable is disapproved of morally. Mullets, socks worn with sandals, and wearing shorts, a baseball cap, and a tie together are all disagreeable but surely not morally wrong. Hume would distinguish here between aesthetic feelings of disapproval and ethical feelings of disapproval. Sometimes, no doubt, the feelings will be almost indistinguishable, but generally we can tell which is which. One might still feel that this is all much too subjective.

If the distinctively moral feeling that Hume has in mind does not exist or cannot be identified, then his talk about virtue and vice is pretty much incomprehensible (unless we disregard his definition, of course). This looks like a problem since we often wonder whether we can really know what others are feeling or whether our feelings are the same as theirs. Ludwig Wittgenstein famously suggested that no word can be defined by reference to a purely subjective object—as we might imagine a feeling to be—since such objects are inescapably private, knowable only to those who have them. So the definition would be no use at all to those who are meant to learn from it. This is his so-called private language argument.[9] The argument is subtle and controversial, and we cannot go into it more here; but whatever we make of it, there does seem to be something suspect (either morally or logically) about defining virtue and vice in terms of a mere feeling or contingent psychological state. If nothing else, a change in our psychology would then mean that what once were virtues might now be vices. If we rule out in advance the idea that cruelty, say, might be a virtue (regardless of how we felt about it), then we must reject this part of Hume's theory.

His moral psychology might be questionable, then; but we can still learn from his analysis of virtue. For instance, Hume seems to be right when he says that we can easily see what qualities lead us to praise people. Benevolence, for instance, or kindness is always highly regarded. It is equally obvious, Hume thinks, why this is. It is useful and makes people happy. It is both pleasant and beneficial for me to have neighbors who will lend me an egg at a moment's notice. So, of course, I prize such neighbors, as everyone does.

Justice, though, and other "artificial virtues" are not quite like this. Neighbors who gave me nothing but what I deserve or what is rightfully mine might not be especially pleasant. But it is certainly useful to have neighbors who do at least this much. This is one difference, then, between benevolence and justice. Justice is not especially pleasant and is valued solely because of its utility. Injustice is certainly unpleasant, and justice might be correspondingly pleasant but only because of what benefits us or what we have learned to expect. It is not, Hume thinks, simply, immediately, or naturally pleasant in the way that the so-called natural virtues are.

Another difference is that warmth and kindness are much the same everywhere, whereas justice will vary depending on the circumstances. For example, we might not have property rules at all if all goods existed in such abundance that I was really not affected by someone else's taking what I had intended to eat myself. In a world overflowing with foods and all kinds of things that we like, there might be no conception of "mine" and "yours" and so no theft as we know it. Similarly, where the rules of marriage are very different, so might be the rights of wives and husbands. So justice, conceived of as having to do with such things as property rules, promises, and rights, is not a natural but an artificial virtue depending on the time and place in question. Consequently, it is not part of human nature as such to be inclined toward one version of justice or another, so just acts do not give rise to the kind of spontaneous pleasure that we get from benevolent ones. They are undeniably useful though. It is because of this that pressure is put on people to keep their promises, respect private property, and so on. How far this kind of pressure, in the form of anything from criminal law to parental persuasion, is justified depends on whether we are justified in valuing utility.

The Selfish Hypothesis

Why do we value usefulness or utility? The question might not appear to be worth asking since obviously we have selfish reasons for valuing it. But this is only part of the answer, according to Hume. After all, how could we ever have developed and mastered the rich vocabulary that we have for moral values if all this talk were just a cover for straightforward self-interest? Thrasymachus thinks our moral concepts were invented by people in power who want to keep or increase their power. How, though, could such crude motives lead to the creation, retention, and daily use of sophisticated and nuanced notions such as honor and modesty? It seems that these concepts must fit something already in our lives, in the world around us and the way we respond to it, so that we take them into our language quite naturally. They are not just artificially imposed on us. If they were, we might think, knowing whom to call honorable or decent or slimy or squirrelly or whatever would be a very complicated matter, instead of something that we pick up fairly easily and take to quite intuitively. Having said that, concepts like modesty and honor have gone in and out of fashion in human history and tend to be rather culturally sensitive. If they seem natural to us, perhaps that is only because we have been so well trained by the power elites that Thrasymachus warns us about.

It is difficult to settle that issue one way or the other, but Hume has other reasons for rejecting the idea that all ethics rests on selfish desires for pleasure and what is beneficial to ourselves. For instance, he points out that we admire virtuous acts done long ago, that do not benefit us in any discernible way. We even admire virtues that harm us, such as the courage of our enemies. At least some people sometimes feel such admiration, and this is all that Hume needs to make his point. (Or is this just more evidence of successful brainwashing?) We also distinguish without too much difficulty between the moral approval and the selfish glee we feel when someone does something morally good that also happens to benefit us. Other qualities, those that Hume calls the "selfish virtues," of hard work, frugality, and the like, are approved by others even though they benefit directly only their possessor. And we approve of cleanliness, wit, politeness, and dignity, to name a few, immediately, without having to stop and calculate how these traits will affect us. It appears, in short, that we are not *purely* egoistic or selfish, even if selfishness is an important *part* of our makeup.

As Hume says,

> It is sufficient for our present purpose, if it be allowed, what surely, without the greatest absurdity, cannot be disputed, that there is some benevolence, however small, infused into our bosom; some spark of friendship for human kind; some particle of the dove, kneaded into our frame, along with the elements of the wolf and serpent.[10]

Is and Ought

At least up to a point, as we have seen, Hume would happily accept that ethics is subjective. Knowing what is right and wrong does depend on having certain feelings. Science and logic cannot help us much here. This has to do with the distinction between facts and values, which Hume helped to make famous. The passage in question is as follows:

> In every system of morality, which I have hitherto met with, I have always remark'd, that the author . . . makes observations concerning human affairs; when of a sudden I am surpriz'd to find, that instead of the usual copulations of propositions, *is*, and *is not*, I meet with no proposition that is not connected with an *ought*, or an *ought not*. This change is imperceptible; but is, however, of the last consequence. For as this *ought*, or *ought not*, expresses some new relation or affirmation, 'tis necessary that it shou'd be observ'd and explain'd; and at the same time that a reason should be given . . . how this new relation can be a deduction from others, which are entirely different from it. But as authors do not commonly use this precaution, I shall presume to recommend it to the readers; and am persuaded, that this small attention would subvert all the vulgar systems of morality, and let us see, that the distinction of vice and virtue is not founded merely on the relations of objects, nor is it perceived by reason.[11]

We might, perhaps, be able to prove that something is natural, say; but it does not follow logically that it is good (unless we define "natural" so as to ensure that we reach the conclusion we want). We might prove that something always makes people unhappy, but it does not follow that this thing is bad (unless we build badness into the definition of "unhappy"). From the fact that something is the case, Hume argues, nothing follows about what we ought to do. Judgments of value are not empirical facts. Many philosophers have concluded from Hume's reasoning that facts and values are logically distinct.

Is this right? Suppose we argue as follows:

Murder generally makes people unhappy.

It is bad for people to be made unhappy.

Therefore, murder is generally bad.

Don't we here have an evaluative conclusion following from two facts? Someone might argue that values have been smuggled in, that the second premise of our argument is not a statement of fact but a judgment of value. Of course it is, but what justifies the idea that it is not also a fact? Does empirical science discover it to be true? I would say not, but if "bad" means "tending to produce feelings of disapproval in the non-psychopathic" (which is roughly what it does mean according to Hume), then perhaps it does. Does logic prove it to be true?

If we analyze the concept of unhappiness, thinking carefully about its precise meaning, isn't it possible that badness might turn out to be one of its ingredients? Unhappiness certainly feels bad and is generally shunned (which would fit with the account of "bad" given by Thomas Hobbes).

However we define "bad" or "unhappy," if, the first time we ever met, you spat in my face (which would then be a fact), then you would have been rude to me (a value judgment). Whether you care about rudeness is a subjective or personal matter, but there are public, shared, and perhaps objective standards of what counts as rudeness. And the same might be said of cruelty and injustice or virtues such as courage and honesty. Whether courage really is a virtue might be disputed, but it rarely is; and its status as a virtue might seem to some people to be definitional, or at least close to being so. Consider another example. It is a fact that the deliberate judicial conviction of a person known to be innocent is unjust. This is part of the meaning of injustice. Is it part of the meaning of injustice also that it is bad? We might certainly doubt, with good reason, that someone understood the concept of injustice if he or she did not accept that it was bad (in general—there are always going to be exceptional cases that can be dreamed up). Or, again, could we define "murder" without reference to wrongfulness, innocence, or some other morally loaded term? I doubt it very much.

It would be going too far to pretend that all ethics is analytic, that we can figure out what is right and what is wrong just by analyzing concepts; but the idea that there is a logical or conceptual gulf between statements of fact and judgments of value is somewhat implausible. For instance, it makes sense to say that you support abortion rights, so abortion is not wrong *by definition*, if it is wrong at all. On the other hand, it makes little sense to say that you support murder. The very concept of murder seems to include the idea of wrongness. So if it is a fact that an act is murder, then it looks as though it is a fact that the act in question is wrong. But from the fact that an act is one of abortion, it does not logically follow that the act is wrong. It appears then that there is not an absolute difference between facts and value judgments but, rather, a fact/value continuum or spectrum. "Taking drugs is illegal" (factual) and "Taking drugs is morally wrong" (evaluative) are importantly different kinds of statements, but questions of value cannot be completely separated from questions of fact. So ethics is not as subjective as Hume makes out. This is just as well considering that he reduces vice to those traits apt to produce a particular kind of feeling in a large class of people. If that were all there was to it, we might be best advised to follow a sort of Freudian path of therapy designed to cure us of our "negative" feelings. There seems to be something wrong with the idea that vice could be removed from the world by changing the way that people feel about murder, theft, and so on, whether by brain surgery or extensive psychotherapy. Moreover, if vice and virtue are matters purely of particular subjective feelings, then there would be the problem of knowing that we had correctly identified our disapproval as specifically moral and not, for instance, aesthetic.

The General Point of View

We should note, though, that even Hume considers ethical evaluation to be somewhat objective. If someone hurts me, then I am likely to feel that what he or she did was wrong. But I might have deserved it, or my pain might have been necessary to achieve some greater good. So to judge properly I need to see things with a certain kind of distance. I also need to be well-informed about whatever it is that I am judging. And I need to be nonpsychopathic. A morally wrong act is therefore an act that came from a character tending to produce feelings of moral disapproval when considered by sane, well-informed, impartial people.

If we were utterly self-interested, incapable of impartiality, then perhaps there would be no such thing as morality or ethics or even such concepts as these. After all, what I like is a matter of my personal taste, and it is not likely to be exactly the same as what anyone else likes or finds useful. But the concepts of virtue and vice are not the concepts of what this person or that finds good or bad—that is, what she likes or dislikes, is helped or harmed by. A good character trait or virtue is one that is good objectively or according to some general standard such as the typical, ideal, or reasonable human being. The word "good" implies that something more is meant than an expression of merely personal taste.

> [When a man] bestows on any man the epithets of vicious or odious or depraved, he . . . expresses sentiments, in which he expects all his audience are to concur with him. He must here, therefore, depart from his private and particular situation, and must choose a point of view, common to him with others; he must move some universal principle of the human frame, and touch a string, to which all mankind have an accord and symphony.[12]

The very notion of ethics implies such a general or objective standard. If none exists, then ethics makes no sense, which is not to say that there *is* a standard like this to be found. If we are to defeat Thrasymachus, then we cannot simply *assume* that ethics really does make sense. Indeed, finding a standard of the kind described might seem especially challenging for Hume since he denies that vice and virtue are to be found outside our own hearts. Surely, this makes it all subjective. It is just as well, then, that ethics seems to require only a general standard, not an objective one. (Notice that I said above only that the "notion of ethics implies . . . a general *or* objective standard." Notice also that I have said only that ethics *seems* to require only a general standard. We will see in the next chapter reason for thinking that ethics actually requires universal standards and that these cannot be merely subjective.) And Hume finds, or claims to find, the necessary generality in a feature of human nature. The foundation of morals, he says, is the "principle of morality." From this principle come sentiments that are the same for all human beings, leading to the same moral assessments. They also apply to all human beings, so they are applied by all to all.

Adopting the appropriate, ethical point of view involves engaging one's sympathy with the viewpoints of others and correcting for any natural biases in one's own sympathy. So the point of view of all relevant parties to the action being judged must be considered sympathetically. This is one place where reason comes in because finding out who the relevant parties are and how they are (likely to be) affected by the act might take some research. It would hardly be surprising if different people had different information or different abilities to correct their own biases or to sympathize with others. So it is not surprising that we do not always agree on moral issues. But that is all there is to moral disagreement, according to Hume. We judge subjectively, it is true; but our feelings are all fundamentally the same. If feelings have a biological basis, then there is some reason to believe that this is true, although of course no two people are identical, however similar we may all be. This raises the question of whose judgment we should regard as correct when there is disagreement, once differences of knowledge, bias, and sympathy have been corrected as much as possible. Hume really offers no answer to this question, but then perhaps nobody can really answer it in a very satisfactory way. Perhaps that is just part of life.

After all, the problem of whose judgment to trust in cases of disagreement seems to arise inevitably if value judgments are subjective. And, Hume might ask, how could they possibly be anything else? The very same act, killing one's father, say, is wrong when done by a human being but not when done by an insect. But what is there as an objective fact about humans that makes us moral creatures while plants and animals are not? Especially bearing in mind our close biological relation to apes. Perhaps they are moral too, but then what about monkeys, dogs, cats, mice, and so on? If ethics applies only, or even just primarily, to humans, then it is hard to imagine what objective fact about us could be the basis for this situation. The obvious answer might be that we have souls, but this is hardly a scientific fact; and if by "soul" we mean simply a nonphysical object associated somehow with the physical body, then there is nothing of obvious moral significance about that. It is only if we think of the soul in religious terms, and smuggle ethics in that way, that its existence would be relevant to ethics in any readily apparent way. But then we would need some other fact to base this religious idea on, if it was to have the kind of objective justification that Hume is concerned with. And what fact that might be is hard to imagine. The existence of God, perhaps, but then we would face the *Euthyphro* dilemma if we wanted to justify ethical judgments on the basis of God's existence.[13] There is just no way, Hume argues, to reach a conclusion about what one *ought* to do from premises about what *is* the case. Purely factual or positive premises do not logically lead to ethical or normative conclusions. To get values out, you need to put values in; or, to use the Humean slogan, you cannot derive an *ought* from an *is*. Ethics cannot be anything but subjective at its foundation. As we have seen, though, Hume's radical distinction between ought and is, factual and evaluative, objective and subjective, is open to question.

Why Be Good?

Let us consider how well Hume has answered Thrasymachus. Hume seems to be concerned with our question about moral skepticism right from the start of his

Enquiry on morals, as he begins the book with an attack on it. However, this attack consists largely of the claim that it is hard to imagine anyone really having the kind of doubts about all ethics or morality that Thrasymachus expresses:

> DISPUTES with men, pertinaciously obstinate in their principles, are, of all others, the most irksome; except, perhaps, those with persons, entirely disingenuous, who really do not believe the opinions they defend, but engage in the controversy, from affectation, from a spirit of opposition, or from a desire of showing wit and ingenuity, superior to the rest of mankind.[14]

Rather than try to answer what he takes to be imaginary people, Hume suggests that one simply ignore any pretend Thrasymachus. His prediction is that after a while they will admit that they were only pretending. Surely everyone makes *some* distinction between right and wrong, even if he or she does not make the distinction in the same way as we do.

This is a point worth considering, but it is hardly very satisfactory. No doubt, many self-proclaimed moral skeptics are just seeking attention or trying to be artificially controversial. There is a deeper worry that Hume seems to be overlooking however. After all, the point is not so much how to deal with a Thrasymachus if one should come along. The point is that even fairly normal people can wonder whether they are making a mistake in trying to be good. If an opportunity for fun or profit comes along and you pass on it because of your conscience, you might well have some feelings of regret, even if these are outweighed by feelings of having done the right thing. The regret will not simply go away, as a real-life skeptic might, if we ignore it or if we remind ourselves that we do believe in right and wrong. We know that already. What we want is some assurance that this belief is right or good, that we are not wasting our lives because of pointless conscientiousness. Hume offers no immediate answer to this concern.

But what he does say is promising. He is interested in the psychology of moral belief, in the nature and origin of feelings of right and wrong, for instance. And that is highly relevant to Thrasymachus since it is part of his skeptical theory that these feelings are planted in us by people who basically want power over us, as the owner of a dog wants control over the dog. Indeed, Hume has much to say on this subject that has to do with our question.

Why should we try to do the right thing? Because, Hume might say, that is what people of good character will do. Why then should we want to have a good character? Well, what is a good character? One that will cause feelings of a particular, nice kind in right-minded people (including ourselves if we are virtuous). Why should we want or care about that? Because such a character is useful or agreeable to oneself or others. OK, but why should I care about others? No reason; but you do, don't you? It is natural, Hume argues, to feel others' pain and pleasure, through the faculty that he calls "sympathy." This might not be a good thing in itself; it just exists. But because of it, it makes sense to want others to be happy. This does not apply if you are psychologically deformed in such a way as to lack all sympathy, but few people are so deformed. Those who are will not care about benefiting others, but most virtues will still be useful for them. And that's it. Ethics does all come down to how we feel, for Hume. Lacking the appropriate feelings, or the capacity for them, the whole thing loses its appeal or point. *C'est la vie*, Hume might say.

It is hardly as if ethics does have the same kind of objective status as mathematics and the natural sciences. There really is moral disagreement (whether for the reasons Hume identifies or not), and we can worry about what this means. How can we be sure that our judgment, whether we think of it as objective or subjective (or something else), is right? This brings us back to the amoral skeptic. Hume seems to believe that some virtues are natural to all people and universally recognized, but even he admits that the goodness of artificial virtues can be lost from view. That is to say, society's rules against theft, for instance, do benefit all of us; but not all people will necessarily see clearly that it is against their own interest to violate these rules. I am better off if nobody steals my stuff, of course; so a world in which there is the concept of theft and rules against it is preferable, other things being equal, to a world in which theft is not understood or outlawed. And I am certainly better off if I am not caught and punished for stealing than if I am. That much almost everyone can see. But what is harder to see, and may in fact be impossible to see, at least for some people, is why they should not violate the no-stealing rule in situations where they can be certain that they will not be caught. Society will not collapse into anarchy, and they will personally be richer. Hume concedes that, from a purely rational (i.e., amoral) point of view, such a "sensible knave" might be right to behave viciously. A knave, though, would care more about material gain than about other people (most notably his victims) or his or her own character. This kind of person is hardly enviable and would seem likely to be friendless, at least at anything more than a superficial level. Knaves, Hume says, are dupes:

> How little is requisite to supply the *necessities* of nature? And in a view to *pleasure*, what comparison between the unbought satisfaction of conversation, society, study, even health and the common beauties of nature, but above all the peaceful reflection on one's own conduct; what comparison, I say, between these, and the feverish, empty amusements of luxury and expense? These natural pleasures, indeed, are really without price; both because they are below all price in their attainment, and above it in their enjoyment.[15]

Why we should not be knaves, in other words, is hardly a real problem. We just need to protect ourselves from people who are. The best things in life, after all, are not only free but priceless.

Objections

It is sometimes objected that Hume's theory would count immoral acts as right if somehow sane people worldwide one day woke up and felt differently about them. Imagine that somehow our brain chemistry changes so that when we consider acts of murder, rape, and theft, we feel, instead of a sense of outrage and disapproval, a warm glow of moral approval. We still might well not like suffering such things, but we will feel good about them in a moral sense if only we can get ourselves to take an impartial view of them. It is very hard to imagine this though. It is difficult to make sense of the idea of morally approving of murder. Perhaps that is because the very word "murder" implies something morally bad. But what about approving of the killing of an old woman in order to take her money? I can imagine someone taking sadistic pleasure in such an act but not feeling moral approval. Since I do not know what you can imagine, I will not dwell on this point. But it might lead us to think that this objection to Hume is not straightforward. Perhaps the very idea of the world changing in this way is literally inconceivable. Or, alternatively, perhaps this shows that ethics cannot simply be a matter of feeling this or that in response to certain facts, that concepts such as moral approval simply cannot be applied meaningfully to just any act.

Two other major objections to Hume's theory are that it is subjective and that it values the useful and the agreeable above all else. I have talked already about some of the problems with Hume's subjectivism, but some people object that ethics cannot be just about feelings. If Hume is right, then "Murder is wrong" means something like "Murder is the kind of act that characters of a certain type produce, and characters of that type make well-informed, sane, impartial people feel moral disapproval when they think about them." It is not a statement merely about murder, in other words, but (also) about the psychology of a certain class of people. It is often objected that "Murder is wrong" is about *murder,* though, not human psychology.

This raises the question of what "wrong" means, which is by no means easy to answer. Virtue ethics largely avoids this question since it focuses not on what acts are wrong but on what character traits are desirable, but the link between acts and the character of the agent (i.e., the person who does the acts in question) cannot be denied. Part of Hume's point is that only a person with a particular kind of character would commit an act like willful murder. Vice (perhaps the vice of murderousness) leads to such acts, and this trait is a vice because of how certain people feel about it. But they feel that way (i.e., disapproving) because the trait is not useful or agreeable, and this is surely at least in part because it produces such acts as murder. Now, what exactly is wrong with murder?

Hume's answer would surely be that murder itself is not useful or agreeable. We do not like it. Does evil reduce then to mere dislike? Not quite. First, we dislike murder not in itself, if Hume is right, but because we see it as a symptom of moral sickness. This sickness is bad for no deeper reason than that we dislike it—true—but each disapproved act brings with it (or in a sense is) the threat of more such acts. Second, moral disapproval is basically just a form of dislike, but it feels different (and since what it *is* is a feeling, it is therefore essentially different) from other kinds of dislike (of raisins, e.g.). This theory of moral psychology strikes me as being somewhat misguided for the reasons outlined above: the differences between dislike of raisins and disapproval of murder are what we might call logical or conceptual, not merely subjective or qualitative. But at least Hume has an answer to the question of the meaning of "wrong." Others have treated it as irreducible, inexplicable, and thus (arguably) incoherent. What meaning can a word have whose meaning cannot be explained? We will consider the question of the meaning of "right" and "wrong" further in Chapter 7.

Before that we should consider the final objection to Hume, that he values nothing more than, and nothing but, usefulness and agreeableness. We can immediately ask what usefulness could be, except a tendency to promote the agreeable. What is useful is instrumental but instrumental to what? Something we want or like, presumably. Hume's ethics seems to reduce to a theory of the agreeable, the pleasant, the satisfying. An image of Hume, fat and on a sofa after a large meal, comes to mind. "Good" is the news in the paper that brings a small smile to his lips; "evil" is what brings a frown. This is a caricature, of course, but not a million miles from the truth. Hume's depth seems rather too easy to plumb, his values bourgeois, as Nietzsche complained. This could be a matter of Hume's character or the character of the culture of which he was a part, but it could also be linked with his attempt to offer a scientific account of moral psychology. To his credit, he offers a relatively simple explanation of previously underexplored territory. To his discredit, his explanation seems a little too simple. But it is easy to accuse someone of superficiality, quite another thing to prove that the charge sticks, that life is more complicated, richer, or deeper than has been alleged. From a religious point of view, Hume is missing rather a lot by making the agreeable the pinnacle of all that is good. But we should not criticize him for this if we cannot prove that God, or Plato's form of the Good or some other, "higher" good, really exists. If there is no higher good, then Hume is not shallow but realistic.

Conclusion

Hume's defense of friendship and the other good things that a complete moral skeptic would seem likely to miss out on is a nice response to Thrasymachus, but it might still not be completely convincing. We do not know what Thrasymachus' life would be like, and Hume, however plausibly, is engaging in mere conjecture. We have also seen reason to question his other views on ethics, on what being good really means. So Hume's is hardly the last word on ethics generally, and we should not stop here if we want to know how we should live and why.

Questions for Further Thought

1. Can we separate questions of meta-ethics (about the meaning of such words or concepts as "good" and "bad") from questions about normative ethics (i.e., about what we ought to do, about what things are good and bad)? Think of the idea that talk about morality or ethics is really about human psychology. If you

believed this, might it change what you regarded as good and bad? Would you be able to take ethics seriously?

2. Compare and contrast ethical judgments and aesthetic judgments (judgments of taste).

3. Could you morally approve of eating toast rather than cereal for breakfast or disapprove of people with blue carpets? Does your answer show anything about the nature of moral approval and disapproval?

4. Must a knave be a dupe?

5. How can we decide which virtues are merely "monkish" and which are genuinely good?

Notes

1. See David Hume, *Enquiry Concerning the Principles of Morals,* included in *Enquiries Concerning Human Understanding and Concerning the Principles of Morals,* 3rd ed. Edited by L. A. Selby-Bigge and P. H. Nidditch (New York: Oxford University Press, 1975), 270.
2. Written by Ludwig Wittgenstein (who was not a natural law theorist) in a letter to Paul Engelmann, quoted in Ray Monk, *Ludwig Wittgenstein: The Duty of Genius* (London: Jonathan Cape, 1990), 187.
3. Hume, *Enquiry,* 270.
4. David Hume, *A Treatise of Human Nature,* 2nd ed. (Oxford: Oxford University Press, 1978), 415.
5. Ibid., 398.
6. Ibid., 365.
7. Ibid., 469.
8. Ibid., 471.
9. See Ludwig Wittgenstein, *Philosophical Investigations,* trans. G. E. M. Anscombe (Oxford: Basil Blackwell, 1958), §§243ff.
10. Hume, *Enquiry,* 271.
11. Hume, *A Treatise,* 469–470.
12. Hume, *Enquiry,* 272.
13. See Chapter 3 for more on this.
14. Hume, *Enquiry,* 169.
15. Ibid., 283–284.

Suggestions for Further Reading

Hume's main work on ethics can be found in David Hume, *Enquiry Concerning the Principles of Morals,* included in *Enquiries Concerning Human Understanding and Concerning the Principles of Morals,* 3rd ed. (New York: Oxford University Press, 1975), and in Books II and, especially, III of David Hume, *A Treatise of Human*

Nature, 2nd ed. (Oxford: Oxford University Press, 1978). The *Enquiry* was written after the *Treatise* had not found the large audience that Hume had hoped for. The *Enquiry* is more readable, but both are important sources for serious study of what Hume thought.

   Two good introductions to Hume's thinking on ethics are James Baillie, *Hume on Morality*, (London: Routledge, 2000), and J. L. Mackie, *Hume's Moral Theory*, (London: Routledge, 1993).

CHAPTER 7

Kant

Unlike most of the philosophers we are looking at, Kant is not concerned much with character. His theory does have some key elements in common with those of Plato and Aquinas, however. Like Plato, he believes that reason should rule over the passions. Like Aristotle, he emphasizes the importance of moral education.[1] Like Aquinas and others in the natural law tradition, he believes that human beings should be as human beings are. Again, reason is the key idea here as far as Kant is concerned. Not only is it traditional to base ethics on ideas about reason, but we saw in the last chapter that attempts to reduce ethics to matters of what happens to be true, like how we happen to feel about cruelty, face serious problems. If we cannot base ethics on our changeable psychology, perhaps we would be better off trying to base it on timeless principles of logic or reason. It sometimes seems as though Kant believes that reason alone can answer Thrasymachus' question. In the end, though, he appears to recognize that this is not really possible. What we need ultimately is faith. This idea, too, has its problems, but Kant's defense of it is original and worth examining closely.

Acting and Willing

One way to understand Kant's ethics is to think of him as profoundly nonvegetarian.[2] Some people today like to emphasize our close biological relation to other animals, the signs that other species show of intelligence and the use of language and tools, the fact that all (or almost all) animals feel pain, and the fact that animals can be our companions or even friends. For these reasons, people today tend to oppose various kinds of cruelty toward animals, some people will not eat animals killed for food, and some will not use animal products such as leather or fur. Kant has nothing against animals, but his attitude is quite different. He emphasizes the difference between human beings and other animals. As has traditionally been the case, he locates this difference not in accidental differences of furriness or number of legs, for instance, but in the fact that we alone (he believes) are rational. This is not to say that all people behave rationally all the time but that, basically, reasoning with people is (almost) always an option, whereas with other animals it is not. Human beings are *capable* of being rational, that is to say, and can be judged according to how rational or irrational their behavior is.

Now, what does this have to do with vegetarianism or wearing leather shoes? Just this: many people do wear leather shoes and eat meat, but even vegans (people who will not wear leather) do not consider using animals in these ways as being nearly as horrifically evil as treating human beings like this would be. Some extreme animal rights supporters might claim to believe that animals are exactly equal with humans, but few if any wage the kind of war against butchers and shoe shops that we might all engage in if it were human beings that were raised and slaughtered to provide meat and shoes.[3] So, although the degree to which this is true varies, we all believe that human beings have more moral value than other animals. If the relevant difference between us and them is our rationality or capacity for reason, then reason itself might seem to be what really has moral value. This certainly is Kant's view. It is rationality, which Kant sometimes calls "humanity," that adds this great worth to the relatively insignificant value of what we have in common with other species. Hence, Kant's ethics can be seen to be all about reason and, in particular, about the connection between reason and action. So from Kant's ideas about the value of reason we turn now to a brief look at his thinking about action.

In Kant's view, there are two kinds of things that we do. The first kind is mere behavior—for instance, sneezing, blinking, and so on. These "acts" are not deliberate or voluntary; they simply happen without our choosing them. This kind of thing has nothing to do with ethics, even if my sneeze spreads an illness that has terrible consequences for humanity. It does not, as Hume might say, reflect at all on my character (unless I could have controlled or redirected the sneeze, that is). Behavior like this is instinctive or a matter of reflex, like animal behavior. Ethics, as Kant conceives it at least, does not apply to animals. Ethics, he argues, requires responsibility, which requires choice. Animals, being ruled by their instincts, have no real choice in what they do. What matters for ethics, then, is the second category of things that we do, the chosen or voluntary.

His point here is not only that voluntary acts are more important than nonvoluntary or involuntary ones (more important morally, that is, precisely because they alone can be assessed morally and so have a moral dimension). It is also that ethics belongs to our lives or world precisely insofar as we engage in voluntary acts. When I sneeze, even if my sneeze has terrible consequences, I am not thinking about, and so cannot be guided by thoughts about, what I should do. Voluntary action, though, even if free will turned out somehow to be a myth, is action under the idea of freedom. It is behavior conducted as if free will were not a myth. We seem to be able to choose what we do, and ethics is concerned with what choices we ought to make. It is a concern only of those who think they can choose, and it is a concern about what to choose. What we should choose will be easier to see after we have looked at the nature of action.

Voluntary acts (or just "acts" for short) also come in two kinds, depending on the reason they are performed. Most acts are done in order to achieve some goal. For example, if I really want a pie, then I might go to a bakery. When we perform an act like this, Kant believes, our will, having chosen the act, makes our body carry it out (unless we are paralyzed or fall down along the way, etc.). Orders that we give ourselves Kant calls "imperatives." In this case, the order given to my legs and the rest of my body would be something like "Go to the bakery!" but this particular command is a result of a more general policy along the lines of "If (or whenever) you want a pie, then go to the bakery!" This kind of order Kant calls a "hypothetical imperative" because it depends on some particular desire (in this case for pie) that I might or might not happen to have (just as a hypothesis might or might not happen to be true). These hypothetical imperatives will be different for everyone (some people do not like pies or have their pies brought to them or else have been forbidden by their doctors to eat any more pies, and so on). Partly for this very reason, hypothetical imperatives are not what Kantian ethics is about. Ethics, as he sees it, must not be optional and, thus, must be the same for everyone. So we must turn to the other kind of imperative that he identifies.

The Categorical Imperative

Hypothetical imperatives deal with one kind of acts. The other kind of acts, though, does not result from any merely hypothetical imperative. There are some things, Kant believes, that simply must be done, regardless of what you (or anyone else) happen to want. These acts are commanded by categorical imperatives. And it is these acts that are morally good. Why is this?

Kant agrees with Hume that what we morally approve of is not any particular deed or consequence of a deed but something within the person who does the deed, the agent. He rejects the idea that what we approve of are virtues however. A mere tendency to perform good acts, or a character trait that gives rise to such a tendency, is not morally praiseworthy, Kant would say. The acts must be voluntary or willed, not lucky or done while sleepwalking, for instance, to count as morally good. What matters, then, is not character but will. Now, these might amount to the same thing. A person of good will might have internalized various moral laws so that acting on them becomes second nature, or what Aristotle might call that person's "character."[4] Kant regards it as impossible for a human being to have a perfect character though. All we can do is try to progress toward having such a thing. In the meantime, the essential thing is to have a good will, to be committed to doing what is right, whatever that might be. Indeed, he famously says that "Nothing can possibly be conceived in the world, or even out of it, which can be called good, without qualification, except a Good Will."[5]

If a good will is so important to ethics that nothing else can conceivably be called absolutely good, then we had better try to understand exactly what it means to have a good will. It is not enough merely to strive to do the right thing. One cannot be moral by accident. Imagine that Reese Witherspoon has lost her watch and I have found it. I do not know it is her watch but want to give it to her anyway just because I want to meet her and think my chances are better if I have a gift to give. Since it is her watch, the right thing to do is to give it to her. So, what I want to do is the right thing, but I want to do it not *because* it is right but just for my own selfish reasons. I do not even know that what I plan to do *is* the right thing, and I might not care that it is even if I did know it. All I want is to meet Reese Witherspoon. Therefore, Kant argues, if I give her the watch, my act will not be morally worthy, even though it is the right thing to do. To be moral you must will to do the right thing just because it *is* the right thing, even if this does get you what you want. Willing is enough, as long as it is sincere. If you fail to do the right thing because you are physically incapable of it, say, or because of bad luck, that is not your fault. Your will is still good, and that is what counts:

> Even if it should happen that, owing to special disfavour of fortune, or the nig-gardly[6] provision of a step-motherly nature, this will should wholly lack power to accomplish its purpose, if with its greatest efforts it should yet achieve nothing, and there should remain only the good will (not, to be sure, a mere wish, but the sum-moning of all means in our power), then, like a jewel, it would still shine by its own light, as a thing which has its whole value in itself. Its usefulness or fruitfulness can neither add nor take away anything from this value.[7]

And if this is true, that the usefulness or fruitfulness of a will can make no difference to its goodness, then it cannot really matter, from the point of view of moral judgment, what the results of my willing and my actions are. Thus:

> an action done from duty derives its moral worth, *not from the purpose* which is to be attained by it, but from the maxim by which it is determined, and therefore does not depend on the realization of the object of the action, but merely on the *principle of volition* by which the action has taken place, without regard to any object of de-sire.[8]

If we were God, judging souls at the end of time, we should judge them, Kant implies, not by what good they brought about during their lives, nor by any harm they might have done, but by the maxims or "principles of volition" on which they acted, or even just tried to act. A **maxim** is a kind of policy for action that a person adopts and lives by. These principles are central to Kant's thinking about ethics, and we will consider several examples of them below. For now, the impor-tant point is that, for Kant, the will is judged by how it wills and not by what, if anything, such willing causes to happen.

So what exactly does a good will will? Well, Kant might say, in the spirit of Aristotle and Aquinas, what is a will? To know its nature or essence is to know its proper function. The will is the internal legislator. It gives orders and makes laws for the human being to follow. So a good will is one that makes good laws. And what is a good law? Well, what is a law? A law is a general rule concerning con-duct. So a good law is a very general rule concerning conduct. The best law will be one that is so general that it allows no exceptions at all, a completely universal law. And the best will is the one that makes such a law and chooses to obey it. And this, Kant thinks, is just about all that we need to know in order to know what is right and what is wrong. Any law, command, or order that *can be* universal and that can be willed (i.e., chosen) is a good one and breaking it must be wrong.

So far, this is all very abstract, but Kant assures us that it will work in practice as a test for which acts we must not commit. It will not tell us what to do, but everything that is not forbidden is all right (e.g., in most circumstances, eating pie). If we ever have any absolute moral duties, things that we simply must do, then it will be forbidden not to do these things; so Kant's rule will tell us this. He uses four examples to demonstrate what he has in mind, simultaneously explaining how we are to use this theory in practice and proving that it will bring us to satisfactory conclusions. These examples cover cases of **perfect duties** (acts we must do at all times), **imperfect duties** (acts we must do but only some of the time), duties to self, and duties to others.

Let us first consider a perfect duty to others. We have, Kant argues, a perfect duty never to make a false promise. That is to say, we must never pretend to be promising to do something when in fact we have no intention of doing it. Kant's theory of the categorical imperative ("I am never to act otherwise than so *that I could also will that my maxim should become a universal law,*"[9] which means, roughly, act on no policy that cannot be willed universally) shows why not. What would the maxim be in the case of a false promise? Something like, whenever it suits me, say "I promise" but never actually keep the "promise" in question. Could this rule be followed universally? It never will be, of course, because some people cannot speak English, or speak at all, and some have too much integrity to do such a thing. But that is not the point. The point is, *could* there be a universe in which everyone followed this rule? Does this policy have what it takes to be universal, to be a perfect example of a law?

Kant argues that it does not. You say "I promise" because you count on a certain response from your audience. For instance, you count on them believing you and therefore lending you the money, the key to the drug cabinet, or the cop-killer bullets that you promised just to look at. In a universe in which "I promise" meant something like "Yeah right," saying it would not produce the desired effect. Therefore, you would not bother saying it. In fact, not only would you not bother but you *could* not bother. Saying "I promise" would not *be* making a promise if the words meant only something along the lines of "I am not going to pay you back but want your money all the same."[10] So you would not make false promises (or any promises at all, in fact). The idea of a universal following of the rule "Make false promises when it suits you" thus contains a kind of contradiction. Kant's point is not that the rule would have *bad* consequences if carried out on a universal scale. It is that it *could not be* carried out on such a scale. The policy cannot be a universal law. So it is not very law-like, and it is not the kind of thing that a rational will (a good will) would will. Therefore, it is a bad rule and should not be followed. Ever.

Our next example concerns what Kant thinks is a perfect duty to oneself—namely, not to commit suicide. If suicide were ever acceptable, he thinks, then there would be some acceptable principle or maxim that tells us when to kill ourselves. This maxim would be something like "Whenever my future looks like offering more pain than pleasure, out of concern for myself I will kill myself." Could this be a universal law? No again, or so Kant thinks. Could there be a universe in which all beings capable of reason reasoned in this way? You might think so, but Kant does not. There would be a kind of contradiction, he believes, if concern for oneself led to destruction of oneself. And a contradiction cannot possibly be true since it would then make itself false. In this case, it is hard to put into words any literal contradiction involved in suicide, but Kant seems to have in mind the idea that a suicidal person is thinking both "Up with me!" (having concern for oneself) and "Down with me!" (wanting to kill oneself). There are not two contrary facts being asserted here, but there is what we might call a contradiction in attitude (if this is really what all suicidal people think, which is debatable). So we might agree that there is a *kind* of contradiction here. And contradictions cancel themselves out. Thus, this could never be a universal law: no good will would ever will it, so it is bad. Before we consider objections to this line of thought, let us briefly look at Kant's other two applied cases.

These concern imperfect duties. Let's start with imperfect duties to others. Kant's example is about helping people. We must have a duty to do this, at least some of the time, he argues, because the maxim "Never help anyone else" cannot be willed universally. Why not? Not, this time, because it could not be a universal law. We can imagine a miserable universe of rugged individuals steadfastly refusing to do anything but respect the rights of other rugged individuals to be left alone. But we could not rationally will to live in such a universe. Kant thinks that we all need someone to lean on, sooner or later. Imagine that your stack of libertarian books and privately published pamphlets together with your hardback copies of Ayn Rand's longest novels all tumble down on you one day, breaking your legs. Perhaps you have no right to help from others, but you could not help wanting it, Kant believes. And accidents do happen. So you could not (rationally, and we are rational beings after all) will to live in such a universe, a universe in which nobody ever helps anybody else. Therefore, a good will (or any rational will for that matter) would never will a law of not helping others. A good will must will a law of helping others, at least some of the time. We do have, in other words, an imperfect duty to help other people.

Finally, let us consider whether we have any imperfect duties to ourselves. Kant thinks we do. What if we all just neglected ourselves? Could there be a universe like this? Well, if you are lucky, then you might just be able to imagine it. There could be a universe in which we all just lay around while delicious food and drink fell into our mouths and somehow we never got sick or sore from lying on the sand. But could we want to live this kind of life? "Boy howdy!" might be your initial response. But think about it. Your muscles would all waste away while your body fat grew and grew. You would become a fat wimp, flopping on the sand like a beached whale. And, perhaps more importantly, the same kind of thing would happen to your mind. Without mental exercise (such as can be had by reading Kant's books), you would become dull, stupid, and unimaginative.

Mentally and physically you would be a blob. You cannot rationally will that, or so Kant thinks, so it must be wrong to allow yourself to become such a blob.

In some ways more appealing than the version of the categorical imperative that we have been discussing up to now is the second version, that we should never use people (in a certain bad sense of "use") but always treat them (and ourselves) with respect. What Kant says is this: "So act as to treat humanity [i.e. rational nature], whether in thine own person or in that of another, in every case as an end. . . never as means only. . . ."[11]

This is supposed to mean exactly the same as what the first version of the categorical imperative means, but it certainly sounds different. What exactly does it mean? For Kant, humanity means rationality, which is connected with autonomy (self-rule). The distinctive feature of all moral agents—human, angel, or alien—is that they are capable of acting, not just behaving.[12] They are capable, that is to say, of doing things for a reason. This capacity, Kant says, ought to be respected at all times, in ourselves and in others. Treating someone as a punching bag, for instance, is not respecting his or her humanity. More generally, we might say that Kant is against exploiting people—indeed, that he defines this as the essence of immorality. If I murder someone just to inherit his or her fortune, for instance, I am using that person as a mere means to an end. Arguably, the same might be true if I use pornography or treat an employee badly.

Some instances of using people are perfectly acceptable though. Imagine I am at the supermarket and cannot reach the tortilla chips on the top shelf. A very tall woman comes by, and I ask her to help me. I am basically using her height to get the chips that I want. But I am not treating her "as a means only." I recognize that she is a human being and make no attempt to coerce her into helping me. I ask politely and would not become violent if she said no. In other words, although I do use her as a means to my end, I also treat her as something much more than that. I respect her humanity. This is obviously an important aspect of ethics, but it is not completely free of problems, as we shall see.

Why Be Good?

Now we can ask, how well does Kant provide a response to Thrasymachus? Why should we obey Kant's categorical imperative? Kant provides two kinds of answer to this question. Perhaps the more distinctively Kantian of the two is the brusque riposte that we *just should*. We should do the right thing just because it is the right thing to do. Ethics for Kant is not at all a matter of prudence. Whether doing the right thing will get us into heaven or not, make us happy or not, make us rich or popular or not, make society better off or not—all such considerations are irrelevant from the moral point of view, Kant believes. All that matters is whether an act is right or wrong. If it is right, we should do it; if it is wrong, we should not. End of story. This will not satisfy Thrasymachus, of course; but that should not bother us. He is clearly an enemy of morality, and good people should not compromise their principles in order to win his approval or acceptance.

The second kind of Kantian answer is more complicated. We should do the right thing because it is the rational thing to do and we are rational beings. One might ask, however, why we should try to conform to whatever our nature happens to be, especially if we do not believe that this nature was chosen for us by God. If it just so happens that we have evolved to be rational, how on earth can this make it *morally right* for us to behave rationally? Evolution, after all, if not guided by God, is just a matter of which random mutations happen to survive best in whatever environment they happen to find themselves. How could this possibly make certain actions right and others wrong in a moral, non-survival-focused sense? Kant would say that this question misses his point.

It is rational, he believes, to value reason or rationality. Choosing to commit irrational acts, therefore, goes against our nature. His point is not so much that this is wrong (that point would require some separate argument) but that it goes against ourselves. Like Plato, Kant believes that we have a kind of inner, true self and that this self is essentially rational. We should not do irrational acts because these are not really consistent with our will, deep down inside. This is a kind of argument that Thrasymachus might listen to. He cares about getting what he wants. But why should he, or anyone else, believe that this "true self" exists?

Kant identifies the rational self with the will, but there is more than one will here. After all, we are aware of desires within us to do all kinds of irrational and immoral acts. It is not this will that Kant has in mind. That is what he calls the "phenomenal" will. This is the will that appears to us, that we experience, that we are conscious of. It is the will considered as a phenomenon or thing that appears. The true will is the "noumenal" will, the will as it is in itself. Unfortunately, according to Kant, we can know nothing at all about things in themselves. We can only know objects as we experience them (i.e., phenomenally). So we cannot know that the true will, the noumenal will, is rational or moral.

His thinking here can be understood in terms of the movie *The Matrix*. In *The Matrix*, people have experiences of other people, food, streets, and so on. These would be what Kant calls "phenomena."[13] But underlying these experiences is a computer program, computers, and so on. In short, underlying these experiences is the Matrix. So the apple that I bite and taste in the Matrix is really some strings of code, not a three-dimensional object at all. This code is the noumenal apple, the apple as it is in itself. Now, Kant believes that behind the you and me that we are aware of, that we experience, there is a noumenal you and a noumenal me. Even when I look into my own mind, what I experience is a phenomenal me, not the noumenal me. This noumenal self *might* be just like the self that I am consciously aware of. Kant does not insist that we are living in the Matrix or anything like it. But he allows for the possibility that we might be. We simply cannot know the nature of our noumenal selves because by definition they are not something that we will ever be conscious of. They lie outside our minds and so outside our possible knowledge or understanding.

It seems then that the real me might be rational, but it also might be some computer code, or a Chinese butterfly, or anything at all that we can imagine (or even something that we cannot imagine). Why believe that it is rational? Because, Kant says, this is what ethics requires. If we think of ourselves or other people as acting just on instinct, like cows, say, then we will see no reason not to treat people the way we treat cows. But this would be monstrous! So if we wish to be sane, or perhaps just if we *are* sane, then we will acknowledge some important difference between human beings and other animals. This difference might not be so great that we are prepared to eat animals—vegetarians are not insane—but it will exist, as far as we are concerned. Traditionally, the difference has been thought to be that we are rational while other species are not. Whatever intelligence animals might have, this does seem to be the most obvious difference between us and them. So it is hard, if not impossible or insane, to reject the belief that we really are rational beings.

In case the reference to animals here is misleading, let me put the point another way. Kant claims that we do not think of ourselves as mere objects, behaving in ways caused by instinct or some other nonrational force. As Christine Korsgaard puts it,

> insofar as we are rational, we ... regard ourselves as *active* beings, who are the authors of our thoughts and choices. We do not regard our thoughts and choices merely as things that *happen* to us; rather thinking and choosing are things that we *do*. To this extent, we must view ourselves as *noumena*.[14]

So what exactly our noumenal selves are might be a mystery, what being rational means exactly might be a mystery; but we do think of ourselves this way. If we are rational in Kant's sense, then we must be capable of doing things for reasons, not just instinctively. We must be able to choose these reasons. Otherwise, they will never be *ours*. You do not buy, inherit, or find reasons, after all. The way something gets to be *your* reason for doing something is that you *choose* to do the thing in question for that reason. You choose your reasons, that is, your goals and purposes in life. For instance, say I decide to swim every day to keep healthy. Keeping healthy is then the reason that I have chosen for spending my time this way. Now, you might think that I am really swimming because I am biologically programmed by my genes to want to stay healthy or perhaps to make myself attractive to potential mates. If so, you are thinking of me the way we think of animals, as a slave to biology. But ethics (and perhaps common sense and perhaps sanity) require that we do not think this way, at least not all the time. So Kant rejects this kind of deterministic account of human behavior and insists that we have free will. We cannot prove that we have free will, that our actions are freely chosen; but we must believe it if we are to be ethical. It also seems as though we *just do* treat ourselves and others as responsibly choosing what we do. Treating people as mere objects governed by laws of nature, the way we treat not only animals but trees and rocks, seems to be not only insane but impossible. So we have little choice but to believe in our own rationality.

This does give us a reason to believe that the noumenal self is rational, despite the absence of proof. But it is not of the kind that would move Thrasymachus. Ethics itself can justify faith, according to Kant. It can justify faith in God (so that we do not despair of justice), faith in an immortal soul (so that we can understand when justice might ultimately be handed out), and faith in free will (so that we can make sense of holding people responsible for their actions). Perhaps it can also justify faith in our own inner rational selves. But if this belief is justified by ethics, then it cannot itself justify ethics. Otherwise, we would just go round and round in a circle.

Going round like this might be inevitable though. Kant certainly does not believe that we can justify our ethics by appeal to experience. He blames the principle of empiricism (that all ideas must be derived from experience, which leads Hume to reject as illusory any pseudoidea that cannot be traced back to experience) on mere laziness. In the case of ethics, he appears to think that empiricism will play directly into the hands of the likes of Thrasymachus. Why should this be so? Perhaps simply because experience is not the basis of ethical ideas. That is to say, Kant's understanding of duty and its requirements is not a matter of hypothetical imperatives or ways of getting people what they want. Rather, duty is a matter of acting out of respect for the moral law. This law comes before any experience. We do not discover that murder, say, is wrong by trying it and finding that people do not like it. It would be wrong even if they did like it. Any attempt then to base ethics on what has been found to work will produce something that Kant would not recognize as ethics. And any attempt to base ethics on what has been found simply to be true (that people often lie, e.g., or sometimes commit murder) will likely be even worse. So Kant relies on reason, not experience. But reason, as Kant did much to show, has its limits.[15] In particular, it cannot provide the faith in free will, immortality, and divine justice that Kant believes is vital for the ethical life. If we are not free, then ethical judgments about what people should or should not do seem to make little sense. And, although Kantian ethics is not self-interested or egoistic, without faith in ultimate justice he thinks we will lack the necessary wind in our sails to steer toward what is right and away from what is wrong. So ethics needs reason for any attempt at justification, and in turn reason needs the faith that ethical commitments provide. Hence, the apparently inevitable circle in Kant's work.

This circularity need not be considered fatal though. After all, Thrasymachus does not want to reject reason. If Kant is to be believed, then reason shows what we ought and ought not to do. All that it cannot do is give us the moral energy or motive to do what is right. It does not follow that a cynic like Thrasymachus is right. It simply follows that he will be unmoved by rational argument on its own. Unfortunately, that seems to be true; cynics are not generally improved through argument alone. Yet, according to Kant, rational argument is all that can be offered here. Faith might underlie the practice of ethics, but it has no place in the working out of what we ought to do:

Even the Holy One of the Gospels must first be compared with our ideal of moral perfection before we can recognise Him as such. . . . Imitation finds no place at all in morality, and examples serve only for encouragement, i.e., they put beyond doubt the feasibility of what the law commands, they make visible that which the practical rule expresses more generally, but they can never authorize us to set aside the true original which lies in reason and to guide ourselves by examples.[16]

The Kantian moral law belongs purely to reason (including the rational will). What appeals to the heart, whether it be a religious appeal or an imaginative one, has no place except in helping to get the law put into practice. What Thrasymachus wants, a purely rational motive for what Kant believes is rational action, cannot be found—at least not in the works of Kant.

It is worth looking at this a little closer. Kant believes that the only ethically valuable motive for action is the will to do one's moral duty. This duty is not a matter of doing what parents, teachers, or police officers tell you to do. That is how Thrasymachus would see it and how some Nazis regarded their duty, but it is not how Kant or anyone he would recognize as moral would see it. The will to do one's duty is the will to do what is right, to obey the moral law. It is an almost religious obedience, complete obedience, willingness to obey the moral law whatever it might command. This is the defining characteristic of the good will, the only absolutely good thing that we can conceive of either in or out of the world. It is like an arrow trained on a target or a panting dog ready to fetch at its owner's command. Two questions need to be asked about it: Will it actually fly (thinking of the arrow) or run (in the case of the dog)? Should it?

Let me explain these questions. Kant's idea of the rational will implies the existence of a kind of true self. Indeed, his distinction between noumena and phenomena implies that there is a true self about which we can know nothing. In this sense, at least, it is distinct from the phenomenal self that we know through the senses and through introspection (ordinary self-awareness). We cannot know what this self wants, if it wants anything. So perhaps I can have noumenal desires that are unknown to me or even completely opposed to the desires that I think I have. Ever since Sigmund Freud, we have been familiar with the idea that our subconscious desires might be quite different from our conscious desires, but the Freudian subconscious is at least theoretically accessible to us. Subconscious desires can show themselves in our behavior and dreams and could become conscious. Noumenal desires, by definition, can never be known at all. It is hard to accept, or even understand, the idea that we might "really" hate the people we "think" we love or dislike the pizza that we spend so much time drooling over. Perhaps in the end we cannot make sense of noumenal psychology. But for the purpose of his ethics, Kant does not really need this idea. All he needs is the idea of a rational self, capable of desiring its own obedience to the moral law. Even this self, though, might be at odds with other selves. Remember Plato's division of the self into three parts—the rational inner person, the spirited lion or dog, and the appetitive monster. The Kantian rational will is like the inner person, or that person's will. What if one of the other selves—the monster, let us say—desires something else?

This is an entirely Kantian scenario. He knows that we are human. He does not expect any human being to be able to go through life without ever willing something morally bad. The important thing for him is to be able to overcome such desires and act instead on the rational will. But this raises Thrasymachus' question right away: Why should I? And it is no answer at all to say simply that that is what one's rational will wills. Why listen to that will rather than others? This problem is complicated by the fact that there is no obvious reason Kant should agree with Plato that there are only two other inner selves or wills. There could be countless wills, including some that desire obedience to something very like, but not quite the same as, the moral law. For example, we have seen that Kantian morality is not about giving people what they want. But we could will such a thing. Why listen to what Kant identifies as the rational will rather than, say, this altruistic desire-satisfaction will? A different version of reason, such as Hume's or the utilitarian one that we will look at in the next chapter, might favor obedience to a different, and arguably equally rational, will. In fairness to Kant, we should not try to consider the merits of every conceivable kind of will before deciding which is best. But we do need to consider *some* alternative ideas about both rationality and morality. Kant's theory is not so good as to be necessarily the last word on ethics.

The other problem I mentioned is whether the willingness to obey the moral law will actually be acted on. This is a problem recognized by Kant himself. He says that without faith in ultimate justice, with rewards in the life to come for good people and punishments for the bad, we will not have what it takes to obey the moral law. The will might be there, recognizing that what is right must be done for its own sake alone and not for the sake of any reward that might be attached (or the avoidance of any punishment that might be threatened). But that in itself will not, as a matter of regrettable fact, be enough to get the right thing done in the absence of faith in life after death and a god to deal justice. Why not? It is hard to say. Kant seems to be guessing somewhat about human psychology, although his guesswork is quite plausible. He gives no real evidence to back it up. But it is also hard to say precisely because we are no longer dealing with the rational will here. *It* is all set and ready to go. What is lacking is something else, something non-rational. It is not the physical ability to do what is right. Rather, it is what I have called "the wind in one's sails." You might call it the absence of despair or, more positively, hope. It is something like psychic energy, the energy or drive to make the effort to do right. It is precisely what Thrasymachus seems to be lacking. So Kant has not so much failed to explain to Thrasymachus why he should be good. Rather he has admitted that, in his opinion, reason alone cannot bring him over to the right side. You got to have faith.

Kant says something similar about love. The Bible says that you should love your neighbor, but love, or even liking, seems to be beyond our control. The novelist and philosopher Iris Murdoch has argued that, in fact, we can work to make ourselves feel more positively about other people; but Kant treats feelings as beyond the scope of the rational will.[17] The moral law, he thinks, cannot tell us what to feel, whether the feeling in question be love, outrage, or anything else. It can only tell us what we are to do or not do.

One of the main complaints about Kant's ethics is that he downplays feeling and focuses exclusively on action, as if it were not wrong to be filled with hate, say, or to be indifferent about other people. An ethics of feeling would certainly not be Kant's, but the criticism is otherwise perhaps a little unfair. He does not celebrate the absence of sympathy but suggests instead that the unsympathetic should be judged by their actions, not by their feelings, since they cannot help these feelings. This is actually rather sympathetic on Kant's part toward people who lack good feelings. To the extent that they can help these feelings, he might say, people should be held accountable for what is in their hearts. Disagreeing with him on this point would involve either claiming that people should be held responsible for things that they cannot help (which *might* be true if people can be born with bad characters, e.g., as Schopenhauer thought)[18] or else claiming that we *can* control our feelings, at least to some extent. The latter would be a disagreement about fact, not about ethics, however.

Another problem comes from the Christian point of view. Not every Christian would agree with Kant's interpretation of the Bible. It commands us, after all, to believe in God. This is not something that reason can help us with, according to Kant. Faith lies beyond the limits of reason or rational argument, as he famously insists. Kant appears to believe that, as philosophers like to put it, "ought" implies "can". If something is one's moral duty, what the moral law requires, then it must be something that one is able to do. Otherwise, the law would seem to be unreasonable or unfair. (And how rational or moral would such a law be then?) Yet, Kant believes that we will only obey the moral law if we have faith in God and divine justice in the hereafter. In what sense then can someone who lacks faith obey the moral law? Is it any more fair or reasonable for the law to presuppose some state of the heart (faith or love, e.g.) than it is for it to command such a state? Perhaps it is, but the answer to this question is hardly obvious. In short, Kant's theory faces problems in connection with his views on the relation between reason, action, and some third unnamed thing that we might call motive, faith, or heart. He has gone perhaps as far as it is possible to go in the attempt to show just how rational ethics is, but he still seems to need something more than, or at least other than, reason itself to explain what it takes to do the right thing or simply to be good. The attempt to generate an ethics of reason, which is done partly to win over skeptics like Thrasymachus, leads to the following view:

> it is the simple conformity to law in general, without assuming any particular law applicable to certain actions, that serves the will as its principle and must so serve it, if duty is not to be a vain delusion and a chimerical notion.[19]

There is a lot at stake, in other words. Either ethics can be made purely rational or else it is an illusion, as Thrasymachus assures us it is. Fortunately, Kant does quite a good job of showing how ethics can be rational. Unfortunately, he also shows the limits of reason. It is not clear that his particular conception of reason is the best one available. He does not show that reason itself can always figure out what the right thing to do is. And he admits that the motivation to do the right thing in some sense cannot be purely rational. A kind of religious faith is also, he thinks, necessary.

Objections

So much for Thrasymachus. What about the merits of Kant's theory otherwise? Many objections have been made to Kant's categorical imperative, in both its main versions. Let us start with the first version. Is he right to think that it is irrational to want the easiest, laziest life imaginable or that any of his examples supports the conclusion he draws from it? His ideas about what is right are quite traditional and so might simply seem like common sense to you. But their very traditional nature has led some people to wonder whether all Kant is doing is rationalizing the cultural beliefs he happened to grow up with. Certainly, his theory does not seem right to everyone who studies it. So regardless of what common sense might seem to tell us at first sight, we must ask: Is his theory right? Is it true that we have a duty to act only on maxims that could be willed as universal laws? Is a good law necessarily a very law-like law, universal and without exceptions? Is a good rational being necessarily a very *rational* rational being, willing to obey universal laws?

I do not see why it should be. With Aquinas we considered the idea that human beings, for instance, ought to be rational because that is what God wants. If that is what God wants, then this is fair enough. But why on earth should God care whether the laws we make for ourselves are very law-like? Indeed, we can ask whether the most law-like law is really the one that conforms most closely to Kant's ideal of a law. It might be, but it might instead be the law that is most typical of human laws, an imperfect average rather than a perfect ideal. And, besides, Kant's theory is meant not to rely on any belief in God's existence, let alone on any belief about exactly what God values. So the question of why we should be rational, or have the kind of will that he describes as good, is a problem for Kant.

His answer to the problem has to do with autonomy, or self-rule. We are, and want to be and should be, free beings, Kant thinks. No rational person wants to be a slave to someone else or to an addiction or to anything else. As we have seen, Plato thinks much the same thing. Even Thrasymachus wants to be free and so does not need to be convinced that freedom is a good thing. So we can take this as our starting point. Now, what does it mean to be free? It cannot, Plato and Kant would say, mean simply being able to do whatever we want to do. Addicts are not free just because they are able (if they are) to get whatever drug it is that they crave. True freedom means not only freedom from interference by other people but also freedom from one's own inner enemies or rivals (think of the monster and the lion/dog that Plato describes). A free person is not ruled by her addictions or anger or love for somebody else. She does not do, that is to say, things that she would never have done were it not for some moment of madness or weakness. She is, on the contrary, in control of herself at all times. In short, she is rational.

This is very similar to Plato's answer to Thrasymachus, and it faces the same challenge: Why should Thrasymachus accept that the rational thing to do is to be good or to obey the moral law? Kant's answer is that it is rational to value reason. Being rational does not mean simply figuring out the best way to get whatever it is that you happen to want, as Hume suggested. Instead, there are certain things that it is rational and certain things that it is irrational to seek. The desire to become more stupid than you are is irrational. The desire to be left in pain is irrational. On the other hand, the will to be rational, and for other people to be rational too, is rational. Valuing reason is itself rational. This is controversial and seems to depend on what conception of reason or rationality we adopt. Hume's is rather thin, being only about means to ends. Kant's is richer, including its own ends. If we prefer Kant's version, then we will probably accept that we should value reason. From this Kant believes it follows that we should obey the categorical imperative, which is derived (supposedly) from reason alone.

A problem with the categorical imperative, though, is knowing what the relevant maxim is in any particular case. This comes out in Kant's suicide example. His argument against suicide depends on taking the suicidal maxim (or policy) to be about what is to be done out of concern for oneself. Remember that he thinks it is contradictory, and hence irrational, to destroy oneself out of a concern for oneself. But why bring in this reference to concern for oneself? If the maxim had simply said "Whenever life looks like offering more pain than pleasure in future, I will end it all to avoid the pain," then there would seem to be no contradiction anymore.[20] This might not be a *good* principle to live by, but it seems quite *possible* to will it and, indeed, to will it as a universal law without contradiction or irrationality. The very same act (in this case, suicide) might turn out to be either wrong or perfectly acceptable, by Kant's test, depending on the wording of the maxim. Dishonest people, like skillful lawyers, might seem to be able to justify almost any immoral act if their powers of redescription are good enough. Murder could be presented as ending the victim's misery, theft as redistribution of wealth, and so on. Then how can we know what is allowed and what is not? Of course, Kant is counting on our honesty in using his theory. It is not meant to provide excuses for those who are not sincerely interested in doing the right thing in the first place. But surely a decent person might be sorely tempted to end his or her life. And it can be very hard to know whether one's ultimate motive is concern for oneself or something else, such as not wanting to be a burden on others, say. Without perfect self-knowledge, we might be unable to say what our maxims are and, hence, unable to use Kant's theory to figure out what we ought to do.[21]

Finally, Kant not only derives moral conclusions from the categorical imperative, but also judges the categorical imperative by the conclusions that it produces and whether these match our preexisting beliefs. So there is an inherent conservatism or conformism here, and it brings with it a certain rigidity. Kant says that it is never all right to make a false promise or to lie. Even if the lie is told to a would-be murderer in order to save the life of his potential victim, Kant says it is still wrong to lie. This does not mean, of course, that you have to help the murderer. It would not be wrong to slam the door in his face or to fight with him. But you must not do wrong, even in order to bring about good. The Bible says the same thing (see Romans 3:5–8). So this should not be an unusual view in a historically Christian society, but it is. Very few people agree with Kant on this point. Those who do are perhaps influenced more by their adherence to the Bible and traditional values than by Kant's arguments.

If you do not like the first version of the categorical imperative, you might prefer the second. Certainly, respecting people's humanity and not using them merely as means to our own ends sounds good. Some consequentialists will disagree though. Imagine that an innocent person has some information that we want to get from him. He will not tell us what we want to know, perhaps believing that other innocent people will be harmed if he talks. So we torture him until he tells us what we want to know. This seems to be a clear case of using the man as a mere means to the end of gathering information. We are not inflicting pain on him as a punishment for anything he has voluntarily done. Kant's theory implies, therefore, that torturing in cases like this is always wrong. Yet not everybody shares that view.

Even if we do agree with Kant and the major ethical traditions that injustice must never be done deliberately, whatever the consequences—"though the heavens fall," as the Romans used to say—we might still have trouble knowing how to apply Kant's rule. What exactly does it mean to treat someone else with due respect? Part of it is respecting the rational decisions of others. But what are these? Is it rational to choose to become a prostitute or a porn star? Is this ever a free choice, or is it forced on people by poverty, addiction, brutal pimps, or low self-esteem? These are partly empirical (scientific) questions, of course, but there is a purely philosophical or ethical aspect to them as well. Some Kantians will insist that we must treat all people, rich or poor, as making free choices, whatever the empirical evidence. Others will insist that no rational being would choose to be a drug-addicted prostitute, no matter what evidence to the contrary there might seem to be. The decision to take drugs such as heroin or crack cocaine can be thought of as being like the decision to commit suicide. One's maxim will presumably reflect a concern for pleasure and a readiness to risk death (just one dose of heroin can kill, after all), perhaps something like "Whenever a drug looks like offering more pain than pleasure, out of concern for myself I will risk ending it all." If Kant is right that such reasoning is irrational, then his argument will go against using hard drugs. We have seen already, though, that it is debatable whether Kant has shown that reasoning like this is irrational. If reason is all about finding means to ends, as Hume thinks, and if you really want to be high on heroin, then taking heroin is a perfectly rational thing to do. This does not mean that Kant is wrong, but it shows how hard his theory can be to apply in practice.

A second controversial feature of this second version of the categorical imperative is that it requires us to respect our own humanity by not treating ourselves as mere means. But again, what does this mean in practice? Is smoking cigarettes so disrespectful of oneself that it is *morally* wrong? (Maybe, but why exactly?) Or working as somebody else's servant? (Probably not but, again, why?) To repeat, Kant might well be right, but the practical implications of his theory are hard to discern. The most practical solution might be to interpret the second version of the categorical imperative by means of the first. But then we will be back with all the problems that it faced.

Conclusion

Kant's ethical theory is justly regarded as one of the best ever devised. It still faces quite a number of objections however. Many people who reject his theory prefer some version of utilitarianism. Perhaps the most famous such person is John Stuart Mill. In the next chapter, we will look at his view, which is almost diametrically opposite to Kant's, and see whether it can do any better at providing a persuasive response to our challenge.

Questions for Further Thought

1. Can torturing the innocent ever be justified?
2. Do we have moral duties to ourselves or only to others?
3. Do only rational beings have moral status?
4. Is religious faith psychologically necessary for ethical behavior?
5. Is ethics a matter of reason, feeling, both, or neither?

Notes

1. On this, see his *Doctrine of Virtue*, the second part of his *The Metaphysics of Morals*, ed. Mary Gregor (Cambridge: Cambridge University Press, 1996).
2. I should emphasize two points here. Firstly, this is one way to get into Kant's ethics, not an idea that Kant himself made much of. Secondly, I am not denying that a Kantian argument for vegetarianism could be constructed.
3. In a similar way, few people who say that abortion is murder would support the death penalty for women who have abortions, even if they support capital punishment for both murderers and those who hire people to carry out murder on their behalf.
4. Barbara Herman points this out in *The Practice of Moral Judgment* (Cambridge, MA: Harvard University Press, 1993), 26. It follows that Kant is not guilty of "rule-fetishism" (p. 27). We are not to obey rules in a spirit of checking off a list of required acts. Rather, he thinks, we should act out of respect for humanity.
5. Immanuel Kant, *Groundwork of the Metaphysic of Morals*, in *Kant's* Critique of Practical Reason *and Other Works*, trans. Thomas Kingsmill Abbott (London: Longmans, Green and Co., 1909), 9.

6. This word sometimes causes confusion and offense. It comes from the Norwegian dialect word *knika* or *gnikka,* meaning "to pinch or be mean," and means stingy or cheap.

7. Kant, *Groundwork,* 10.

8. Ibid., 16.

9. Ibid., 18.

10. The meaning of the words "I promise" seems to depend on what use we make of them in our lives. If we just ignore, or always fail to do, the thing we have said we "promise" we will do, then "I promise to. . ." would seem to mean something like "I am not going to. . ." Promising as we know it in such a universe would be nonexistent, not just pointless.

11. Kant, *Groundwork,* 47.

12. Of which creatures the moral law applies to, Kant says this: "unless we deny that the notion of morality has any truth or reference to any possible object, we must admit that its law must be valid, not merely for men but for all *rational creatures generally."* Ibid., 25.

13. What I say about Kant's theory here will not actually be strictly correct, but it is close enough for our purposes. Computers and their programs can be perceived, after all, while Kant's noumena or things in themselves can never be perceived, by definition.

14. Christine M. Korsgaard, *Creating the Kingdom of Ends* (Cambridge: Cambridge University Press, 1996), xi.

15. His classic work on this subject is the forbidding *Critique of Pure Reason.* His shorter *Prolegomena to Any Future Metaphysics,* written as a guide to the longer work, is slightly easier to understand. Jonathan Bennett has made available an accessible translation of this work at http://www.earlymoderntexts.com/f_kant.html, and Roger Scruton has written a good introduction to Kant's work generally in his book *Kant: A Very Short Introduction* (Oxford: Oxford University Press, 2001).

16. Kant, *Groundwork,* 25.

17. See Iris Murdoch, *The Sovereignty of Good* (London: Ark Paperbacks, 1985), 17–18.

18. See Arthur Schopenhauer, *On the Freedom of the Will* (Oxford: Blackwell, 1985), 55: "virtues and vices are inborn." Schopenhauer also holds that a person's character can never change, so those born bad cannot become good. It does not follow that we should condemn, or even criticize, those born with more than their fair share of vices. But we *might* agree with Aristotle that people should be held responsible for their own characters. Vice is bad, after all, and we might believe in judging characters rather than any particular acts or choices that are believed to create or shape characters.

19. Kant, *Groundwork,* 18.

20. There does need to be some reference to why the act is being done, for example, "to avoid the pain." This is an essential feature of maxims as Kant understands them but is often overlooked. Herman points out (*The Practice,* 218) that maxims are to present actions "as they are or are believed to be good." Korsgaard makes a similar point (*Creating,* 9).

21. The importance of knowing how to articulate one's maxims is one of the reasons Kant stresses the importance of moral education. See Herman *The Practice,* 109–110. No education can guarantee that one will become perfect at doing this however, as Kant would admit.

Suggestions for Further Reading

Kant's main works on ethics, which are by no means easy reading, are *Groundwork of the Metaphysics of Morals*, ed. Mary Gregor (Cambridge: Cambridge University Press, 1998); *The Metaphysics of Morals*, ed. Mary Gregor (Cambridge: Cambridge University Press, 1996); and *Critique of Practical Reason*, ed. Mary Gregor (Cambridge: Cambridge University Press, 1997). The *Groundwork* is the one to tackle first.

Two excellent books on Kant's ethics are Barbara Herman, *The Practice of Moral Judgment*, (Cambridge; MA: Harvard University Press, 1993), and Christine M. Korsgaard, *Creating the Kingdom of Ends* (Cambridge: Cambridge University Press, 1996).

The best general introduction to Kant is Roger Scruton, *Kant: A Very Short Introduction* (Oxford: Oxford University Press, 2001). After that, you could try Paul Guyer, *Kant* (London: Routledge, 2006), and Sebastian Gardner, *Kant and the Critique of Pure Reason* (London: Routledge, 1999). Unlike Scruton's and Guyer's, Gardner's book is about only one of Kant's works; but it is Kant's most important work, and one that has implications for his theory on ethics, even though it is primarily concerned with questions about knowledge and the ultimate nature of reality.

CHAPTER 8

Mill

Like Kant, John Stuart Mill (1806–1873) is usually considered something other than a virtue theorist. His famous essay in defense of utilitarianism makes him a prime advocate of one of the main theories that virtue ethicists like to attack (Kant's being the other one). However, if we look at Mill's version of the utilitarian theory, we will see that he is part of the same tradition as Aristotle and has some insights that are original and important.

An Introduction to Utilitarianism

Mill defends a version of utilitarianism; but his is only one version of this kind of ethical theory, and there are people who deny that Mill was really a utilitarian at all. It might help to look first at the generic theory. Then, we can compare Mill's theory and see what labels we want to apply to it.

Utilitarianism is a combination of several ethical theories. The first is *consequentialism,* the idea that what really matters, from the ethical point of view, is the consequences or results of what people do, so that, for instance, good ends can sometimes justify bad means. This idea is at least as old as the Bible, which quite specifically asserts that we are not to do bad in order that good may come of it. Even Christians, though, are likely to believe that *sometimes,* when the consequences are important enough, we should do bad in order to bring about good. Telling a white lie to save someone's feelings is an obvious example of such an occasion.

The second component of utilitarianism is **hedonism**, the idea that the only good is pleasure or happiness and the only evil is pain or unhappiness. This idea is at least as old as Epicurus (341–270 BCE), who, despite giving his name to the epicurean lifestyle of good food and drink, recommended living a very simple life with minimal risk of unhappiness.

Finally, utilitarians believe that each person is of equal moral importance. This makes utilitarianism, while not completely self-sacrificing (you count too), one of the most altruistic theories of ethics imaginable. If it turns out that the best way to do good is for each of us to take care of his or her own soul first and foremost, then we will not need to give much thought to the distant souls of unknown people; but that is a very big "if." Note too that my reference to souls here should not be taken too literally. Utilitarianism has no commitment to religious beliefs or any particular theory about whether immaterial objects exist. In fact, it is often thought of as a particularly secular ethical doctrine.

We turn now to some particular variations on the general theme of utilitarianism. Modern utilitarianism began with Jeremy Bentham (1748–1832), a strange man[1] who, while perhaps lacking in imagination or sensitivity, was full of zeal to reform ethics, law, and politics and to make them all more rational. Like Hume, Bentham was an empiricist, believing that knowledge is based on experience; and his idea of ethics was that it should be all about maximizing good experiences and minimizing bad ones. Good experiences, as he thought of them, are sensations in the mind that feel good to the person having the experience. He was also like Hume, therefore, in tying ethics to psychology, defining right and wrong in terms of certain types of mental event—namely, the experiences he called pleasure and pain. We have seen some problems with this idea as it appears in Hume's ethics, and we shall see more later in this chapter too.

Bentham was a friend of John Stuart Mill's father and he shaped Mill's education. Bentham's influence helped Mill to become one of the great philosophers of the nineteenth century but also led Mill to an emotional collapse at the age of 20. Mill eventually escaped from his nervous breakdown with the help of Romantic literature, especially William Wordsworth's poetry. This gives us an important clue as to the differences between Bentham and Mill.

On the third, altruistic element of utilitarian doctrine, Bentham and Mill were agreed. On the first two, they were not. The most striking difference between them lies in their conceptions of happiness. Bentham valued pleasure alone and held that all pleasures were of essentially the same kind. They differ with regard to duration, intensity, and so on, he believed; but none is intrinsically better than any other. On this basis, he developed a "felicific calculus" to work out what was the right thing to do. Ideally, as Bentham saw it, a numerical score could be given to the intensity and duration of a pleasure; and then other factors, such as the likelihood of this pleasure occurring and its probable effects on others, could be taken into account. We could then compare the scores of different courses of action and read off from the numbers what we ought to do. If bowling gives the world more pleasure than does the music of Beethoven, then bowling is better, for instance.

Mill disagreed. He argued that some pleasure is inherently superior to other, lower kinds. Consider the pleasures of virtue. People who value justice get a certain satisfaction from knowing that justice has been done. This is not a very intense pleasure. It does not tend to make us deliriously happy, but it is important. Those who value justice would not want to cease valuing it, even if they were compensated with greater pleasures of some other kind. The same kind of thing can be said about the pleasures of the intellect. Solving some mathematical problem might be satisfying, but it is unlikely to have one punching the air in triumph.

Still, would anybody willingly give up his or her intelligence for a more pleasurable life?

Mill says no. "It is better to be a human being dissatisfied than a pig satisfied; better to be Socrates dissatisfied than a fool satisfied," he says.[2] His point is not simply the Bentham-friendly idea that intelligence and moral virtue (the things that Socrates has and that a fool lacks) are useful and likely to generate happiness for ourselves and others. His point is that intelligence and moral virtue are better than their opposites even when or if they do not bring pleasure.[3] There is more to life than pleasure, in other words. Hedonism, or at least simple hedonism, is false.

What, though, is good aside from pleasure? Mill calls it "happiness." But Mill's idea of happiness is not the subjective feeling that Bentham valued. Being a human being rather than a pig is not just a feeling, and it is not subjective. What Mill calls "happiness" is really a way of being, a quality that we might, thinking of Aristotle, call *eudaimonia*.

This brings us to consequentialism. Elizabeth Anscombe, who coined the term "consequentialist," did not apply the label to Mill because she thought he believed that there are certain things that simply must not be done, no matter what the consequences.[4] Most people who read his work, though, think that Mill is a consequentialist. Since he values being like Socrates, however, he would not advocate un-Socratic actions. And Socrates was not a consequentialist. There are two main views on what to make of this apparent tension in Mill's thought. One is that Mill believes in ethical rules that should always be followed, even if breaking one might seem on occasion more likely to bring about a good end than adhering to the rule would. This is still a form of consequentialism because the rules to be followed are those that generally have good consequences, but it is not as strictly consequentialist as Bentham's view. This helps Mill's version to avoid some of the criticisms that have been leveled at classical utilitarianism. The other view, though, is that Mill allows for both improving rules in the light of new information and making exceptions to them when this is necessary for the greater good. For instance, he suggests that it might be justifiable sometimes to force a doctor to work against her or his will in order to save somebody's life. Emphasizing this strain in Mill's thought would lead to regarding him as a standard kind of consequentialist. In order to decide what kind of utilitarian he was, it will help to look more closely at his theory and how he justified it. We will do this in the next section, but of course there is no substitute for a careful study of his own words.

Happiness

Mill begins his essay "Utilitarianism" by noting that no progress seems to have been made in ethics since the time of Socrates. In science we can make progress by discovering this or that fact, without having to worry too much about the big philosophical questions, such as "What is truth?" or "How can we really know anything?" Ethics is not like this. "All action is for the sake of some end," says Mill, echoing Aristotle; and to know which actions are right, we need to know what this end ultimately is.[5] This raises questions about the point of life and how we can settle disputes about what it might be. In making his argument, then, Mill could hardly avoid distinguishing his position from others' and arguing against what they believed.

Mill was opposed primarily not to Bentham or to Kant but to moral sense theorists or intuitionists, who said that we know about good and bad by means of a mysterious special power, like a sixth sense. Against them, Mill claimed that only the intellect and the five known senses are necessary to tell what is right and what is wrong. However, it can be argued that Mill is an intuitionist himself at heart, regarding facts about value as ultimately indemonstrable yet facts nonetheless, discernible by the right character.[6] In this, as in much else, he is like Aristotle. His failure to see this clearly, though, led him to an at times reductive account of what morality is. Thinking about ethics scientifically can make it seem to be a matter of feelings of a certain kind, as we saw in our discussion of Hume, which perhaps might be produced by our brain chemistry. Empiricist attempts to take the mystery out of ethics are likely to present morality as something amoral, something biological or naturalistically determined, as if there were no point even trying to think about it. If ethics boils down to brain chemistry, after all, which we cannot really do anything about, then what point is there in thinking about it? We can alter our brain chemistry, of course, but a conversation conducted solely with this goal in mind would be very different from one in which people tried to argue rationally for what they actually believe in. Philosophical discussion of ethical questions would seem to be pointless if ethics is not rational but somehow merely biochemical. We will return to the idea that we really are purely biological beings and that ethics, therefore, must somehow be reducible to biology later in this chapter and see how it has been used as a deliberate attack on morality (of a certain kind) in the next chapter. For now, though, we should return to Mill's rejection of moral sense theory.

Some people, like Hume, believe in a kind of natural moral sense that will tell us what to do. But there is disagreement about whether such a thing exists, Mill points out; and even if it does, it does not tell us what is right in particular cases in the way that the sense of sight tells us what colors things are. Otherwise, we would not disagree so much. To know whether a particular action is right or wrong, Mill thinks, we cannot simply perceive that it is one or the other. Instead, we have to apply some general law to the particular case.

Most philosophers agree on what these laws are (it is wrong to lie, e.g.), but disagree about whether it is experience or pure reason that teaches them to us. If there is a science of morals, if there is some truth about what is right and wrong that we are to discover by objective principles, then we need to know what the fundamental principle is from which the others are derived. We also need to know which principle should take precedence when two seem to conflict—for instance, when keeping a secret means telling a lie. But there is no recognized, agreed-upon, ultimate principle or standard that settles all moral dilemmas.

Philosophers (and others) tend to agree on what is right and what is wrong, Mill says, not because they derive their principles from a common fundamental idea but because philosophy has tended merely to be "a consecration of men's actual sentiments."[7] In other words, philosophy so far has only taken what people already believed about ethics and stamped it with the seal of approval. Mill thought, though, that philosophy should be a guide, not a codification or celebration of what we already believe.

Since so many people care so much about happiness, the principle of utility has influenced every moral philosophy that has merely consecrated existing sentiments. Everyone takes happiness and the consequences of actions into account in thinking about right and wrong, even those who do not admit it. This is true, he says, even of theories that claim to *oppose* utilitarianism.

Consider Kant, whose primary rule of morality is (in Mill's words) "So act, that the rule on which thou actest would admit of being adopted as a law by all rational beings."[8] No act would prove illogical, irrational, or impossible by this rule, Mill claims. Bad acts are simply undesirable as universal laws because of the consequences that they would have for our happiness. That is Kant's real reason for condemning them as wrong, according to Mill. For example, consider a rule that tells everyone to do all they can to destroy the earth. Is it logically possible for this rule to be adopted by everybody? Mill, like Hume, would say yes. Logic does not prevent us from desiring the destruction of the earth. There is no contradiction involved in the idea of having this as our goal. It is not too hard to imagine a world in which everyone did have this suicidal and genocidal aim, although they would surely achieve their aim quite quickly, and so cease to have any goals at all, given access to enough nuclear weapons. In what sense, then, is this goal impossible for rational agents to adopt? In the sense that it would be *stupid* to adopt it. And that is *not* because of pure reason or logic but because we do not *want* everything to be destroyed. No matter what he might say, Kant is in fact concerned with the effects of our actions on our happiness. He is a kind of utilitarian despite himself. Or so, to repeat, Mill claims.

Mill's aim is to defend utilitarianism and to prove it true as far as that is possible. However, he says "Questions of ultimate ends are not amenable to direct proof. Whatever can be proved to be good, must be so by being shown to be a means to something admitted to be good without proof."[9] We cannot prove that health, say, or pleasure is good. Fortunately, we do not need to since everyone agrees that they are good. It is a kind of proof of the goodness of a thing, then, if we can show that it is a *means* to such goods as health, pleasure, and so on.

Mill points out that utilitarians do not favor usefulness over pleasure, as when someone describes a building's facilities as merely "utilitarian." Utilitarians value precisely pleasure and exemption from pain:

> The creed which accepts as the foundation of morals, Utility, or the Greatest Happiness Principle, holds that actions are right in proportion as they tend to promote happiness, wrong as they tend to produce the reverse of happiness. By happiness

is intended pleasure, and the absence of pain; by unhappiness, pain, and the privation of pleasure.[10]

When we think of pleasure, Mill says, we should bear in mind that human beings have "elevated" faculties and appetites. This is one of the greatest points of disagreement between him and Bentham. Once we are conscious of these faculties, we do not consider anything to be happiness if it does not include the gratification of our elevated appetites. These pleasures are longer-lasting, cheaper, and safer than animal pleasures. But they are also just plain better. They are, after all, "elevated." Why higher pleasures are better cannot really be explained since there can be no rational dispute about ultimate ends, according to Mill. Nevertheless, we might want a bit more explanation of what this means.

What makes one pleasure more valuable than another? "Of two pleasures, if there be one to which all or almost all who have experience of both give a decided preference, irrespective of any feeling of moral obligation to prefer it, that is the more desirable pleasure."[11] This is not Mill's *definition* of higher pleasures. The majority of competent judges is not *necessarily* right about which pleasures are higher. But he does think it reasonable to respect the majority verdict. This is true even if the preferable pleasure brings more *discontent*. Higher pleasures are better than lower ones no matter how intense they may be.

This judgment is not meant to be merely Mill's opinion or a reflection of his personal taste. It is an "unquestionable fact," he writes, that people who enjoy both higher and lower pleasures prefer the kind of life that gives them the former.[12] No one would choose to be less intelligent, less knowledgeable, or less virtuous than they are, even though a lower life might be simpler and more satisfying. We have a sense of dignity that we will not sacrifice—even for more pleasure—unless we are in such despair as to be virtually suicidal. Fools know only the lower pleasures. Better people know both kinds and prefer the higher. Or so Mill says.

People still tend to pursue lower pleasures, though, just because they are often the easiest to get. Giving in to such temptations does not show that we do not know what is better. Sometimes, also, the capacity for higher pleasures is killed off by lack of sustenance. If we keep bad company, for instance, or get into bad habits, we might find that we really cannot any longer enjoy the things we used to regard as finer. Still, higher pleasures are better, as the majority of competent judges affirms. Both quality and quantity of pleasure matter, to be sure; but quality matters more. And it is not just our own happiness for which we should strive but that of all people, indeed of all sentient creatures. Some of the most prominent animal rights supporters today, such as Peter Singer, are utilitarians.

Some object that we have no right to happiness or that happiness is unattainable. The aim of Mill's kind of utilitarianism, though, is not constant ecstasy but a life that contains a lot of pleasure, relatively little pain, and some moments of sheer bliss. We should not expect too much from life but should actively enjoy it to the best of our ability.

Better education and social arrangements should allow most people to enjoy the combination of tranquility and excitement that makes for a happy life.

Selfishness can lead to boredom and despair at the prospect of death, but the more we care about other things and other people, the more interesting we will find life and the less death will bother us. A lack of mental cultivation is the second main cause of dissatisfaction with life, Mill believes. A cultivated mind is alive to the world and rarely bored. Almost everyone, therefore, is capable of the moral and intellectual virtue required for a happy life. What we need to do is fight poverty, disease, and lack of fellow human feeling. This we can and should do, making happiness possible (although not guaranteed) for all. This is the only worthy goal of action. Self-sacrifice for the sake of others' happiness is noble (for any other goal, it is folly). We should love others as ourselves, neither more nor less; and education and public opinion should encourage thoughts of the general good as harmonious with our own individual good.

Motives

The motive of one's actions shows one's worth as a human being but has nothing to do with the worth of the actions themselves, Mill says. This is somewhat puzzling, but what he means is that a happiness-producing act is good, regardless of motive, and a pain-producing one is bad. We do not need to *think* of the good of all, except in rare circumstances. But what we do should *be* for the overall good. Otherwise, it is not good, regardless of why we do it. An example might help to make the point. Say I give you a book because it is yours and you have asked to have it back. I am not thinking of anything so grand as the good of all humanity or indeed of all sentient beings. I am just thinking that I should give back the book that I borrowed. That is fine with Mill, so long as giving you the book does not somehow make the world a worse place. If the book teaches you how to make bombs and you go off to commit terrorist outrages, then I have done a bad thing in returning it to you. Similarly, if the book, unbeknownst to me, carries a deadly virus, then it is bad that I have given it to you.

Mill makes an important distinction between motive and intention. My motive is unimportant in determining the goodness or rightness of an action, but, "The morality of the action depends entirely upon the intention—that is, upon what the agent *wills to do.*"[13] Clearly, Mill means different things by the terms "motive" and "intention." Elsewhere, he says that intention is the foresight of consequences.[14] The example that he uses to make the distinction involves saving a drowning man in order to torture him and then kill him later. To judge the act of saving, Mill says, you have to take into account the torture that is going to happen. And to judge that, you have to consider the consequences of saving the man, not the motive for doing so, if by "motive" we mean simply some psychological factor that caused the act of saving. In other words, when Mill says that the morality of an act depends on the intention but not the motive, what he means is that what matters is what you are doing, not why you are doing it. And "what you are doing" needs to be understood in some sort of context. I can no more justify part of a plan to torture someone by saying that I was saving him from drowning than I can justify shooting someone by saying that I was simply pulling a trigger. If I foresee the consequences of my action (e.g., someone's being shot), then that is what needs to be judged, not the act itself of pulling the trigger. Indeed, for a strict consequentialist, it hardly matters whether I foresee the consequences or not. In that sense, intention is irrelevant to the morality of an action. Since that is the opposite of what Mill actually says, though, we should hesitate to call him a strict consequentialist. The belief that the morality of an action depends on the agent's will is not, after all, compatible with our earlier definition of consequentialism.

We might think that this is good for Mill. Consequentialists are often criticized for thinking that good consequences can justify bad acts. This, though, is not exactly what Mill believes. Bad acts should not be done, he says, even if the consequences on one occasion would be good because they belong to a class of acts that is generally harmful. So Mill appears to be what is called a "rule utilitarian." Lying, for instance, weakens one's tendency to tell the truth and makes one more likely to lie again. It thus lowers the liar (makes him or her less like Socrates) and tends to hurt others, making it wrong on two counts.

There can be exceptions to this rule though, and these should be judged by the general principle of utility, according to Mill. But, we might complain, the principle of utility judges rules or types of acts. How can we use it, then, to judge particular exceptions to rules? Should we consider each possible exception as itself following a kind of sub-rule? If so, how specific should each rule be? Where do we draw the line between considering each individual act, as Mill seems to think we should not do, and considering kinds of acts? Will rule utilitarianism collapse into act utilitarianism (with one very specific rule for each particular act)? The answer seems to be that Mill really is an act utilitarian after all, judging each act by the principle of utility.

But the very act of stopping to judge each possible act can itself be judged by this principle and found to be a waste of time. So Mill recommends instead following general rules of a familiar kind: do not lie, do not steal, and so on. The question now is when to follow these rules and when to make an exception. That is to be determined by the principle of utility. But when should we stop to think about whether we should *perhaps* make an exception? For this, it seems, we must use our judgment or simply go by those times when we simply do find ourselves wondering what to do. This is the limit of the usefulness of the principle of utility. Whenever we are judging actions, though, Mill believes we ought to do so on the basis of this principle.

Other critics of utilitarianism say that there is no time to calculate the effects of actions, but human history shows the usual effects of all kinds of actions. Humanity learns what it likes and passes this knowledge down from one generation to another. Of course, we can make improvements, but the general guidelines are pretty much set for us. We know, for instance, that people do not enjoy being robbed or murdered. Some cases are hard to decide, but at least utilitarianism gives us a standard to (try to) judge by.

If utilitarianism is the product of human history in this way though, why is it that we feel as though we must not rob or murder but not that we must promote the general happiness? Even if we agree with Mill that that is what we should do, we do not have the same *sense* about it that we get with the moral values that we learned as children. Why is this? Because we have not been raised to have a feeling of unity with our fellow creatures, Mill says. Feelings of obligation come from our upbringing and education, so we can be raised to feel obliged to do all kinds of things. The feelings we end up having will depend on the reasons we are given for acting this way or that.

Reasons for trying to do the right thing, Mill says, are sanctions, penalties for not doing it. These are all either external or internal. External sanctions are (1) God (the desire to get rewards from him, to avoid punishment from him, to serve him out of love or awe) and (2) other people (the desire to get favors from them, to avoid their displeasure, to help them out of sympathy or affection). These can all be reasons (i.e., motives) to promote the general happiness. Since Mill does not believe in God, he would hardly say that getting into heaven is a good reason to do anything; but he recognizes that this is what motivates some people to do good deeds. That is all he seems to mean when he calls these things "reasons."

The internal sanction is duty, a feeling in our own mind that hurts us when we do whatever we believe to be wrong and even makes some acts unthinkable for us. Conscience can be shaped in various ways, as Aristotle argued, by religion, experience, and so on; but its essence is the feeling of duty. "The ultimate sanction . . . of all morality (external motives apart) [is] a subjective feeling in our own minds."[15] It is perhaps worth noting that this analysis of conscience is amoral, it comes from outside the conscience. The theory says "We must do x or else feel y." Conscience says "We must do x because it is right." Mill is offering an amoral account of morality. It is possible to wonder whether such an account or explanation will ever be able to be squared with our moral beliefs. That is to say, can we regard our own conscience as nothing more than a subjective feeling in our own minds? Isn't that exactly what Thrasymachus wants us to think? If so, then it seems reasonable to ask whether Mill's empirical psychology is as simply objective as he means it to be or whether, on the contrary, something subversive of morality has slipped in disguised as admirably dispassionate objectivity. This might not matter very much. It could be a blunder in Mill's account of meta-ethics, his theory about the general nature of ethics, that does not affect his particular ideas about what actually is right and wrong. On the other hand, this kind of reductive talk about ethics hardly seems likely to strengthen "the feelings of virtue" in those in whom they are weak, which Mill says is the purpose of writings on ethics.[16]

There is no reason, according to Mill, that the mechanism of conscience should not be converted to utilitarian ends. No reason, that is, children could not be raised to have utilitarian consciences, ones that pained them when they failed to maximize the general happiness. Indeed, our own consciences are at least somewhat like this already. Those who believe conscience to be merely a subjective feeling might be thought to be more likely to ignore their consciences. But, Mill assures us, this *is* all that conscience is, and people often ignore their consciences anyway. As Mill sees it, no moral principles are innate, and people can be brought to believe in almost any set of principles; but utility fits particularly well with our natural desire for unity with others. So utilitarianism fits our nature well and is likely to survive as a principle.

The altruistic element of utilitarianism, he argues, is also likely to survive and, indeed, to grow. Society is natural, necessary, and habitual for human beings: "Society between equals can only exist on the understanding that the interests of all are to be regarded equally."[17] So we have self-interested reasons for regarding others as our equals. As society becomes more unavoidable, as the world gets smaller, and as equality increases, it becomes more natural for us to think of the welfare of others. Sympathy and education can do the rest.

Proof

Can any of this be proved? Can we prove, for example, that the general happiness is the ultimate good? Famously, Mill declares that the only proof that can be offered that something is desirable is that people actually desire it. He is often taken to think that "desirable" means "able to be desired," as if some people's desire for crack cocaine or child pornography or the elimination of all Jews meant that those things must be desirable. But of course "desirable" means "such as ought to be desired" or "desired by right-thinking people." I think that Mill knows this and is not making a stupid mistake. He means that he can't prove to us that happiness is desirable except by appealing to our belief that it is so. "You want proof that happiness is desirable? Well, don't you desire it? Do you regard that desire as on a par with a crack addict's desire for crack? No? Well, there's nothing more I can say." His point seems to be something like that. After all, what proof can there be that something is worthy of desire except an appeal to the reader's feeling or belief that the thing is worthy of desire?

He goes on to say that each person desires his or her own happiness; therefore, the general happiness is "a good to the aggregate of all persons."[18] It is not therefore a good to each individual, but it is in so far as each individual identifies with the whole, as Mill thinks good people do and will increasingly do in the future. This argument too has been much criticized. Just because each of us wants something, whether a banana or the general happiness, it does not follow that we want all of us together to have it. We might be purely selfish, or even hostile to other people. Again, I think Mill knows this. He believes that good people identify their own interests with those of the whole society (see earlier) and that in future more and more people will see things this way. Those who do will value the general good. His critics say that he is just not thinking straight on this point. Certainly, he does not spell out his argument as fully as he might have done, but it does seem possible to construct one for him that makes a certain amount of sense. Since Mill was no fool, it is probably wise to interpret him as making as much sense as possible, consistent with what he actually says.

But is happiness all that we desire? What about virtue and the absence of vice? Mill's doctrine "maintains not only that virtue is to be desired, but that it is to be desired disinterestedly, for itself."[19] It is not an end in itself (only happiness is), but it should be regarded as such. This is because the *belief* that virtue is an end in itself tends to promote happiness and because virtue is part of happiness, that is one of the things that make for a high grade of existence. It is thus like music or health—to have these things is to be happy, as long as one is suitably appreciative.

Development of one's character and of one's feelings is important to Mill not only because a good character is more likely to produce actions that produce happiness but also because educated sentiments are necessary in order to understand what happiness is (contrary to Bentham's view) and because part of what it is to be happy, according to Mill, is to have a well-developed character (i.e., to be like Socrates).

What if someone does not want to be like Socrates? Thrasymachus is a prime example of such a person. The only way, Mill says, to get someone to care about ethics is to make him or her "think of it in a pleasurable light."[20] "Will is the child of desire" and we cannot will something without desiring it.[21] What we consider good, we will; and what we will, we desire. Since the only thing that we desire as an end in itself is happiness, only happiness can be willed as an ultimate end. But if we can persuade others that Mill is right about the importance of society, then even completely selfish individuals will come to desire the happiness of others as well as their own happiness. And if we can educate people to appreciate the higher pleasures of virtue, the arts, and so on, then they will not think of happiness as crude pleasure.

Why Be Good? The Problem of Justice

What about justice, the virtue that Plato focuses on in the *Republic* in response to the challenge from Thrasymachus? We might have a natural sense of justice, but a natural feeling is not always a good feeling (i.e., one that we should act on). Justice, Mill says, being a general term, is best understood by looking at a range of particular things that are considered to be just. And what is unjust is easier and better to consider for this purpose than what is just. It is generally unjust to violate legal or moral rights, for people not to get what they deserve, to break faith with someone (as when one breaks a promise), to be partial when one should be impartial, and for there to be inequality, except where it serves a purpose.

Mill allows for poetic justice. We might not like the idea of a government so intrusive in everyday life that each single act of injustice, however small, is investigated by the police, brought to trial, and punished by the state. And with certain very large injustices we might not like the idea of the state inflicting suitable punishment. For example, it is common to feel that there is something fitting about the ancient *lex talionis*, the law of an eye for an eye. But many people would shudder at the thought of the state appointing someone to gouge out the eyes of a criminal, even if he had done the same to one of his victims. If he somehow accidentally, or at the hands of an enraged victim, suffered the same fate, then he would, we might feel, have got what he deserved. But this is not the same thing at all as feeling, and still less *thinking*, that the state ought to inflict such barbaric punishments on people. Mill puts it this way:

> Duty is a thing which may be *exacted* from a person, as one exacts a debt. . . . Reasons of prudence, or the interest of other people, may militate against actually exacting it; but the person himself, it is clearly understood, would not be entitled to complain.[22]

There is more to justice, though, than matters of crime and punishment. Duties of perfect obligation (things one must do all the time) correspond with rights, and this is what justice is all about, Mill thinks. The rest of duty is duties of imperfect obligation (things one must do only some of the time, e.g., duties of gratitude and beneficence). "Justice," though, "implies something which it is not only right to do, and wrong not to do, but which some individual person can claim from us as his moral right."[23]

The feeling of justice, Mill says, is the desire to punish those who do wrong plus the belief that some definite individual(s) has been harmed. Justice itself is a rule of conduct sanctioned by this particular feeling. The desire to punish is basically the instinct of revenge, which does not sound very ethical. It becomes moral, according to Mill, when a sense of human sympathy is added to this instinct—not sympathy for the one to be punished but sympathy for the victim of the original crime. We can see here again something like the moral psychology that Hume introduces, especially in the importance given to the notion of sympathy; and we will see it attacked in the next chapter, precisely on the grounds that our supposedly noble ideal of justice often seems to be nothing more than the desire for revenge, or even just for violence, dressed up.

For now, though, let us continue with Mill's view of justice, to which rights are essential. What, we might ask, is a moral right, as distinct from a legal right, which is something defined by the government? "To have a right . . . is . . . to have something which society ought to defend me in the possession of."[24] Why should society defend me in this way? Mill's answer is "general utility." There is little agreement about the justice of punishing someone in order to make an example for others, punishment in general if our characters are not ours to make, the idea of justice as retaliation, whether taxes should be flat, or a host of other things. The solution is to apply the principle of utility to these questions.

Justice is about rules concerning "the essentials of human well-being."[25] Peace requires social feelings, and social feelings require some noninterference by others (i.e., freedom); thus freedom (which essentially involves rights) is essential to peace and happiness.

But the protection of individual rights is not an absolute value. "[T]o save a life, it may not only be allowable, but a duty, to steal, or take by force, the necessary food or medicine, or to kidnap, and compel to officiate the only qualified medical practitioner."[26] How can we decide when rights may be violated in this way? By appeal to the principle of utility, of course. We should always act in ways that promote the greatest happiness of the greatest number.

Objections

One complaint made about utilitarianism is that it seems to require that we be able to see the future. If right acts are those that produce good consequences, then we cannot know what is right unless we know what the consequences of any conceivable act will be. But we cannot know this, so we cannot know what is right. As a practical guide to life, then, it might seem that utilitarianism is useless.

There is something to this. We do not know the future, and it is often hard to know what is right. But generally this is not the case. Only someone trying to make a point would insist that we really do not know what the consequences will be if I start slapping people at random. We do not know the exact consequences, true, but we do know that a decrease in happiness will occur, unless something very bizarre happens. And we know that this is not likely. Mill points out that we have had the whole of human history to see which kinds of act generally make people happy and which make them unhappy. Murder, lying, and so on have bad consequences; acts of courage, justice, and the like have good consequences. Yes, there are exceptions; but this a problem for everyone, not just utilitarians. And since Mill mostly believes in following general rules, we do not need to worry too much about these exceptional cases.

A second complaint is that utilitarianism values justice too little. If all we care about is making people happy, it is said, then sometimes we will trample on the rights of the unpopular individual for the sake of the greater happiness. Totalitarian regimes have shown how much evil can be done in the name of the greater good (of the Aryan race or the proletariat or whatever). But history has shown that totalitarian regimes and their oppressive disregard of justice and individual rights do not make people happy. Mill foresaw this. He argues that only a society in which individual liberty is protected will promote happiness successfully. He seems to be right.

We could say the same kind of thing about giving people what they deserve. Perhaps on occasion a person will be so unpopular that a society as a whole would be happier if he were framed for a crime of which he is innocent, but certainly as a general practice this kind of thing will not help anyone to sleep easily. Even if the event were a one-off, the truth could be very unsettling if it ever got out. Similarly with letting a guilty person go. When President Clinton was being investigated over his affair with Monica Lewinsky, some people argued that his guilt or innocence was irrelevant since he was doing so well in all the other areas of his job. This is clearly a kind of utilitarian reasoning, but it is not at all clear that Mill would have agreed. In general, he might say, the guilty should be punished and the innocent left free, not out of any desire for retribution but because justice so defined makes people happy or at least less fearful than the alternative. Here again, we face the problem of what kind of utilitarianism we should prefer. Should we stick with certain general principles, or should we always be prepared to break these rules when making an exception seems to promise greater happiness? The more we make maximizing happiness our sole concern, the less likely we are to treat justice as an absolute value.

The final objection to utilitarianism that I will look at here comes from Bernard Williams. Williams argues that utilitarianism ignores the value of integrity. Say you object very strongly to killing innocent people but you find yourself held at gunpoint by terrorists who demand that you shoot an innocent woman. If you shoot her in the head, they assure you (and you have read that they are reliable in both their threats and their promises) that they will free you and their other 19 innocent prisoners. If you refuse to shoot her, they will kill her and the other 19 too. A standard utilitarian would say not only that you should overcome your scruples and shoot the woman but that it is *obvious* that this is what you should do in the circumstances. Williams' objection is not so much to the idea that you should shoot one person in order to save 19 others but rather to the idea that this should be an easy decision. Indeed, a standard utilitarian would say that here your scruples are bad, that they detract from the total amount of happiness in the world and should be abandoned or minimized if at all possible, at least for a while.

Mill's version of utilitarianism, though, seems to avoid any such problem. For one thing, as I have said, he believes that (for the most part) we should follow general rules, and "Do not kill innocent people" is likely to be one of these rules. For another thing, he thinks that what we should promote is not happiness in any obvious sense but happiness in the sense of being like Socrates. Would Socrates kill one person in this situation with scarcely a second thought? Surely not. Would anyone's killing an innocent person increase the "Socrates-ness" of anyone in the world? Again, probably not. Integrity is surely a key feature of what Mill means by "happiness," and he would be unlikely to sacrifice it for the sake of mere life. Life on its own, without happiness, he says in his essay on capital punishment, is not valuable. Mill respects certain feelings or sentiments. But it is these sentiments that prompt us to reject the idea of maximizing happiness in the kind of case that Williams describes in connection with integrity. So, arguably at the cost of really being a utilitarian, Mill seems able to avoid the main objections that have been leveled at utilitarianism. This does not mean that his theory is without flaws however.

Think again of Thrasymachus and the question of why we should behave as Mill says we should. What's in it for me? As far as being like Socrates goes, Mill's answer is interesting. For any two pleasures, he suggests, if you want to know which is better, you can simply apply the following test: find people who appreciate both and then ask them which they value more. This seems entirely reasonable. If we want to evaluate professional wrestling objectively, it would be foolish to appoint as judges people who hate wrestling and see nothing in it. It obviously has some appeal and should be judged by those capable of appreciating this. Now, if we want to compare professional wrestling with Shakespeare's play *Hamlet*, should we just ask the wrestling fans which they prefer? Of course not. The competent judges are those who are able to appreciate both the thrills of wrestling and the drama of *Hamlet*. If these people value *Hamlet* more highly, even if wrestling gives them more pleasure, then *Hamlet* is better. (Just don't tell The Rock.)

This seems fair enough, but it raises some questions. For one thing, where are we to find such people? There probably are a number of people who like Shakespeare and wrestling, but can we be confident that they find in wrestling what the typical wrestling fan likes about it or that what they value in *Hamlet* is what other theatergoers like about the play? Perhaps they just like seeing men in tights. And where will we find the people to judge the relative merits of Sufi mysticism and crack cocaine, or quantum physics and badger-baiting? Mill's test might not work in practice.

Even if we find competent judges, we might not trust their judgment. This could be because they are eccentric and unrepresentative, or it could be because they have been debased by the lower of the two pleasures into valuing it more highly. Mill is confident that a human being would not prefer to be a pig or that Socrates would not prefer to be a fool. He implies that Socrates knows what it is like to be a fool and is therefore competent to judge. But we do not know what it is like to be a pig, surely. And what if the lower pleasure in question is addictive or satisfies some primal instinct? Can we be sure that Shakespeare-loving heroin addicts would value *Hamlet* more than their next fix? If they did not, what would this prove? That heroin is better than *Hamlet* or just that their addiction had clouded their judgment? If we assume the latter, then the test is starting to look biased against the so-called lower pleasures.

Perhaps more seriously, how confident can we be that all or even most of the qualified judges will value the same pleasures? Are all human beings constituted the same way so that we will all, with the right education, have the same tastes? It seems doubtful. Mill appears to be counting on there being some common human essence that will ensure that, at least largely, on the important things in life, we will all agree. There is some evidence for this. It is generally agreed that *Hamlet* is a good play, that Bach was a good composer, that torturing innocent people is wrong, and so on. But not everyone accepts Mill's view.

How might they be converted? One way is by asking them whether they would gladly trade their "higher faculties" (their capacities for the "higher" pleasures of morality and the intellect) for lower ones if guaranteed more pleasure. Unfortunately, some people say that they would indeed make such a trade. Others say that they would not but also have no desire to move any higher on the faculty/pleasure ladder. One suspects that either ignorance or a lack of imagination is at work here, but even so, Mill has not yet won, and seemingly cannot win, this debate outright. So, perhaps it is better to be like Socrates than a fool, but some people remain unconvinced and seemingly unconvinceable.

What then of Mill's further idea that ethics is about promoting Socrates-ness in others as well as in oneself? Why on earth should we want to do that? Well, as a matter of fact, we do tend to want others to be like ourselves; and if we are going to be like Socrates, we might well want others to be so too. Then we will have people we can talk to. Mill famously argues that the only test for whether something is desirable is whether it is desired, for which he is often criticized. He has a point, however. If *nobody* desires a certain kind of thing, then it is hard to make sense of claims that it is desirable. Who would make such a claim if they did not in some sense desire it? And what, as Aristotle observed, do all people want but happiness? If happiness is the only thing that anybody ultimately wants, as Aristotle argued, then it is the only thing that can conceivably be desirable. And that, I think, is what Mill means to say, combined, of course, with the further argument that true happiness, what everybody in a position to know really wants, is happiness in the sense of being like Socrates. Therefore, happiness so conceived is the only end to seek. If we do not seek it for ourselves, Mill thinks, it is because we are ignorant. And once we are like Socrates, we will care about others too.

Are we, though, better off being utilitarians? Possibly not. We might be happier being prepared to sacrifice ourselves for others, but actually doing so, making the sacrifice, could presumably make us less happy. (Unless Mill's conception of happiness is radically divorced from Bentham's.) Most of the time, for most people, being like Socrates might be the best option—but not necessarily always.

And why should we want this kind of happiness for others, indeed even at the possible expense of getting it for ourselves? It is the greatest good of the greatest number, not oneself, that Mill enjoins us to seek, remember. Companionship is one possible reason, but one still might want some others to be slaves. Aristotle wanted philosophical friends but still supported slavery, after all. Mill's defense of liberty is surely relevant here. If anybody is enslaved, then people will never be certain that they or their children or friends will not some day join the ranks of the slaves. A happy society will have to be one of free people. Mill takes this idea farther. A happy society will have to be one of free, well educated people. People, that is, like Socrates.

Conclusion

There is some reason to think that Mill has an answer to Thrasymachus' challenge. It is in my own self-interest to become like Socrates and to want to live in a society of similarly cultivated people. Should I sacrifice my own cultivation for the sake of others? In some circumstances, almost certainly yes. Will Thrasymachus accept this? Not at all. But Socrates, understood here as a generic wise and good person of taste, probably would. And such a person would, we can imagine, support the production and protection of a society of free, wise, and good people of taste. We are back in a way to Aristotle's emphasis on education and upbringing. Thrasymachus might not see why he should want moral and intellectual improvement, but all those who have undergone it agree that it was for their own good and that it is bad to be like Thrasymachus. Or so Aristotle and Mill would seem to think. The remaining question would then be why Thrasymachus should listen to these people, why the opinions of the experienced should be thought relevant to him. Should he trust experience to educate rather than corrupt them? Should he trust *their* experience to be relevant to his life?

Most of the time I think we would be inclined to answer both of these questions affirmatively, although not necessarily all the time. Indeed, a refusal to listen to those with experience might be regarded as irrational. But reason thus far has seemed incapable of *proving* that it would be wrong to ignore the wise (those who have learned from their experiences which experiences and faculties they value most). Perhaps we have reached the limits of reason. Perhaps we are all too different to learn much from each other.

In the next chapter we will look at the ideas of Friedrich Nietzsche, a great champion of individual differences and, some would say, an enemy of reason. As we shall see, Nietzsche strongly rejects the idea that Socrates represents the ideal of humanity and uses something like Mill's moral psychology deliberately to subvert traditional values. This makes him an interesting critic of the British empiricist tradition that includes both Hume and Mill. Nietzsche is also an innovative thinker with a competing vision of his own to promote. Whatever flaws there may be in the work of Hume and Mill, Nietzsche's rival theory has not yet received as much admiration from professional philosophers as theirs have. But there are signs that this is changing and, of course, you should not judge him until you have seen what it is that he has to say.

Questions for Further Thought

1. How well can we understand what happiness is or measure it?

2. Is sex a higher pleasure or a lower pleasure? Would most people value it or, say, charity more? Should we distinguish between casual, meaningless sex (a lower pleasure perhaps) and sex as part of a loving relationship?

3. Should society aim to improve its members' tastes? How could it best do this?

4. Can a utilitarian consistently value justice?

5. Is utilitarianism consistent with integrity? Does it matter?

Notes

1. For instance, instead of being buried, he had his body stuffed and put on public display, where it remains in London, in order to encourage people not to be afraid to donate their bodies to science. He was eccentric but not irrational.

2. John Stuart Mill, *Utilitarianism and Other Essays,* ed. Alan Ryan (London: Penguin Books, 1987), 281.

3. This is my interpretation of what his point is, at any rate. Not everyone agrees since Mill explicitly says that what he means by happiness is pleasure and the absence of pain. This does not tell us, though, what he means by "pleasure." It is clearly not the same thing as satisfaction. His valuing of "higher pleasures" over animal pleasures suggests to me that he is not really a hedonist after all. It is possible that

he was in two minds about this, though, and you should bear in mind that other readings of Mill are possible.

4. As we shall see, Mill believed something like the opposite of this as well. Anscombe's implicit conclusion is that his theory has no content whatsoever. See *Human Life, Action and Ethics: Essays by G. E. M. Anscombe*, ed. Mary Geach and Luke Gormally, (Exeter, UK: Imprint Academic, 2005) 172. She also accuses him of failing to see how hard it is to understand what pleasure is.
5. Mill, *Utilitarianism*, 273.
6. See Roger Crisp, *Mill on Utilitarianism* (London: Routledge, 1997), 132.
7. Mill, *Utilitarianism*, 274.
8. Ibid., 275.
9. Ibid.
10. Ibid., 278.
11. Ibid., 279.
12. Ibid., 280.
13. Ibid., 290 footnote.
14. See Crisp, *Mill*, 100.
15. Mill, *Utilitarianism*, 301.
16. See John Stuart Mill, "Remarks on Bentham's Philosophy," in *Collected Works: Essays on Ethics, Religion, and Society*, Vol. 10, ed. J. M. Robson (Toronto: University of Toronto Press, 1963–1991).
17. Mill, *Utilitarianism*, 304.
18. Ibid., 308.
19. Ibid.
20. Ibid., 313.
21. Ibid.
22. Ibid., 322.
23. Ibid., 323.
24. Ibid., 327.
25. Ibid., 333.
26. Ibid., 337.

Suggestions for Further Reading

Two useful collections of primary readings are John Stuart Mill and Jeremy Bentham, *Utilitarianism and Other Essays*, ed. Alan Ryan (London: Penguin Books, 1987), and John Stuart Mill, *Utilitarianism, On Liberty, Considerations on Representative Government*, ed. Geraint Williams, (London: Everyman, 1993). The former has interesting selections from Bentham, while the latter includes Mill's important essay on liberty.

Some of the best secondary literature on Mill and utilitarianism can be found in Roger Crisp, *Mill on Utilitarianism* (London: Routledge, 1997); Samuel Scheffler, ed., *Consequentialism and its Critics*, (Oxford: Oxford University Press, 1988); Amartya Sen and Bernard Williams, eds., *Utilitarianism and Beyond* (Cambridge: Cambridge University Press, 1982); and J. J. C. Smart and Bernard Williams, *Utilitarianism: For and Against* (Cambridge: Cambridge University Press, 1973).

CHAPTER 9

Nietzsche

Friedrich Nietzsche (1844–1900) was certainly not a utilitarian. Nor was he a Christian or a Kantian or a Platonist. But like all virtue ethicists, Nietzsche was concerned with what kind of person one should be, with character. One of the reasons for emphasizing the importance of character is the belief that life is too complicated or unpredictable for ethics to be reducible to a set of rules for conduct. Rather, one should become the right sort of person and then, more or less, do as one sees fit. Nietzsche goes one step farther than this. He thinks that life is too complicated or unpredictable for ethics to be reducible to a set idea about what sort of person one should be. As he says in *Twilight of the Idols*, "Reality shows us a delightful abundance of types."[1] A one-size-fits-all morality cannot do justice to this richness. That is not to say that it is of no use to anyone, only that it is not for everyone. Nietzsche writes elsewhere that "The ideas of the herd should rule in the herd—but not reach out beyond it."[2] So ethics as we know it, or traditional morality, might be all right up to a point; but it is beyond that point that Nietzsche's interest lies, beyond the morality of good and evil.

"God Is Dead"

Past philosophies and religions, Nietzsche felt, had characters of their own. Platonism, for instance, reflected a kind of disgust with the body and a romantic longing for another, purer realm. It was admirably idealistic but unacceptably blind to the value of reality, of the flesh, and of nature in all its glory and violence. Christianity, Nietzsche famously remarked, was Platonism for the masses. At least since Augustine, Platonic ideas had infiltrated and informed Christian thinking, giving it the same faults as Platonism proper without the intellectual credentials. Nietzsche claimed to admire Jesus but considered Christianity, what Jesus' teachings had become, a slave morality, full of resentment. The Bible says that the last shall be first and the first shall be last. Nietzsche would want the first to be first. The Bible says that the poor and the lonely and the miserable are blessed. Nietzsche would say that they are poor and lonely and miserable and that conditions of this kind should not be glorified (although they might be inevitable, even desirable—would we have blues music if nobody ever felt blue?).

God is dead, he declared, in the words of a fictional madman. Having a madman speak for him acknowledges that Nietzsche saw the paradox involved in asserting the death of an immortal being. What he seems to have meant is that the world has changed, that the time when belief in God was both good and possible is now past. Since Martin Luther (1483–1546) split the Christian church in western Europe in two (albeit against his will), it has become unbelievable that there is one true faith. After all, which one would it be, Protestant or Catholic? And if Protestant, then which kind: Methodist, Baptist, Presbyterian, Anglican, or what? Can anyone truly believe that one sets us on the path to heaven and the others damn us to hell? If not, then we cannot believe that the differences between these denominations matter. If we ignore the differences, though, we end up with a generic, seemingly watered-down faith. If we do not ignore them, we must decide which is right. This is no easy task, and yet our souls are allegedly at stake. Nietzsche's response seems to be that the whole business is no longer credible. Nobody really has faith any more; we just have not all realized it yet. Thus, God is dead, and we have killed him but do not recognize our crime.

Belief in science has replaced faith in God, not necessarily for the better. Trust in science is not groundless, of course. Scientific methods have been shown to work again and again. But it does not follow that science is better than religion. The aims of science are not the same as the aims of religion. That is to say, science tells us about the natural world and allows us to develop new technologies and medicines. Religion is more concerned with the supernatural and with salvation. It seems quite possible to many people, therefore, to accept the findings of science without this affecting one's religious beliefs. Nietzsche, however, seems to think that it is not so simple. Rightly or wrongly, we now believe in the doctrines of Nicolaus Copernicus (1473–1543) and others who supported theories that the Church taught were false. Copernicus was a scientist, not a theologian; but the Catholic Church of his day, the only Christian church in western Europe at the time, taught an entire worldview, including scientific doctrines. Some of these doctrines have now been proved false, so at least some of what the Church used to teach is now no longer believed by anyone. Copernicus, Galileo, and Darwin have shaken people's faith that the Church is 100% believable. Luther made people wonder which church (if any, of course) we should listen to in the first place. As Nietzsche apparently sees it, there is no going back to any true faith in the Church. Once questions have been asked, they cannot be unasked. Doubt cannot be removed. Faith cannot be restored. The only thing to do is to boldly move into the future.

What does this mean? One thing it means, Nietzsche says, is that we cannot cling to the old ways, the old beliefs, any longer. If God is dead, then so is Christianity and we cannot rely on Christian ethics. We need new values. But where are we to find them? We must reevaluate all values. If you think about it, you will see that this is impossible. We cannot just make up new values. Values are things we have, not things we choose. I cannot make myself value something simply by willing to value it, just as I cannot make myself fall in love with someone. Most people do have loveable (or at least likeable) features, and we can make ourselves focus on these and thereby, often, come to like or love them. But for this to happen (and it cannot be counted on to happen in every case) we must first value the loveable features in question. It is doubtful that you could, by sheer act of will (rather than, say, complicated processes of association), make yourself feel sexually attracted to someone not of your preferred sex, for instance.

Similarly, it is doubtful that you could make yourself value dishonesty or treachery. Indeed, as we saw when looking at Hume, it is doubtful that this idea even makes sense. To value treachery, one would have to be able to say *and mean* "Oh good, I've been betrayed," which is very hard to imagine except possibly in rare circumstances. So it appears that our values cannot be evaluated except in terms of those that we already have. Doing so might well weed out some misfits, but it will not create new values. Nietzsche's project seems to be more of a weeding one than a grandly transformative one, his rhetoric notwithstanding. He even compares one's character to a garden that must be landscaped and tended, removing the bad stuff that can be removed and making lemonade out of the lemons or beauty spots out of the warts, to mix a few metaphors. He is thus perhaps better thought of as the gardener of the soul than as the hammer of the gods, although all religiously based beliefs would seem to be among the weeds, as he sees it.

The main values that remain are ancient Greek and aesthetic ones. Nietzsche values nobility, beauty, pride, and the like. But he does not generalize too much. Like a good Victorian, Nietzsche wants us to make ourselves into works of art. In art there are certain criteria that can be used to distinguish the good from the bad, but there are no formulae for creating masterpieces. Each individual character must express itself and create itself in the process. As we attempt to articulate our deepest, strongest beliefs harmoniously in our words and deeds, we both reveal what was inside and define who we are for ourselves as well as for others. What these beliefs are will vary from person to person, and what constitutes harmony will be determined not by universal, objective rules but by the standards of the individual. How should we live then? In a word, beautifully. Plato would have approved.

Of course, though, Nietzsche's idea of beauty is quite different from Plato's. For Plato, beauty was whatever resembled, in an objective way, the absolute, otherworldly form of Beauty. The standard of taste, in other words, was absolute, universal, and objective (it actually is a kind of object, according to Plato). For Nietzsche, the standard of taste is the individual. It is relative, particular, and subjective. But if Nietzsche's injunctions are to have any meaning, then the standards to which he refers cannot be *utterly* relative. Not just anything can go, or else there would be no point at all in praising courage, nobility, and the rest. If Nietzsche's work is to make any difference at all, as it is surely meant to, then he cannot mean that it is fine just to go on as before, perhaps claiming that one's Christianity or Platonism is indeed beautiful or noble or whatever. To be Nietzschean means being oneself but not just any self.

Against Others

I have already made comparisons of Nietzsche with several other thinkers, as he himself did; but his views on other thinkers are hard to know even in cases where he makes them quite explicit. For instance, he expresses admiration for Jesus, seemingly thinking that Jesus' teachings have been perverted by Christians. No doubt there have been some changes over the years, but Jesus' praise of such Christian virtues as meekness hardly seems very Nietzschean. Nietzsche holds what he calls "slave morality" in contempt, and by this he means the morality of such religions as Judaism and Christianity.[3] According to Nietzsche, these religions appealed to slaves in the Roman Empire because they made virtues of suffering and being downtrodden. This enabled the slaves to feel a spurious superiority to their masters, whom they resented. In the allegedly healthy, if primitive, morality of the masters, good is contrasted not with the sophisticated and twisted concept of evil but with simple badness. Good and bad in the master morality are quite straightforward terms. It is good to succeed, to be healthy, to live long, to be good looking, to conquer, to be rich, and so on. In short, it is good to win, to be one of the masters. Similarly, it is bad to lose, to be a slave, to be ugly or deformed, to be weak, and so on.

In their resentment, Nietzsche suggests, enslaved people not only looked for an alternative morality but embraced one that was precisely the opposite of their masters'. According to slave morality, it is *good* to be weak, oppressed, suffering, passive, and so on. And to be the opposite is not bad (who could claim that with a straight face?) but *evil*. Nietzsche does not advocate going back to the old-fashioned, simple morality of the masters. It is too late for that; we have become too sophisticated. But he certainly opposes the now dominant slave values. It is this opposition that is hard to square with his professed admiration for Jesus, who preached in his Sermon on the Mount the very values that Nietzsche reviles.

In *Ecce Homo*, Nietzsche describes the point of his main work on ethics, *On the Genealogy of Morality*, as showing the origin of morality in *ressentiment*, internalized cruelty, and the will to power.[4] By morality here he means traditional Christian morality (importantly related to Kantian and utilitarian ideas about ethics), not absolutely everything that might be called ethics. Roughly, *On the Genealogy of Morality* argues that slave resentment created the dichotomy of good and evil out of the old one of good (high, in both a spiritual and an aristocratic sense) and bad (low, base, common). This was taken up by the masters, with encouragement from priests, who were admired for their ascetic toughness, as a way to regard their suffering as meaningful or valuable. The will to power (which it might be helpful to think of here as a will to make sense of things) thus embraces asceticism as the best it can do in the circumstances. Our natural sadistic tendency cannot be destroyed though, only redirected. Under the influence of priests and slave morality, it is redirected against the self in the form of bad conscience. Instead of inflicting pain and humiliation on others, our consciences inflict pain on ourselves in the form of guilt. This is "moral" but not healthy. Christianity encourages people to revel in such pain. The original masters were "Roman, Arabian, Germanic,

Japanese nobility, Homeric heroes, Scandinavian Vikings," who murdered and raped like lions in the wild.[5] Social life requires the taming of such beasts, so Christianity is not responsible for the internalization of cruelty. What it is responsible for is the triumph of asceticism and an especially antilife, antiself, masochistic form of it.

In other words, as Nietzsche sees it, human beings are naturally cruel, but cruelty to others makes social life unbearable or impossible. So we have little choice but to turn our cruelty on ourselves. We cannot simply turn it off. The problem with Christianity is not that it endorses internalized cruelty but that it goes too far in this direction. It exaggerates the goodness of self-cruelty. Is Nietzsche right about all this? Is this the nature or origin of Christian ethics? It is hard to say. Brian Leiter puts it mildly when he writes that "Speculative, historical moral psychology of the kind Nietzsche is practicing here is not, it is fair to say, a developed field."[6]

Not only Christians but other philosophers are also treated to Nietzsche's scorn, usually for offering as objective truths beliefs that are in fact, if Nietzsche is to be believed, merely expressions of their own personality and culture. British philosophers such as Mill and Hume are derided for their complacent, bourgeois values, such as happiness. In Nietzsche's view, it is not happiness that is good but, as he says in his *Antichrist*, "What is good?—Whatever augments the feeling of power, the will to power, power itself, in man."[7] The more rigid Kant is dismissed also (too rigid), as is Plato (too idealistic). It seems that we are to create ourselves but that any past philosopher who has created a vision of his own is to be rejected for having believed in it. Perhaps Nietzsche is simply encouraging us to think for ourselves. After all, he says in *The Gay Science* "*What does your conscience say?*—'You shall become the person you are.'"[8] This is itself a somewhat anti-Kantian point since Kant's ethics are about one part of ourselves, the rational part, overcoming or subduing another part. Nietzsche believes in self-affirmation, at least for a certain type of person, not self-overcoming or self-denial.

Free Will

Then again, perhaps there is little point in offering such encouragement since, according to Nietzsche, we have no free will. This appears to be a belief he picked up from Arthur Schopenhauer, whose work he at one time admired. Schopenhauer was an anti-Christian, post-Kantian naturalist with leanings toward Asian philosophy. His philosophy held that reality consists of both will (specifically the will to live, a blind but immensely powerful force that manifests itself in all living things) and representation (little more than a kind of illusion, consisting of all things that are not pure will). There was no room in such a world for individual free will. The individual is hardly real at all. Everything that happens, Schopenhauer assures us, happens necessarily and cannot be helped. Nor should it be regretted. It simply is and we must accept it, including all the pain and boredom with which life is filled.

Nietzsche took from this little except the idea that free will is an illusion, one that he considered a little too comforting. Schopenhauer thought that life was pretty dreadful but that it could be at least tolerated if we realize that we are all part of something much bigger and that there is no point in feeling bad about anything. Individuals have no power to change the course of events. At the same time, though, he thought that we cannot necessarily avoid feeling bad. Nietzsche sees no comfort in determinism and seems almost to embrace determinism for this reason alone. Even if we have free will, we should not enjoy this thought. Our pleasures should come from achievements of our own, not the idle contemplation of our metaphysical condition.

In *Philosophy in the Tragic Age of the Greeks*, he writes "Man is necessity down to his last fibre, and totally 'unfree,' that is if one means by freedom the foolish demand to be able to change one's *essentia* arbitrarily, like a garment."[9] Schopenhauer was led to say no to life, so Nietzsche investigates and perhaps purposely sets out to undermine Schopenhauer's philosophy, which is largely based on belief in the value of compassion or pity. Yet Nietzsche praises Schopenhauer's views on determinism, saying that "we can only *dream* ourselves free."[10] Elsewhere he says that we should reject both the ideas of "free will" and "unfree will."[11] It is hard to know what to make of this. Surely, we might think, the will is either free or unfree? Robert C. Solomon's view is that Nietzsche allows for two perspectives.[12] From one we are free and responsible, from the other we are the product of biology and circumstance. It is part of the human condition that we see ourselves both ways. They do not need to be resolved. This is a difficult issue though, and we will return to it below.

Nietzsche's Point of View

On the other hand, Nietzsche is a more optimistic philosopher than Schopenhauer. Schopenhauer sought a way to bear this awful life. The poet Philip Larkin once memorably wrote (not wholly seriously, I suspect) that "life is first boredom then fear."[13] Schopenhauer, entirely seriously as far as it is possible to tell, thought that this was right except that it overlooks all the pain that goes along with the boredom. Nietzsche would have none of this. Anyone who deserves to live does not just tolerate life; he or she loves life. Indeed, one should love life so much that the prospect of it recurring again and again, just as it is and has been, through all eternity, should be one's idea of heaven. You should love this experience so much that you wish it could be repeated endlessly, and the same goes for every other experience you have ever had. There is a whiff of madness about this,[14] but the enthusiasm is refreshing. Nietzsche's alternative offers no sense of meaning but merely gives us something else to will: eternal recurrence. (Few people, as he sees it, are likely to be up to the task of embracing the world in all its meaninglessness.)

All of this dogmatism from Nietzsche seems a long way from the perspectivism and relativism with which he is generally associated. **Perspectivism** is the idea that we see things and think about things from a particular perspective. This point of view will inevitably be historically, geographically, and culturally conditioned, so we are bound to have various limitations and biases in our views and should not pretend to be able to discern universal, objective, timeless truths. This sounds almost like common sense in today's postmodern world. There are two apparent problems with it however.

The first is the fact that Nietzsche uses this perspectivism as a reason to criticize other philosophers when perhaps he would be more consistent if he used it to argue that they could hardly have thought otherwise than they did. In other words, if perspectivism is true, then nobody should be *blamed* for thinking only from a particular perspective. Moreover, perspectivism itself should not be treated as an absolute truth. Presumably, Nietzsche was aware of this, but it is something that some of his would-be followers might do well to keep in mind.

The second problem is that perspectivism implies something on which to have a perspective.[15] It does not deny the existence of reality or say that every perspective or interpretation is as good as any other. So the implication is that, while we might never know the whole, unbiased truth, there is nevertheless such a thing out there and some people might have a better understanding of it than others. Indeed, Nietzsche seems to believe himself to be such a person, but he could be wrong. Perhaps Plato saw more clearly. From Nietzsche's perspective, it is very hard to know; and all he can really offer is a kind of rhetoric that we may or may not find moving. There is no definitive answer to Thrasymachus here, as Nietzsche realizes.

Still, there is something to appeal to Thrasymachus in Nietzsche's philosophy. Nietzsche is quite the opposite of philosophers who ask us to deny our own will, such as Simone Weil (see Chapter 3) and, perhaps, Schopenhauer and Martin Heidegger (see Chapter 10). He is by no means antiself, so living as he recommends does not have the paradoxical or masochistic appearance of some systems of ethics. All you need to do, he says, is one thing:

> *One thing is needful.*—To "give style" to one's character—a great and rare art! It is practiced by those who survey all the strength and weaknesses of their nature and then fit them into an artistic plan until every one of them appears as art and reason and even weaknesses delight the eye. Here a large mass of second nature has been added; there a piece of original nature has been removed—both times through long practice and daily work at it. Here the ugly that could not be removed is concealed; there it has been reinterpreted and made sublime. Much that is vague and resisted shaping has been saved and exploited for distant views; it is meant to beckon toward the far and immeasurable. In the end, when the work is finished, it becomes evident how the constraint of a single taste governed and formed everything large and small. Whether this taste was good or bad is less important than one might suppose, if only it was a single taste![16]

Once your character has been given style, thereafter you must do what you will. This "must" is deterministic (since Nietzsche denies that we have free will), not moral, because he rejects what we would ordinarily regard as morality altogether. In his determinism he is close to Schopenhauer, but he rejects the latter's pessimism in favor of bold (sometimes seemingly forced) gaiety or joyfulness. The individual will is to be celebrated in its triumph, not itself triumphed over.

Twilight of the Idols

What I have said so far is a kind of general overview of Nietzsche's thinking, especially as it relates to the challenge of Thrasymachus. However, Nietzsche wrote his own introduction to his philosophy, and it would be foolish to ignore that. This section is devoted to a critical summary of that book, *Twilight of the Idols*.

On the first page of the book, Nietzsche famously writes "Whatever does not kill me makes me stronger." This might seem to be an obvious lie and evidence of Nietzsche's hysteria, which we will discuss later. But the idea is presented not as a simple truth but, rather, as a kind of motto from what Nietzsche calls "the Military School of Life." His thought seems to be that this is a possible belief to adopt, not an objective fact. The Stoics thought something very similar. You have the power to choose your attitude toward events. Any setback can be regarded as nothing but a setback, but it can equally be regarded as a challenge or as a kind of test that one has already passed by not being destroyed. It might be very helpful to try to adopt this attitude when faced with misfortune. On the other hand, it would hardly be a very sympathetic remark to make to someone who has undergone a trauma. Nietzsche is not interested in pity but in turning muck into gold. This, it seems, is something that one can only do for oneself.

His goal, he tells us, is a reevaluation of all values, a thorough checking of the old inherited beliefs. He is not rejecting all old values but sounding them out to see which ones are hollow. He writes in *Daybreak* as follows:

> It goes without saying that I do not deny—unless I am a fool—that many actions called immoral ought to be avoided and resisted, or that many called moral ought to be done and encouraged—but I think the one should be encouraged and the other avoided *for other reasons than hitherto*. We have to learn to think differently—in order at last, perhaps very late on, to attain even more: *to feel differently*.[17]

Notice here that the goal is to feel differently, an inner thing. This is what Nietzsche means when he talks about "doing philosophy with a hammer." Like Mill, he suspects that much, if not all, past moral philosophy has merely dressed up unquestioned values in the language of reason. So we need to be more critical.

The same goes for the attitude of nonphilosophers toward their values. Consider the following quotation, from *Thus Spoke Zarathustra*:

> . . . there are [those] who call it virtue when their vices grow lazy . . .
> And there are others who are like cheap clocks that must be wound: they tick and they want the tick-tock to be called virtue. . .

And then again, there are such as to consider it virtue to say, "Virtue is necessary"; but at bottom they believe only that the police is necessary.[18]

Like Søren Kierkegaard, who thought that many so-called Christians had little real faith or enthusiasm for what they professed to believe, Nietzsche thinks that many people's ethics are the kind of self-interest disguised as values that Glaucon described in Plato's *Republic*. Unlike Mill, Nietzsche thinks that what people really want is not pleasure but some sense of meaning in life. For this, they will suffer almost any hardship or pain.

Anyone who is envious of what bad people get (money, sex, power, etc.) has not renounced worldly advantages. Such envy is a sign of hypocrisy. The true Christian, for instance, does not want such things.

Nietzsche also criticized people's desire for a system, a consistent theory (e.g., utilitarianism), a kind of neatness not found in oneself. It is a fantasy, and a hypocritical one at that. "The will to system is a lack of integrity," Nietzsche tells us.[19] Integrity here, I take it, means honesty to oneself. Nietzsche is perhaps implying that the self is not systematic or, at least, not obviously so. We do not really want consistency; we want exceptions. That is, philosophical theories and systems are based, ultimately, on our intuitions or feelings about what is right and true. But these feelings are not systematic and can only be made into a system by ignorance or distortion. And to ignore or distort one's own most basic feelings is to fail to be true to oneself, to lack integrity. Integrity, then, seems to mean acting only on the basis of what Mill calls "internal sanctions." For instance, Nietzsche says, it is honorable to be honest because one hates dishonesty but cowardly to be honest because God forbids dishonesty. (So much for Mill's first external sanction.)

This is not a rejection of all sanctions, of all sense of right and wrong. Morality must not be rejected, Nietzsche claims, but challenged in order for it to stay healthy and strong. (Mill argued something similar about true beliefs in his book *On Liberty*.) In a sense, it needs to be worldly. An inactive life, passively withdrawn from the world, is "the *sin* against the holy ghost."[20] It might sound odd to hear a man who called himself the Antichrist talking about sin and the holy ghost. In its context, though, this remark is about which of our thoughts have value, and it rejects those that come from sitting down in favor of those that come from walking. It is also possible to infer, although perhaps this is a stretch, that Nietzsche means both that (1) Christians are hypocritical if they claim that God's creation is good and yet turn away from it as a place of sin and (2) the only kind of acceptable religion (if there were such a thing) would relish the world and life.[21]

In this, he stands against a formidable tradition. For ages, wise men have said that life is no good. Should we accept this, Nietzsche asks, because they are so wise or, on the contrary, should we question their wisdom because what they say is so sick? Socrates and Plato thought that it was better to be dead than alive. So much the worse for them. How can we even judge life at all since we cannot step outside it to judge objectively? Any philosopher who judges life to be bad is therefore questionable. Indeed, the whole philosophical tradition from Socrates on is questioned by Nietzsche.

Socratic dialectic, Socrates' method of questioning supposed experts in search of a definition they can never find, puts the common person on the same level as the élite. But it is not a powerful tool since it tends to seem sophistical and to be unpersuasive. So why use it? Surely only because one is weak and wants to disrespect those on top who are strong. This is just resentment. Socrates' placing of reason over instinct also suggests that he was sick in some way. Healthy people have good instincts and value them. It is unhealthy to reject this world, the senses, the body, change, and history. We should not crave some supernatural ideal but enjoy what is real. The senses do not lie, as many philosophers have claimed. Rather, it is reason that draws false conclusions from what the senses tell it. "The 'apparent' world is the only one: the 'real world' has just been *lied on*. . . ."[22] The so-called real world is nothing more than a lie that has been added to the so-called apparent world in which we live. This is a rejection most obviously of Plato's metaphysics (and Kant's) but also of Christianity, which Nietzsche called Platonism for the masses. The world rejected by Plato and others is defended by Nietzsche as the only one there is.

Science, he says, comes from accepting the senses. Nothing else, such as metaphysics and logic, has any connection with reality. Philosophers, though, abstract and abstract until all contact with reality is gone. The ultimate abstract concept is God, which is then treated as the most real of all. "I am afraid we are not getting rid of God because we still believe in grammar."[23] What does this mean? Nietzsche seems to mean that we have faith that nouns name objects, so we think of the will as something that causes things to happen. And we think similarly of the cause of all things as the divine will, God. But "will" is only a word (and so, presumably Nietzsche thinks, is "God").

There is no other world more real than the one we sense, he believes. The desire for another world is an insult to the senses, to the world, to life. The healthy thing to do is to accept this world, saying "*yes* to all that is questionable and even terrible."[24] This, he says, is Dionysian; that is, it is the attitude of the passionate, musical, dancing, intoxicated, perhaps even violent side of human nature that we dishonestly and unhealthily deny when we fixate on the rational, the ordered, and the good. This is also the essence of what we might think of as Nietzsche's hysterical stoicism. **Stoicism** is, very roughly, the idea that we should accept whatever happens without complaint combined with the idea that we cannot change the course of events anyway. Stoics believe that we are free only with regard to the attitude we take toward events in the world, and they tend to be somewhat grim, dutifully accepting their fate without complaining. Nietzsche's view is similar, equally denying that we have free will; but instead of merely accepting the world, he revels in it, even in its worst horrors. This is the part that seems hysterical. However, a word of caution is in order here. He does not deny, after all, that the terrible is terrible, even while saying yes to it. This is perhaps not so much hysterical as self-contradictory or, more charitably, as reminiscent of the kind of truth-fitting paradox that G. K. Chesterton finds in Christianity (see Chapter 3).

Unlike the Stoics, Nietzsche is not against passion. The roots of passion, he asserts, are the roots of life. We must not attack them, as puritanical Christians and Stoics have. But we need not just accept them either since they can be stupid and cause us problems. Self-control is possible for the strong and healthy (though we might wonder, given his apparent denial of free will, whether Nietzsche means that we can control what we *do* or only how we *feel* or *think* about things). Temperance can be a value. Indeed we *must* have some values. Life (human nature?) forces them on us. The only question, then, is what values to have. We cannot judge life or humankind in general, as we have seen. We are what we are. Our choice is simply to condemn (which is degenerate, "moral," and sick) or to affirm (which is "immoral," positive, and healthy).

If this is our only real choice, then we control only our attitudes, not our actions, as the Stoics believed. I read Nietzsche as a kind of determinist, like the Stoics, but the best commentators on his work seem to agree that he denied *both* free will and determinism. If by "determinism" we mean the idea that every event has a cause, then Nietzsche might not be a determinist simply because he rejects the idea that there really are such things as separate events. Otherwise, he does seem to be a determinist. Since this is a controversial claim, I need some good evidence. I have already quoted Nietzsche denying the freedom of the will, but here is my reason for saying that he denies events but is otherwise a determinist (like the Stoics):

> The individual is a piece of fate from top to bottom, one more law, one more necessity for all that is to come and will be. Telling him to change means demanding that everything should change, even backwards. . . [25]

If an individual's changing should require or involve everything's changing, even backward in time, then everything is one. Everything is so intimately connected, Nietzsche appears to be saying, that it must all be accepted or rejected together. This includes everything in space and in time. We cannot pick and choose the objects or events that we like or dislike. Change one and you change the whole world, the whole of history. The question of value and life is not which parts of life are good since there really are no parts in any meaningful sense. It is all one big whole, from the beginning of time on.

The question, as Nietzsche sees it, is simply a yes or no one. Or, as he puts it in *The Gay Science,*

> What, if some day or night a demon were to steal after you into your loneliest loneliness and say to you: "This life as you now live it and have lived it, you will have to live once more and innumerable times more; and there will be nothing new in it, but every pain and every joy and every thought and sigh and everything unutterably small or great in your life will have to return to you, all in the same succession and sequence—even this spider and this moonlight between the trees, and even this moment and I myself. The eternal hourglass of existence is turned upside down again and again, and you with it, speck of dust!"

Would you not throw yourself down and gnash your teeth and curse the demon who spoke thus? Or have you once experienced a tremendous moment when you would have answered him: "You are a god and never have I heard anything more divine." If this thought gained possession of you, it would change you as you are or perhaps crush you. The question in each and every thing, "Do you desire this once more and innumerable times more?" would lie upon your actions as the greatest weight. Or how well disposed would you have to become to yourself and to life to crave nothing more fervently than this ultimate eternal confirmation and seal?[26]

Crucial to this view that ethics can be reduced to one question about everything is the metaphysical issue of relations between events. I have suggested that Nietzsche believes that there really are no events as such or perhaps that history is just one big event. Connected to this there are, he says, "four great errors:" (1) confusing cause and consequence, (2) false causality, (3) imaginary causes, and (4) free will. The "real corruption of reason" is the mixing up of cause and effect. For instance, religion and morality say "Do this and you will be happy." Nietzsche says "Be happy and you will do this." Virtue is the result of happiness, not vice versa.

We have no reason, Nietzsche agrees with Hume, to believe in causality. All we see, according to Hume, is one event *happening* after another, not one event *making* another happen. Nietzsche believes that we get the idea of causation from how things seem to us. It *seems* that we cause our own actions by means of the will. But the will does not cause events (it is not an object that could cause events, according to Nietzsche; rather, willed actions are simply those (whose true causes may be unknown) to which we consent). It is fear of the unfamiliar that leads us to think of events as acts and, hence, to believe in God as the agent behind all events. A desire to explain leads us to think we must *deserve* all our suffering. "The Entire Realm of Morality and Religion Belongs Under This Concept of Imaginary Causes," as he titled one chapter.[27]

Free will is an error, a myth to blame and punish people who can then be held responsible for their acts. The "doctrine of the will was fabricated essentially for the purpose of punishment," he writes.[28] "Christianity is a metaphysics of the hangman."[29] But we are not responsible for our environment or our innate nature or our existence. There is no goal, end, or purpose to life as such. There is simply life as it is, and the whole cannot be changed. Each of us is part of the whole, and the whole cannot be escaped in order to judge it. We redeem the world by denying God. That is to say, we redeem the world by *denying* responsibility, judgment, guilt, and the rest. As Schopenhauer argued, if determinism is true, if we really have no free will worth the name, then we have no reason to feel guilt or regret about our own, or others', deeds. Denial of free will, far from being depressing, can be a cheering, even a redeeming, idea. Or so Schopenhauer and Nietzsche seem to have thought. If there is a difference between them on this point, perhaps it is that Schopenhauer seeks consolation, while Nietzsche rejects anything so weak as consolation and looks for affirmation and joy instead.

For Nietzsche, it is all a question of attitude. There are no moral facts. "Morality is merely an interpretation of certain phenomena, more precisely, a *misinterpretation*."[30] This formulation suggests that there are facts here, after all, but that morality as traditionally understood gets them wrong. As a result, religion and morality *tame* people, but they do not improve us. It is a mistake to claim otherwise. (Here, Nietzsche sounds just like Thrasymachus, but it is not as if he rejects all values, as we have seen.)

Attempts to improve humanity are questionable in Nietzsche's eyes anyway. He makes so many extreme and violent-sounding pronouncements that Nazis have enjoyed quoting him (usually out of context), but some of his remarks about attempts to improve the human race show that he was no Nazi. The ultimate Aryan morality, he says, is breeding for "pure blood," which inevitably treats the "impure" inhumanely. (Nietzsche is clearly not a racial "purist" like his Nazi admirers.) We can see this, for example, in India, where, Nietzsche claims, the "untouchables" were at one time effectively starved, infected, and left to die. Christianity, he says, is the opposite of such cruelty, but it too is a lie. It is the revolt of the poor and downtrodden, disguised as love.

Another way in which Nietzsche was unlike the Nazis is that he was no German nationalist. Alcohol and Christianity, he says, have made the Germans stupid. The science industry (i.e., scientism, infatuation with technology, and the utilitarian idea of progress) has despiritualized Germany. Nietzsche seems to admire science—the discovery of truths about the world—but not scientism—the idea that science can answer every kind of problem. Or perhaps there is no judgment meant here, only description. If your energy goes into the quest for power, money, and military strength, he says, then it will not go into understanding, seriousness, and self-overcoming. So perhaps Nietzsche was a kind of pacifist. He certainly believed in self-overcoming and, hence, going by this last claim of his, not in the quest for military strength. Again, he sounds very unlike a Nazi. We only have so much energy. We have to choose whether to put ours into political success or something else, such as cultural success. In effect, therefore, great culture requires political decline. Presumably, Nietzsche would seek the decline of any German *Reich*, preferring artistic achievement to political and military strength.

Just as he was no Nazi, neither was Nietzsche any kind of socialist or Millian liberal. "All great, all beautiful things can never be common property," he wrote.[31] Nietzsche clearly opposes Mill's ideas about education. Higher education for the masses, he says, is a contradiction in terms. So-called higher education is really just training people to become bureaucrats. Education should not be rushed and should not have pragmatic or utilitarian goals. To become spiritual, you must learn to *see*, to see things as they *are*, not how you want them to be or assume they are. This requires a will that can suspend itself, which requires great strength. The will must have self-control. Without such a will we are slaves to every impulse; we fall into every vice. (This is reminiscent of some of Plato's views on ethics.) Education should teach us to think—that is, to dance with concepts—and to write—that is, to dance with words. Not everybody is capable of this though.

We are not free to have the right kind of will. Some do, some do not. And even those who do need to be trained in the right way, perhaps by themselves. This talk of the will and self-control, then, does not contradict Nietzsche's other remarks about free will's being an illusion.

As well as attacking Germany, Nietzsche was strongly critical of another northern European power: England. As we have seen, he rejected British empiricism and utilitarianism. In England, he says, people reject God but cling to Christian morality. They have no right to do this. Christianity is a system that "stands and falls with the belief in God."[32] God is what justifies Christian ethics. Without God, what sense do the commandments make? What sense can there be in self-sacrifice (e.g., in turning the other cheek)? We might *feel* that this or that is right or wrong, but this is the effect of centuries of Christianity. These feelings will go in time, and then morality—how to live, what to do—will be felt or seen as a problem. The truth is that it is already a problem right now.

So what to do? We should not take nature as our guide, Nietzsche says, if by that we mean whatever we happen to come across when we pay attention to nature. Instead, we should express ourselves, our whole nature, not this or that but the main features or essence of who we are. If we move beyond good and evil to an aesthetic ethic, we should act in a frenzy, an energetic drive to express ourselves.

Today, there is very little hypocrisy, acting contrary to one's beliefs, he says, because so few people have genuine beliefs and act in a consistent, unambiguous manner. This lack of strong belief makes the world ugly. By seeing the world in our own terms, though, we can make it beautiful to ourselves. Nothing can be beautiful in itself, and who knows how things would appear to, say, God? Beauty comes down to us: "Nothing is beautiful, only man is beautiful."[33] Ugliness is corruption, which we both fear and hate. Art praises, glorifies, chooses, prefers. It is the great stimulus to life. Even tragic art is positive: it shows fearlessness in the face of terrors. It is art that can save us.

So we do not need the mediocre and vulgar ethics of philosophers. Kant's ethics is the most boring, he says, teaching us to put duty above all instinctive feelings. This is ethics as taming. In contrast, Nietzsche might seem to be advocating a form of egoism. But he says that self-interest can be unworthy and contemptible. It depends on the self in question. What matters is whether the person is sick and in decay or instead represents a step upward or forward. Sacrifices are worth making for the sake of truly healthy individuals.

Altruism (putting others before oneself) is not necessarily a bad thing, but it is a bad sign. "Instinctively choosing what is harmful to *oneself*, being *tempted* by 'disinterested' motives—this is practically the formula for *décadence*."[34] But Nietzsche is not an all-out egoist. He believes in egoism for a certain type of person, a person who is artistic—that is, frenziedly self-expressive. As he puts it in *The Gay Science*, "'Selflessness' has no value either in heaven or on earth. All great problems demand *great love*."[35] We should love, and in loving, we should love the whole of life, including, perhaps above all else, ourselves. Those who can no longer live proudly should die proudly. Those who think this life not worth living should kill themselves (or rethink).

So what, finally, is Nietzsche *for*? The writer Goethe is the example he gives (adding that Kant is the opposite of Goethe). Goethe, allegedly, said yes to everything. He created himself; he was strong, well-educated, and self-controlled. He despised nothing, seeing each thing as part of the whole and the whole as good. This is Dionysian. Dionysus is all about sexuality—sex, birth, procreation. Dionysian festivals make the mysteries of sexuality and everything connected with them (including pain) holy. It was Christianity, according to Nietzsche, that spread the idea that sex is somehow unclean. This idea is, of course, antilife. The prolife idea is that life is good, what brings life is good, what is necessary for life is good, the whole cycle of birth and death is good. Tragedy celebrates the goodness even of pain and death. Everything recurs, recycles, endlessly, and this is good. So says Dionysus.

Other examples of higher men that he seems to have in mind are Beethoven and himself. More generally, he characterizes higher men as solitary, resilient, life-affirming, different, and seeking responsibilities. This is a somewhat puzzling list of characteristics for Nietzsche to admire since he says we should deny responsibility. It is also hard to imagine a solitary person being life-affirming and embracing the sexual part of the Dionysian cycle of life and death. What he has in mind is presumably someone like himself, someone who enjoys his own company as well as others' and who denies that we have moral responsibility (because we have no free will) but seeks out such responsibilities as taking on the writing of a new book. In *The Will to Power*, Nietzsche says that "The 'higher nature' of the great man lies in being different, in incommunicability, in distance of rank, not in an effect of any kind."[36] The higher man is better than others in ways that even he cannot quite explain. He is superior, almost belonging to a different, more advanced species. This superiority, though, is not a matter of producing any particular effect. Once again, Nietzsche is no consequentialist. Just as Kant thinks a good will shines like a jewel even if nothing comes of it (through bad luck, say), Nietzsche seems to value the nature of great artists, even if their works are never published or are destroyed in a fire. Perhaps their work might even be their own character, and this might be unappreciated by the inferior people all around them.

Why Be Good?

So why should we change? Why should we give up our old ways and take Nietzsche's advice? Nietzsche might give two kinds of answer to this question. The first would be that we should not necessarily but that we will nevertheless. In other words, it is not a question of what we ought to do. Sometimes Nietzsche writes as if he is predicting the future, not advocating anything. He is like Karl Marx in this regard and, like Marx, can barely contain his enthusiasm for the future that he dispassionately predicts. God is dead, the old values have left with him, and new values are arising, as our faith in science attests. So new values will come along, perhaps first in the slightly vapid form of secular humanism but later more vitally as something we can scarcely begin to imagine in this impoverished age. Thrasymachus would then need no answer. He would be right about the current dead morality that we continue to treat, as far as possible, as if it were living. As for the future strong morality, Thrasymachus would judge it and be judged by it accordingly; but how this would be we cannot yet say, not having this morality at all clearly before our minds.

The second kind of answer that Nietzsche might give to the skeptic is that we should change because, deep down inside, that is what we really want to do. We should stop going to church, if we ever went and have not already stopped going, because we do not really believe in it anymore. For much the same reason, we should give up on all moralities, traditional and modern, except Nietzsche's, of course. Our characters lack style and consistency—not in some Kantian, rational sense but in an aesthetic sense. We are, Nietzsche thinks, in a mess and we need to dig ourselves out of it. Nothing objective or universal will do this for us, just as works of art cannot be judged without sensitivity and careful attention to the particulars of each work and its context.

Objections

Thus far, Nietzsche's prediction does not seem to have come true, unless the people of the new morality, the famous Supermen that he predicted, were perhaps the Nazis, the communists, or the whole range of tyrannical dictators the twentieth century threw up. Nietzsche's language is certainly violent at times, and his work was often quoted by the Nazis. On the other hand, Nietzsche was strongly opposed to anti-Semitism, and his high valuation of the individual makes it very unlikely that he would have sympathized with any totalitarian or despot. So he might not be evil, but he does seem to have been wrong. Once again like Marx, though, he gives no firm timescale, so his defenders can always still claim that the time is not yet come. We shall see.

Another objection to Nietzsche is that he might seem to assume that he, who has never met me, knows what I believe deep down inside even better than I know myself. This is not very plausible, especially coming from someone who stresses the differences between individuals and their unique styles. It also begs the question of why I should care that I am in a mess. Must aesthetics, Nietzsche's aesthetics at that, rule my life? Can't religious or ethical or logical or selfish reasons (such as laziness) take priority over aesthetic consistency? Or is Nietzsche assuming the existence of an inner aesthete or critic who is my true self, just as Plato and Kant assumed that there is some true, rational self within each of us? If so he might be right, but he might not be. His case remains unproven.

This probably would not surprise or bother Nietzsche though. In *The Will to Power* he writes that "all attempts to give reasons for morality are necessarily *sophistical*."[37] We cannot help *having* values, it seems, but neither this fact nor anything else *justifies* them. Ultimately, we have the values that we have, just as we think the thoughts that come to us. Elsewhere in the same book Nietzsche admits that he cannot rationally justify his own values.[38] They too are a matter of taste.

Conclusion

It is necessary to be hard in order to make an impact, Nietzsche says. And it is blessed to make an impact, "to write upon the will of millennia as upon bronze."[39] He admits, in other words, that he writes as he does in order to try to make an impact, to get through to people. We should not rule out the possibility, therefore, that he sometimes exaggerates for effect. So we should not read him too literally. Perhaps, with Nietzsche's work, there are no facts, only interpretations.

It is possible, though, to draw some more or less reasonable conclusions about what he means. He does not at all claim to be able to offer proof that we should live as he says we should, affirming the world, history, our own lives, and our core selves. Instead, rather like Plato, he offers a moving kind of poetry, a vision of how things are and how they might be or how they might be thought of as being. This vision, unlike Plato's, is very much of this world. It is naturalistic, but it is not scientistic. He does not attempt to apply the methods of science to every problem that interests him. His historical account of the origins of slave morality, for instance, might be intended scientifically, but it is also a piece of propaganda. His goal is to give a plausible explanation of where Christian values might have come from that makes those values appear highly unattractive. If Nietzsche uses the methods of empiricism, he does so tactically, in order to undermine such ethics as utilitarianism (as well as Christianity), not because of any Apollonian (i.e., non-Dionysian) devotion to the Enlightenment's search for knowledge. What he cares about is not humanity but individuals, not politics but culture, not ethics (in a way) but aesthetics (of a very broad, ethical kind). If at the right level you share his taste, then you are likely to be moved by his rhetoric and agree with him. If not, then you won't. And that seems to be about all there is to it if Nietzsche is right. In the next chapter, we will see whether any progress in ethics has been made in the hundred years or so since Nietzsche died.

Questions for Further Thought

1. Is Christianity or Judaism a slave morality?

2. Is God dead?

3. Is giving style to one's character all that is needful?

4. Can we ever know how things are from anything but our own perspective? Does it matter?

5. Do you have any control over your character? How can this be?

Notes

1. Friedrich Nietzsche, *Twilight of the Idols*, trans. Duncan Large (Oxford: Oxford University Press, 1998), 24.
2. Friedrich Nietzsche, *The Will to Power*, trans. Walter Kaufmann and R. J. Hollingdale (New York: Vintage, 1968), 287.
3. Nietzsche first introduces the terms "master morality" and "slave morality" in *Beyond Good and Evil*, trans. Walter Kaufmann (New York: Vintage, 1966), §260. He says there that they can be found within the same person but adds that they originated in different groups, the rulers and the ruled. His hypothesis is not merely historical, therefore, but also psychological.
4. *Ecce Homo*, trans. W. Kaufmann (New York: Vintage 1967). For more on this, see Brian Leiter, *Nietzsche on Morality* (London: Routledge, 2002), 173.
5. Friedrich Nietzsche, *On the Genealogy of Morality*, trans. Maudemarie Clark and Alan Swensen (Indianapolis: Hackett, 1998), 11.
6. Leiter, *Nietzsche on Morality*, 286.
7. Friedrich Nietzsche, *The Anti-Christ*, trans. H. L. Mencken (Tuscon, AZ: See Sharp Press, 1999), 22.
8. Friedrich Nietzsche, *The Gay Science*, trans. Walter Kaufmann (New York: Vintage, 1974), 219.
9. Friedrich Nietzsche, *Philosophy in the Tragic Age of the Greeks*, trans. M. Cowan (Washington DC: Regnery Gateway, 1996), Section 7.
10. Friedrich Nietzsche, *Human, All-too-Human*, trans. R. J. Hollingdale (Cambridge: Cambridge University Press, 1986), 33.
11. See Nietzsche, *Beyond Good and Evil*, 21.
12. See Robert C. Solomon, *Living with Nietzsche* (Oxford: Oxford University Press; 2003), 181–182.
13. Philip Larkin, "Dockery and Son" in his *Collected Poems* (London: Marvell Press; Faber and Faber, 1988), 152–153.
14. Solomon refers to Nietzsche's "near-hysterical emphasis on *life-affirmation*"; see *Living with Nietzsche*, 116.
15. As Robert Nozick points out in *Philosophical Explanations* (Cambridge, MA: Harvard University Press, 1983).
16. Nietzsche, *The Gay Science*, §290.
17. Friedrich Nietzsche, *Daybreak*, trans. R. J. Hollingdale (Cambridge: Cambridge University Press, 1997), 60.
18. Friedrich Nietzsche, *Thus Spoke Zarathustra*, in *The Portable Nietzsche*, trans. Walter Kaufmann (New York: Viking, 1954), 206–207.
19. Nietzsche, *Twilight of the Idols*, 8.
20. Ibid., 9.

21. Nietzsche seems to have been influenced here by Arthur Schopenhauer, who wrote in his essay "On Thinking for Yourself," that "to banish your own thoughts so as to take up a book is a sin against the Holy Ghost; it is like deserting untrammelled nature to look at a herbarium or engravings of landscapes." See Arthur Schopenhauer, *Essays and Aphorisms*, trans. R. J. Hollingdale (London: Penguin, 1970), 90.
22. Nietzsche, *Twilight of the Idols*, 17.
23. Ibid., 19.
24. Ibid.
25. Ibid., 24.
26. Aphorism 341 in *The Gay Science*, 273–274.
27. Nietzsche, *Twilight of the Idols*, 30.
28. Ibid., 31.
29. Ibid., 32.
30. Ibid., 33.
31. Ibid., 40.
32. Ibid., 45.
33. Ibid., 53.
34. Ibid., 60.
35. Aphorism 345 in Nietzsche, *The Gay Science*, 283.
36. Nietzsche, *The Will to Power*, 876.
37. Ibid., 428.
38. Ibid., 353.
39. Nietzsche, *Twilight of the Idols*, 82.

Suggestions for Further Reading

Nietzsche's main works are *Twilight of the Idols, Beyond Good and Evil, The Gay Science* (sometimes translated as *The Joyful Wisdom*), *On the Genealogy of Morality*, and *Thus Spake Zarathustra*. Several translations are available. I would suggest starting with *Twilight of the Idols*, trans. Duncan Large (Oxford: Oxford University Press, 1998), and *On the Genealogy of Morality*, trans. Maudemarie Clark and Alan Swensen (Indianapolis: Hackett, 1998). Good value are the collections *Basic Writings of Nietzsche*, trans. and ed. Walter Kaufmann, (New York: Modern Library, 2000) (this anthology contains both *Beyond Good and Evil* and *On the Genealogy of Morals*) and *The Portable Nietzsche*, trans. and ed. Walter Kaufmann (London: Penguin, 1977) (this one has *Twilight of the Idols* and *Thus Spake Zarathustra*, among other works).

Brian Leiter, *Nietzsche on Morality* (London: Routledge, 2002), Robert C. Solomon, *Living with Nietzsche* (Oxford: Oxford University Press, 2003), and Keith Ansell Pearson, ed., *A Companion to Nietzsche*, (Oxford: Blackwell, 2005) are useful secondary sources.

To learn more about Nietzsche's life and the development of his ideas over time, see Rüdiger Safranski, *Nietzsche*, trans. Shelley Frisch (London: Granta Books, 2003), and Walter Kaufmann, *Nietzsche: Philosopher, Psychologist, Antichrist*, (Princeton: Princeton University Press, 1975).

CHAPTER 10

Virtue after Nietzsche

We might seem not to have made much progress in answering Thrasymachus. Plato tried but offered little more than a kind of poetry, which might or might not move the moral skeptic. Then, Aristotle criticized Plato's theory, Christians criticized Aristotle's, Hobbes and Hume offered modern alternatives to Christian ethics, Kant rejected the empiricism of Hobbes and Hume, Mill rejected Kant, and finally Nietzsche rejected all of them and offered instead a kind of poetry, which might or might not move the skeptic. Most ethicists since Nietzsche have tried to improve on old theories rather than devising distinctive new theories of their own. This is not to say, however, that nobody has said anything significant about ethics since his day, although for some years ethics was out of fashion.

Twentieth-century philosophy can be divided into two traditions, one called "analytic" and one called "continental." Within the continental tradition (named after the continent of Europe, where most of its practitioners lived), the biggest name early on was Martin Heidegger (1889–1976). He rejected not values but philosophical discussion of values. If we want to understand or to perceive the value of a being, then we need to pay attention to that being, not to theorize about the properties that might give it value, he thought. Think of someone arguing with Hobbes. In a Hobbesian moral theory, the only value that an animal can have is instrumental value. It is hard to see how a Hobbesian objection could be made to people who like torturing animals for fun. After all, animals will surely not be party to the social contract on which Hobbesian ethics are based. Against would-be abusers it is often objected that animals have rights, but this objection raises all kinds of questions. Where do these rights come from? What are their limits? How can it be settled exactly what rights exist? It seems much more reasonable to doubt or deny that animals have moral rights than it does to torture them for fun. In other words, if people deny that animals ought not to be abused, they are highly unlikely to change their minds because of a claim that animals have rights. The claim is less plausible, not more, than the conclusion it is meant to support (namely, that we should not abuse animals).

The problem persists even if we stick to more readily acceptable claims. If I say that tigers should be protected because of their beautiful coats, you might infer that ugly tigers are fair game. If I say that human life is sacred because we are rational beings, then you might infer that it is OK to kill babies or people with Alzheimer's disease. Heidegger says that "precisely through the characterization of something as 'a value' what is so valued is robbed of its worth."[1] Identifying something as "a value" treats it as a kind of ethical option. I have my values and you have yours. Nobody can prove which values it is right to have, nor even that there really are such things as values. In order to save ethics, Heidegger rejects philosophizing about ethics. Instead, he focuses on metaphysics, on the question of the meaning of what he calls "Being." What that means is a very difficult question to answer, and we cannot consider it here. Since it is precisely not a question about ethics, it is not really relevant to our investigation.

Most of the influential early analytic philosophers showed little interest in ethics, partly because they happened to be more interested in mathematics and science and partly because their conception of philosophy did not allow them to answer questions about how we ought to live. If philosophy is the analysis of concepts, then it might tell us the meaning of the concept "life"; but it cannot tell us the meaning of life. One of the leaders of this movement, Ludwig Wittgenstein (1889–1951), said that ethics is transcendental, beyond the scope of what philosophy can deal with. If there is any value in the world, he said, then whatever this "value" is can have no value. That is, it cannot have the kind of value we mean when we talk about ethical value. Perhaps he had in mind something like the value of a human life. Of course, there could be a market for human beings as slaves or organ banks, but that kind of value is not what we mean when we say that you cannot put a price on a human life. The word "cannot" here is not used literally. Any attempt literally to derive ethics from worldly considerations or to justify it in ways that Thrasymachus would accept is not going to be truly ethical. Yet, philosophy cannot be rational and meaningful if it divorces itself from down-to-earth facts. Hence, Wittgenstein and others rejected not ethical behavior but attempts to use philosophy to answer ethical questions.

The Renaissance of Virtue Theory

Wittgenstein and Heidegger were wary of a certain kind of irresponsible talking about ethics. Today, many conservatives also reject talk about values for roughly Heidegger's reasons. But they do not reject all talk about ethics. Instead, they promote the teaching of *virtues*. These are thought to be both more important and more objective, less optional, than mere values. In other words, these people want to return to something like the way Plato, Aristotle, and Thomas Aquinas thought about ethics. Not everyone thinks this way, of course. Utilitarianism and Kantianism have carried on in various forms, but the most dramatic innovation in ethics in the last 50 years has been a return to Aristotelian types of ethical theory. This can be traced back to Wittgenstein's friend and student Elizabeth Anscombe.

She rejected all modern moral philosophy as either morally bankrupt (consequentialism in its various forms, which allows any means necessary to reach a desirable-enough end) or philosophically confused (such as, she argued, Kantian claims that acts are variously permissible or forbidden without anyone—such as God—to do the permitting or forbidding). She suggested that some modification of Aristotle's ethics of virtue might be a better alternative. Anscombe herself was a devout Catholic, but others have taken up her suggestion and tried to devise an adequate moral theory that does justice to our values without smuggling in undeclared references to God. If you read Anscombe's work on the ethics of war or of sex, you will find quite orthodox and traditional Christian ideas, not some radical new post-Aristotelianism. But Anscombe did argue that if you want to do moral philosophy without reference to God or the Bible, then you would be better advised to turn to Aristotle than to either Kant or Mill, or anyone else for that matter. She rejects all subjective ethical theories, such as Hume's, as reducing ethics to a mere matter of feeling. She rejects all forms of consequentialism because they take the end to justify the means, which Anscombe objects is simply corrupt. Utilitarians often try to get us to imagine situations in which they expect us to agree that the ends really do justify the means, such as cases in which torturing a terrorist might enable us to defuse a ticking bomb. Anscombe rejects such arguments as both unrealistic and immoral attempts to corrupt the mind. It is not so much, in other words, that she argues against utilitarianism, assessing the cases to be made for and against it. Rather, she adopts such a strong stance against it that she refuses to listen to the case to be made for it. She is quite openly taking a stance, that is to say, and thus implicitly rejecting the philosophical ideal of dispassionate weighing of logical arguments for and against a variety of positions.

We might be tempted to call this evidence, or a recognition, of the subjectivity of ethics; but Anscombe attacks the idea of subjectivism in ethics. She treats what she takes to be God's laws as perfectly objective. Their defense, though, is not a neutral, impartial, purely logical business. It is itself an ethical act. And the promotion of rival theories is not something to be considered dispassionately, as she sees it. One cannot judge utilitarianism impartially (i.e., really *judge* utilitarianism) if one is committed to Christianity, for instance. This becomes clear if we recall that the Bible itself, as Anscombe notes, says that Christians do not do evil in order that good may come (i.e., justify the means by reference to the end). Any philosopher, then, who invites one to consider such ethical views impartially is presupposing a setting aside of any religious or ethical commitments that one might already have. We cannot evaluate values in a value-free way, without values with which to do our evaluating. Anscombe recognizes this and writes accordingly, without pretense of being value-free.

Utilitarianism belongs to a species of moral thinking that Anscombe recognizes and opposes.[2] The Kantian idea that some acts are just wrong while others are morally obligatory is one that, unlike consequentialism, she cannot oppose because she cannot make out what it is. The idea of a moral law is originally a religious one, with God giving and enforcing the law in question. Kant wanted a rational kind of ethics, one that could be used to judge the commandments of Jesus Christ himself. His ethical theory is meant to appeal to all rational beings, regardless of their religious beliefs. So he keeps the idea of a moral law but ditches the lawgiver and enforcer. Or rather, he ditches God as the lawgiver. Instead, the rational self gives the moral law to itself. As a rational being, he argues, one will want to live rationally, in accordance with universal laws. Think of the way that $2 + 2 = 4$ is a universal law. Now, one cannot live by that law since it does not tell us to do either this or that. But rational rules of conduct, Kant believes, will be equally universal. Any rule that could not be universal must be irrational and, therefore, wrong. In this way, the rational self is meant to legislate its own rules of conduct, or maxims, as he calls them.

But this idea of legislating for oneself is highly problematic, as Kant himself recognized, at least some of the time.

> [c]onscience is peculiar in that, although its business is a business of a human being with himself, one constrained by reason sees himself constrained to carry it on as at the bidding *of another person*. For the affair here is that of trying *a case (causa)* before a court. But to think of a human being who is *accused* by his conscience as *one and the same person* as the judge is an absurd way of representing a court, since then the prosecutor would always lose.[3]

In the same kind of way that it is absurd to think of the accused and the judge as one and the same person, so too it seems absurd to think of the legislator and the one bound by the law as being one and the same person. Kant recognizes this apparent absurdity and yet, as far as he can, embraces it.

When it comes to judging who has obeyed the law and then punishing those who have not, Kant believes that we have to believe in God and an afterlife. Ethics will simply not make sense to us otherwise. In short, he seems very close to relying on the traditional belief in God and his relation to the moral law yet at the same time to be explicitly denying that this is what he is doing. Anscombe's view is that he is simply not making sense. So she is not against what he says. Instead, she observes that he does not seem to be saying anything at all. Indeed, she rejects *all* modern theories of ethics, although she does not bother to say much about theories other than consequentialism and Kantianism since they are by far the most popular and influential of the ideas she urges us to reject.

Inspired by her, many ethicists today have turned to ancient theories, most notably Aristotle's. One of the main such moral philosophers has been Anscombe's former colleague, Philippa Foot. Like Aristotle, Foot wants ethics to fit into our conception of nature. A good person will then be good in the same way that a good dog or rose is good. This is not to say that what is good for a rose (sunlight, water, and lots of manure) is good for people. Rather, it is the idea that there is no special (pseudoreligious) moral sense of "good." Good character is good in exactly the same sense as good fertilizer is good. It promotes flourishing. Anscombe complained that Aristotle's notion of flourishing was hopelessly vague, and recently Foot has struggled to define it. She understands happiness as "the enjoyment of good things" so that, while not identical with virtue (since you might do virtuous things but not enjoy them), it is intimately connected with virtue.[4] She also, though, is reluctant to try to pin happiness down to any one specific definition. The conclusion, in her book *Natural Goodness,* of the chapter on the relation between happiness and the human good, or flourishing, is that "happiness is a protean concept, appearing now in one way and now in another."[5] This is a stumbling block for contemporary virtue theorists. On the one hand, they have a great answer for Thrasymachus: you should be good because to be good is to flourish, to be, in a sense, happy. Don't you want to have a good life, to be happy, to fare well, to flourish?

The answer of course will be yes, but . . . What is at issue with Thrasymachus is precisely what it is that constitutes a good life. He sees it as getting as much as possible of what he wants, the kind of things that money can buy. Foot sees it as possibly partly this but mostly a matter of having a good character, being just, courageous, and so on. Justice is the main problem since it involves treating others with a kind of respect. Why should I do this? What's in it for me? We seem to be right back where we started from. Although not quite, perhaps. After all, Foot points out, we are born into a world and must be raised in its ways if we are to have any meaningful part in it. If we want our children to have friends, we must do our best to encourage in them certain forms of behavior and not others. And most of us do want our children to have friends. These same kinds of behavior, such as playing nicely with others, are likely to be encouraged by the friends themselves too. Thrasymachean egoism is not among them. What goes for friends goes also, to a large extent, for family members. A parent who loves her children will not be Thrasymachean toward them, just as a true friend will not be purely egoistic. So too, good parents will teach their children certain rules, specific rules about not stealing and so on, rather than the general rule of pursuing one's self-interest at all times. This is basically necessary in the kind of society we have, indeed in all societies throughout the world. What follows? That our children have little to no chance if we instill Thrasymachean values into them, that we most likely do not have such values ourselves, and that it is easy to see how those values would be disastrous for humanity. It does not follow, sadly, that we would not be happier being at least somewhat Thrasymachean at times. Whether that is true depends on which conception of happiness we adopt and whether we really prefer the enjoyment of good things to the enjoyment of bad things.

Rosalind Hursthouse has her own answer to the question of what happiness, or *eudaimonia,* might be. She calls it "the smile factor."[6] Happiness is not, she urges, an obscure philosophical concept. It might be more subtle or complex than it seems at first glance, but it must be linked to the ordinary idea that we all share of what it means to be happy. Part of this is the connection with smiling. Do the Thrasymachuses of this world smile a lot? Perhaps some do, but on the whole surely crime and insensitivity to others do not pay. They lead to fear of punishment or ostracism and loneliness. Bad things, on the other hand, *can* happen to good people but *tend* not to. The good are respected and popular, for the most part. They are much less likely to be imprisoned or hated, although of course mistakes can and do happen. They are more likely to be healthy and, in short, happy than the vicious. The best policy for a smile-filled life is goodness. Indeed, Hursthouse goes further than this: "If [a man] never enjoys himself in the straightforward way evidenced by the smile factor then, though his life may be the life of continence [i.e., self-control], it cannot be the life of virtue."[7]

This is not too hard to understand and has an undeniable commonsense appeal. But is it enough? The slogan "Honesty is the best policy" was originally devised to make fun of the kind of amoral pragmatism that Hursthouse might seem to be recommending. Honesty, the idea was, should be valued not because it is useful but because it is right or noble. The "smile factor" might be insufficiently moral a consideration to satisfy us as an answer to the skeptic. We might also wonder about the empirical evidence. Is honesty (and justice and the rest) really the best policy in this sense? What about those exceptional times when we know that we could get away with dishonesty and profit from it? If all I want is smiles, it is far from obvious that I have a reason to be consistently good.

In fairness to Hursthouse, she has much more than this to say about goodness. What she favors is the kind of moral theory that we find in the work of Mill, Foot, and some of the leading Kantians of today. Good people will perform good acts because they are good. That is to say, a properly good person will not need a philosophical reason for being good. Well-raised children will not be told to be just because it will make them happy. They will be taught to value justice because it makes others happy or, perhaps, simply for its own sake. And this is how good adults will think about justice and other virtues too. But if we wonder or come across a doubter, then we have little option but to look for nonmoral reasons for wanting to be good; and here the smile factor comes in. Unfortunately, it faces the problems outlined above. In other words, good people (truly good people, ones better, perhaps, than you and me) do not need to be convinced that goodness is the best path to take. Those who do can only be pointed to plausible but somewhat dubious evidence that they will get what they want most probably by becoming a different kind of person and wanting different things (e.g., justice instead of money). Interestingly, Foot says

> Perhaps there is always a price to pay for wickedness, in real self-esteem or in the possibilities of loving relations with others.
>
> I am, however, dissatisfied with such a solution to [the problem of the relation between happiness and wickedness]. It puts too much weight on a rather uncertain hypothesis. What do I really know about the possibility of combining wickedness and happiness?[8]

Hursthouse does not claim to be able to convert heartless gangsters to the life of virtue. Her arguments are aimed at people who are already reasonably good, and they are intended not to provide motivation to be good but merely rational justification of such a life.[9] Her conclusion, in brief, is that human beings are naturally social and rational beings, just as Aristotle said. And a good human life must therefore be a social and rational life, not the antisocial and irrational life of the criminal. If I want to live viciously, then I am either irrational or not fully human.

But what if I am not a full-fledged human being in the Aristotelian sense? Perhaps another form of moral skepticism is the fear of being some sort of monster (or deviant, creep, weirdo, etc.). Uneasiness about that is quite common, I think. As long as it is, then appeals to what a natural or normal human being will do and value are of limited use to us. An appeal to my sense of my own normality will not be very strong if I have doubts about whether I really am normal or not. Like Foot, Hursthouse does not claim to be able to refute the skeptic. She is confident that she is right and that the immoralists and pessimists are wrong, but it is worth noting that she ends her book not with any proof of this but with a call to "Keep hope alive."[10] That is easier said than done.

This is about as far as contemporary virtue theory has gotten. The tendency to combine Aristotelian and Kantian ideas is promising, but the history we have looked at suggests that we should not be overexcited about the prospects of a really satisfying answer to Thrasymachus (not that this is the main concern of contemporary ethical theorists). Other ethicists are more interested in developing utilitarianism, not in a particularly Millian way in most cases, or social contract theory. Those are families of theories that we have already considered.

Continental Ethics

So much, then, for ethics in the post-Wittgensteinian tradition. What about ethics after Heidegger? Heidegger's followers, or the heirs to his tradition, have gone in different ways. Some have moved toward a Kantian style of thinking. Others have embraced groundless individual choice of values. Others have struggled to develop something more truly Heideggerian, more genuinely concerned with overcoming egoism and seeing things, as it were, in their own terms, not merely in ours. Thus, Jacques Derrida aims at "an openness towards the other"[11] and the ethics of Emmanuel Levinas have been described as "the putting into question of the ego, the knowing subject, self-consciousness."[12] Levinas wants to replace Heidegger's question about the meaning of being with a question about the *justification* of being, giving ethics priority over metaphysics.[13] The writings of such continental philosophers are themselves meant as ethical acts, and the acts in question aim at advancing a seemingly (at least) almost impossibly difficult goal. They aim at something like understanding or acknowledgment without actual understanding or knowledge as we understand these terms. And they aim to achieve this in terms that are not ours, although of course they have to bear at least some resemblance to our terms. Otherwise, nobody could even pretend to understand them.

The results have been controversial. Most of this work goes unread by most philosophers in the English-speaking world. It is accused of fraudulence and willful obscurity. It is accused, more plausibly, of deep confusion. I will not try to show here whether it is fundamentally confused or not as that would take too long. In place of the common, implausible caricatures of it, though, I would like to offer my own rough sketch of the ethics of deconstruction (as Derrida's work in philosophy is called). If it is going to be rejected for simplistic reasons, it might as well be rejected for simplistic reasons that do not involve groundless accusations of phoniness and even malice.[14] Here goes.

On a walk through a park with my 4-year-old son once, he got very excited and shouted "Look! Robin Hood lives in this town! There's Little John's staff!" What he was pointing at was a root twisting out of, and back into, the bank of a stream. It would never have occurred to me to see the root as a staff, let alone as Little John's staff. To me it was just a root. And, of course, it was a root. It isn't a mistake to identify it that way. But it can be interpreted in other ways too. There is something imaginatively closed or dead, something at the very least boring, about seeing it as a root, wholly a root, and nothing but a root. Moreover, to me the root was of no interest at all. I barely noticed it. My view of the world lacks the excitement and possibility of my son's view. It also lacks the poetry of the artist's view, and artists are not as open to the charge of being simply wrong as my son is. The goal shared by philosophers such as Heidegger and Derrida can be seen (of course somewhat simplistically) as getting themselves and their readers to a more poetic or childlike, a more wondering or wonderful, view of the world and the people in it (without, of course, falling into a Disney-ish world "that's full of wonder"—the avoidance of cliché is one motive for writing in a new and difficult way, as continental philosophers often do). This is not because it is so much fun to be a child but because a certain sense of justice requires it. The American poet Wendell Berry makes a similar point quite clearly:

> without its mystery a creature can have no dignity. The presumption of complete understanding is always an affront to dignity. So is the presumption that complete understanding will eventually be realized, or that it is not realizable *yet*. Every creature has an inherent right not to be completely understood. That is the basis of its freedom.[15]

Philosophers in the post-Heideggerian tradition take something like this attitude toward not only living creatures but everything, toward the world and life itself. So part of their goal in doing philosophy is to avoid summing anything up, categorizing it once and for all as this or that. Hence "All . . . statements of the form 'Deconstruction is x' miss the point *a priori*."[16] Nothing is to be labeled; certainty is to be avoided. No wonder, then, that Derrida often seems to want to answer every question with both yes and no.

If we want a simplified version of Derrida's philosophy so that we can begin to understand it, I suggest we start with "yes and no," endlessly qualified. There is even some textual basis for this. For instance, in one interview he gave to a group of philosophers, Derrida begins his answer to a question about Job thus: "First of all, how could we find an echo in Job, but also how could we not find an echo?"[17] Later, he comes right out and says "yes and no" to a question about the philosopher Edmund Husserl.[18] Then, he says "yes and no" again. Of course, there is more to his philosophy than this, but I think the slogan "yes and no" captures something (yet it is precisely such capturing that he wants to resist!)

essential about Derrida's ethics. We must, he seems to think, accept what we inherit, the language we speak and understand, the values we are raised with, and so on; but we must also question or even deny. Above all, we must deny any sense of finality or absoluteness, as when we might think we understand something once and for all, in its entirety. But to put the idea so bluntly is itself to act as if something has been comprehended, grasped, and (in a sense) controlled. This is precisely the kind of act that Heidegger, Levinas, and Derrida oppose. But then saying that is not what they want either. And so on. Derrida's deconstruction emphasizes the importance of the *aporia* (Greek for something like "no through way"), so getting somewhere is not exactly what interests him. Indeed, he writes that "The interest of deconstruction, of such force and desire as it may have, is a certain experience of the impossible."[19] The continental answer to Thrasymachus then might be endless, tortuous conversation in which we struggle to say anything at all with a sufficient lack of hubris. He would most likely not be impressed, even if he stayed to listen.

Ethics and Psychology

Derrida's desire to experience the impossible belongs to a tradition of philosophical thinking concerned with the limits of our understanding. Kant said that he wanted "to negate the impudent assertions of *materialism, naturalism,* and *fatalism.*"[20] He saw himself as living in an increasingly godless world, in which he saw a growing confidence that science tells us all that we need to know. He did not believe that he could prove that anything supernatural did exist, but he tried hard to show that we can never know for sure that it does not. God, free will, and the immortality of the soul can never, he believed, be disproved; and if we need to believe in them, then we may. At any rate, godless materialists have no right to claim that their view of reality has been proved correct. Science might tell us all there is to know, but it cannot ever know that there isn't any more beyond the range of its powers. A desire to bring home the limits of our understanding is common to Kant, Derrida, Heidegger, and Wittgenstein. They want us to be less sure of ourselves and more impressed by the possibility of something greater. What this something is, though, is very hard to say. For Kant it is God, but for the others it is something less precise or familiar. We might call it the wonder of the world or the amazing beauty and complexity of the language we use to talk and think about all the things we care about. Perhaps, like love, it is something you cannot know simply by being told its name.

   This kind of thinking, though, can get very obscure. It aims not to get people to believe this or that but to change the way people think. There can be no guarantee, however, that such attempts will succeed. Nor can the attempt itself be very well justified since it is an attempt whose goal can never be made clear to the uninitiated. Heidegger and Derrida are frequently dismissed as frauds, selling something that does not exist or that is no more valuable than snake oil. The value of Wittgenstein's work is increasingly questioned too, especially in the United States.

Many philosophers today believe that materialism and naturalism are true. They believe in science so much that they share none of Kant's desire for humility on this score. Instead, they are optimistic about future progress and much more interested in practical, quantifiable results than in attempts at intellectual or spiritual transformation. They see no sharp dividing line between philosophy and the natural sciences. To such people, it makes obvious sense to look for connections between ethics, which deals with beliefs and behavior, and psychology, the science of the mind. When we look for such connections, two developments in psychology stand out as being relevant to our concerns.

The first has to do with women. In 1982, the psychologist Carol Gilligan published a book called *In a Different Voice*, in which she argued that traditional thinking about ethics listened to one kind of voice, a voice associated primarily with men, and was deaf to another kind of talking and thinking about what to do, which she associated with women.[21] There are two main claims here. One is that most of what has been accepted as good thinking about ethics is really-only one way of thinking about ethics and that an equally good alternative exists. That has nothing to do with whether you are male or female. The other claim is that in fact it is mostly men who think in the first, recognized way and mostly women who think in the second, downplayed way. This is where feminism comes in.

So, first, what are these two ways of thinking? The first is a legalistic approach to ethics, focusing on inviolable rights and universal principles. It is somewhat abstract and rigid. Social contract theory and Kant's categorical imperative belong to this school of thought. More specifically, it is the kind of thinking held to be at the top of the scale of moral development used by Gilligan's mentor, Lawrence Kohlberg. Kohlberg identified six stages:

1. At the lowest level, children reason, like Thrasymachus, in terms of rewards and punishments, carrots and sticks. They are purely self-interested and not very sophisticated in their thinking.

2. At the next level up, children will bargain or trade for favors with others. They are still fundamentally self-interested but will cooperate with others when they can see that this will directly benefit them.

3. At the third level, people will conform to society's norms in order to get the love and approval that they want. The motivation is still self-interest, but the means–end reasoning is more subtle than at the previous stages.

4. Next comes an internalized sense of right and wrong based on one's place in society. Various roles bring certain duties with them, including the duty to respect people in authority over you. The motivation here is the desire for admiration and respect.

5. Above this is something close to social contract theory. It is a stage at which people believe they should live and let live, so long as one person's idea of living does not cause harm to someone else. Everybody can be expected to benefit from such an approach.

6. Finally, at the top, is the recognition of universal ethical principles of right and wrong. The main concern here is with justice.

This scale makes a certain amount of sense, but Gilligan found that, on tests based on Kohlberg's model of development, men scored much higher, on average, than women did. In fact, women rarely got above stage three, while men routinely reached levels four and five. One possible explanation of these results would be that men are simply more ethical than women. Or they could be more sophisticated in their *thinking* about ethics. Or simply better at taking tests (or smarter). All these explanations seem to imply that men are better in some way than women, either in intelligence or in morals or both. Gilligan smelled a rat. Her alternative explanation was that there was something wrong with the tests, an inherent bias coming from the scale on which they were based. When she researched how women think about ethical problems, she identified another kind of voice, another kind of ethics. This has become known as the ethics of care.

The ethics of care emphasizes people's interdependence. As Plato noted, we need each other in various ways. Without others we would be likely to die, perhaps at the hands of bandits or in the teeth of wolves. As Hobbes pointed out, without others we are deprived of all the advantages of trade and culture. Perhaps, too, Aristotle was right that we have a social nature, one that can only be satisfied if we live cooperatively with other people. This is old news, but the ethics of care emphasizes a different kind of mutual need. Children need the care of parents, and when parents get old, they often need to be cared for by their children in turn. The ones doing the caring are typically women, whether they be nurturing mothers or dutiful daughters. This kind of care is not as dramatic as the dangers envisioned by Hobbes or as speculative as the need that Aristotle hypothesizes about. It is everyday, mundane, and rather foreign to the experience of most philosophers, especially past philosophers, many of whom were unmarried men.

The ethics of care does not reject all past thinking about ethics but seeks to supplement it. In her essay "What Do Women Want in a Moral Theory?" Annette Baier emphasizes that she would "not recommend that we discard categories of obligation, but that we make room for an ethic of love and trust, including an account of human bonding and friendship."[22]

Not all women think this way, and not all who think this way are women. But women tend to emphasize taking care of others and responding to their needs when they think about what they should do. Baier and others do not think that everyone ought to be like this. Instead, they believe that a complete moral theory would include the best of both ways of thinking.

Now, why should we believe them? It is one thing to find out, as Gilligan apparently has, that there are two ways of thinking about ethics. It is another to claim that they are equally good or that we ought to include both in our understanding of what it means to be a good person. Several claims are made on behalf of the ethics of care. One is that when we help others, we should do so because we actually care about them and not because of some impartial principle. Kant famously argued that helping someone when you do not want to, just from a desire to do the right thing, has more moral worth than helping because you want to, because you love the person in need. Many people feel that there is something wrong with this. Isn't the uncaring person heartless and cold? Isn't caring itself morally valuable? Kant might answer yes to both questions but would still want to value the conscientious actions of the person who cannot help being cold. The ethics of care does not disagree with him outright but places the emphasis more on the person who does care.

It is also claimed that only those who do care are likely to understand the real needs of those for whom they care and so are more likely to be able to give the care that is needed. You might know better how to care for your grandmother than I would because you know her better than I do. Now, this might be simply a matter of knowing her likes and dislikes, habits, allergies, and so on; but it could be something more. Perhaps no list that you could ever write out for me would tell me exactly what she needs or wants. Maybe only someone who loves her could ever understand which smiles are real and which are only polite pretences or which sounds she makes mean she's in pain even when she doesn't want anyone else to know. Of course, the more you care about someone, the more you are likely to notice little things about them. But it could even be true that only those who care are capable of seeing everything there is to respond to in caring. And, of course, care itself might be one of the things that a person most wants or needs. It would be very difficult indeed for a sadly heartless yet conscientious person to respond to all the needs of another human being. This would give us another reason to value caring and to emphasize it more than traditional moral philosophers have done.

Another reason might be a desire to redress a perceived injustice done to women throughout the history of ethics. Alison Jaggar says that moral philosophy in the Western tradition has tended to be biased against women in several ways. It has shown little concern for women's interests and rights; it has treated women as less morally developed than men; it has valued allegedly masculine traits such as independence, reason, and transcendence too much and allegedly feminine traits such as interdependence, emotion, and the body too little; and it has valued universal, impartial rules at the expense of particularity, partiality, and relationships.[23] **Feminism**, the idea that women should be equal with men and the movement that pushes for such equality, did not begin to be taken seriously until very late in the history of philosophy and politics. We have seen the apparent bias in Kohlberg's scale of moral development. We have seen also the alleged masculine bias in such ethical theories as Hobbes' and David Gauthier's. Since Plato there has been a tendency among philosophers to value the rational mind or soul above the earthly and corrupt body. This might seem to have nothing to do with feminism, but it is generally men who have been able to be philosophers. The identification of the life of the mind with advanced spirituality and the simultaneous identification of such things as housework and pregnancy with baseness puts men above women almost as angels are thought to be above human beings.

There is not time for us to debate all these issues now, but you do not need to be totally convinced of the truth of Jaggar's case to think that some kind of more feminine ethics is worth considering. If there is any substance to any of her complaints, then the traditional thinking is flawed and might well need to be supplemented, if not overhauled completely. And it is not only women who might be harmed by traditional ethics. Supposedly feminine ways of thinking are actually employed by many men. If caring is downplayed, then we will all be pressed to be less sensitive than we could be. This would distort our natures and make the world a less caring place for us to live in.

Talking of human nature and how we might change it brings us to the other recent development in psychology that is relevant to ethics. This is the rise of evolutionary psychology. If psychology is tied up with the brain and if the brain got to be the way it is through a process of evolution, then it seems reasonable to think that evolution is relevant to questions about human nature and human behavior, including questions about ethics. Evolution has come up before in earlier chapters, so we have already seen some ways in which it is connected with ethical issues. Assuming for now that it is true, if only for the sake of argument, then what follows?

First, we should remember what the theory of evolution says. In fact, there are several competing versions of the theory, but the basic idea is shared by them all. Reproduction is not cloning. Offspring are not exact replicas of their parents, and mutations of various degrees can and do take place. Very rarely, these mutations are extreme, like "Mary-Kate and Ashley," the two-headed snake found by a boy in Centertown, Kentucky, in 2003.[24] More often, they are much less noticeable. Generally, mutations are undesirable. Two-headed snakes, for instance, rarely live very long, although it is not known exactly why. Sometimes, however, the differences between parents and their offspring work in the offspring's favor, making them better suited to the environment in which they live. More importantly, they make them better suited to their environment than their peers. This gives them an advantage when it comes to survival, and those that survive the longest have the best chance of reproducing. Their offspring will not be exactly the same as them, and so their useful mutation might die with them. But it might not. If a useful mutation survives, then those that have it are likely to outlast their peers, and the mutation is likely to become more and more common. Eventually, it might no longer be recognized as a mutation but simply one characteristic of the members of a species.

Which characteristics have survival value depends on the environment. Evolution is not a process of absolute improvement. It is about change brought by the interaction between random biological variations and the environment. Whichever such changes help creatures survive and reproduce in their environment will tend to endure. Changes that are harmful will tend to disappear, along with the unfortunate creatures that suffer them. Brain mutations that produce harmful kinds of behavior will tend to disappear, therefore, while those that produce helpful behavior will tend to survive. "Helpful" here means conducive to survival and reproduction, nothing more ethical than that.

So what is the connection with ethics? According to Charles Darwin, we have certain ethical tendencies hardwired into us because of natural selection (i.e., the survival of the fittest). Individuals that tended not to look after themselves would die out, so we have inherited a certain tendency to be self-interested. In that sense, it is human nature to be selfish. However, we know that people are capable of altruistic behavior too. Mothers make great sacrifices for their children, soldiers throw themselves on grenades to save their comrades' lives, and so on. Perhaps this is because, while pure self-interest seems to make sense if all you care about is survival and reproduction, whole tribes of people who think that way might tend to survive less well than those that cooperate in a more altruistic fashion. The self-sacrificing soldier might not live to pass on his genes, but the tribe that produced him and that he protects might win the war against the tribe of selfish soldiers who all die when a grenade lands in the fox-hole. Taking one for the team helps the team and, thus, the team's genes. This is one theory of how altruism has become a feature of human life. Altruism helps one's genes survive when the others helped are genetic relatives, and there could be times when it pays to help nonrelatives who then help you or your relatives in turn. Evolutionary theory then suggests that we should expect to find tendencies to both selfishness and altruism in human beings. Not that everyone necessarily has both tendencies to a great extent, but we do see both kinds of behavior in human actions. So the theory is not proved but confirmed.

It does not follow that we *ought* to be either self-interested or altruistic or both. Nothing at all follows about how we ought to be. Darwin only tries to explain how we got to be the way we are. If, however, someone supports an ethical theory that is based on some other, incompatible theory of how we got to be this way, then evolution could be very relevant. For instance, it has been argued that human beings are much more closely related to other species than was previously appreciated and that this should make us revise our ideas about what makes things right and wrong. The theory of evolution does not say that we are descended from apes, but it does suggest that we share a common ancestor with apes. After all, there are tremendous similarities between us and the great apes, as well as the very obvious differences. Evolution explains both by positing a species, now extinct, that produced us by one line of descent and the (other) apes by other lines of descent. If orangutans are part of our own family, in this very extended sense, then perhaps we should treat them differently.

It is worth being careful here. Nobody thinks that orangutans are literally part of your family in the normal sense of the word. Even if they were, not much would follow about how you ought to treat them. Perhaps family members who behave like animals deserve to be treated like animals. But if the reason we do not kill people is that people are radically different kinds of being from orangutans and the like, then the discovery (if that is what it is) that we are not radically different from them should give us pause. It has been argued that this invalidates Kant's ethical theory, most forms of social contract theory, and natural law theory. If these arguments are valid, then that would be a very significant contribution from biology and psychology to the study of ethics. How would the arguments go?

The idea is that there is not a fundamental difference between us and other species in terms of rationality. Reason was treated by Kant and the natural law tradition as being *the* differentiating factor that marks human beings off from the rest of the animal kingdom. But apes are fairly smart, and not all human beings are very rational. If we believe the kind of moral theories that emphasize reason or that are based on hypothetical contractual agreements that could only be made between rational agents, we would seem to have to reconsider our attitudes toward other species. If moral rights, such as the right not to be used in medical research, depend on our being rational, then why should we prefer to experiment on a chimpanzee rather than on a mentally handicapped infant? You might splutter, but the question has been raised in all seriousness by intelligent people of good will.

There are two kinds of arguments to keep separate here. One kind is aimed at theories such as Kant's, which start from the idea that reason and rational beings have a special place in ethical thinking. These arguments suggest that reason cannot be so special since human beings are only *relatively* and *usually* more rational than other species, not absolutely and universally so. If they are right, then all that follows is that Kant and company have made a mistake, not that we should change any of our current practices or attitudes (unless they are specifically based on faulty philosophical theories). The other kind of argument is about what we should and should not do to animals. These arguments suggest that animals are smarter than we thought and should be treated better. This view actually presupposes that people like Kant and Aquinas were on to something in valuing reason. Clearly, the two kinds of argument are quite different.

Is either kind correct? With regard to the value of reason, it depends somewhat on the rightness or wrongness of such things as euthanasia and animal experimentation. Some people believe that reason is so important that any being lacking it can quite properly be experimented on or killed. On the other hand, most of us do not think this way. We do value reason very highly, which is why theories such as Kant's appeal to us so strongly; but we have other values too. A mentally handicapped baby might not even have the potential to become a rational being, yet precisely because of this disadvantage some people will feel that it should be especially looked after. This is not to say that euthanasia should not be allowed, only that the issue is more complicated than some defenders of euthanasia believe. Those of us who feel this way will tend to find theories that value reason to the exclusion of everything else unsatisfactory. Kant and Aquinas would surely sympathize, but whether their theories can accommodate this sympathy adequately is another matter.

If we do not base our ethical thinking solely on the value of reason, what follows about how we should treat animals? Nothing at all. It depends on what, if anything, we do base our ethical judgments on. If we base them on the value of humanity itself, then babies will have moral standing and chimpanzees will not. This will strike some people as obviously reasonable, while others will complain that this is just an arbitrary prejudice in favor of one's own species. Such "speciesism," it is sometimes claimed, is little better than racism. Peter Singer is the most famous philosopher who thinks this way. He believes in a form of utilitarianism instead, according to which we should maximize the happiness of all beings that are capable of happiness. That is, we should follow whatever course of action will produce the greatest happiness for the greatest number. Humans have greater capacities for happiness than most other species, so we still come first, as it were; but chimps and other animals should certainly be taken into account more than they currently are.

There are two main problems with this way of thinking. The first is that it leads straight to the highly counterintuitive kind of idea that we encountered above. Singer believes in having the courage to think the unthinkable, following the argument wherever it leads. If babies—not only fetuses but infants too—end up having no right to life, then so be it. Nothing is off-limits for utilitarians like Singer. An important objection to their kind of reasoning is precisely that it does lead to the unthinkable. The second problem is that we cannot pass off the blame for such unthinkable thinking to logic or reason itself. Perhaps it is dishonest to think illogically or to chicken out of a conclusion that reason clearly draws. But reason and logic alone do not tell us that utilitarianism is true, that happiness is the only ultimate value. As Mill observed, there can be no rational proof of any such principle. Happiness is one thing that we value. But so is reason. So is humanity. If it is arbitrary to value humanity above all else, why is it not equally arbitrary to value happiness above all else? Logic does not tell us which values to pick or how to rank them. If we make a choice and *then* apply logic, we must accept responsibility for the conclusions we reach. If they tell us to treat mentally handicapped infants as being close to the bottom of the moral totem pole, then we can go back and try again or else embrace the horrific conclusion. But the latter course of action is no less arbitrary than the other. So we seem to be led back to thinking that evolution really tells us nothing about how we ought to live.

Why Be Good?

Many virtue theorists believe that we cannot answer the question "Why be good?" until we know more about human psychology. What exactly is it to have good intentions or a good will? And does being a person of good will actually lead to happiness? We can, of course, define virtue in terms of things that make people smile; but this proves nothing very much. It is not certain that the people we consider morally good really do smile more than other people. There is no proof that any one way of life reliably leads to more smiles than any other. There is reason to hope, along with Hursthouse, that virtue is a recipe for smiling; but hope is not philosophy. Nor would Derrida and Levinas offer any proof that we should do this rather than that, be this way and not that way.

The ethics of care, though, might have some appeal for Thrasymachus. Stanford University Professor Nel Noddings distinguishes between what she calls natural caring and ethical caring. Ethical caring, she says, is artificial and parasitic on natural caring. That is, it could never exist without natural caring and is a human product. Natural caring is most basic and most important. It is about particular people in particular relationships. It is, for instance, caring about one's own children, not humanity in general. We have at most a constrained obligation to give aid to "the needy in the far regions of the earth."[25] Thrasymachus might agree. He would surely care for his own children but not those of others.

Unfortunately for him, this is not what Noddings means. She does think that we have greater obligations to people we actually meet than to those who are distant and to those we are somehow related to than to those with no relation to us. Active caring involves doing things for people, responding to them as real people. This requires an actual encounter with them. Of course, we can care about a problem and, say, send money to help deal with it. Sending money to a charitable organization, though, is usually a response to a request from someone working on behalf of that organization. We are responding to a direct encounter with someone in our immediate environment, not to a person we have never met at all. You might think that we should care about everybody equally, but Noddings argues that this is simply impossible. In order to care about anyone, we have to make choices, and the caring choice is in favor of the calls for help that we can actually hear. We could choose to go elsewhere and respond to voices we know about but cannot yet hear, but our obligations are to what we are actually called to do. Utilitarians who think we can and should care equally about everyone regard this position as not moral enough. Any apparent lack of morality is likely to appeal to the skeptical Thrasymachus, but Noddings is not advocating an amoral bias against foreigners and in favor of one's own family, friends, and tribe. Nor are other proponents of the ethics of care. They believe in doing all that we can. They disagree with utilitarians largely about how much that is, how much we are capable of truly caring for people who are not part of our lives. Thrasymachus, who does not care for anyone much except himself, is unlikely to be impressed.

Evolutionary psychology is not likely to move him very much either. For one thing, evolution is a theory about how we got to be the way we are. It does not judge what is right or wrong. It might lead us to give up on certain ideals as hopelessly at odds with human nature, but in fact there is room within evolutionary theory for both Thrasymachean selfishness and more idealistic altruism. There is also room for enlightened forms of self-interest that are perhaps more sophisticated than Thrasymachus' version. If we have certain ethical views based on false ideas about the differences between humans and other species of animals, then evolution might lead us to give up those views; but Thrasymachus is simply skeptical about all ethics. He has no such beliefs to revise in the first place. And if he sees no reason to care about other people, then he will surely see no reason to care about pigs or pigeons either, no matter how much we teach him about biology. Whether evolution is true or false appears to make no difference to whether we should try to be good. And it is not as if Thrasymachus would be likely to have faith in creationism or intelligent design instead.

Conclusion

I think it is fair to conclude that we have yet to find an answer for good people who want to satisfy their inner Thrasymachus. Wittgenstein, Heidegger, Anscombe, Foot, Hursthouse, Derrida, and Levinas would agree that the moral skeptic cannot be refuted. This does not mean that their work is devoid of interest or value though. The ethics of care and evolutionary psychology do not seem to offer an answer to our question either. But we have also seen reasons for thinking that Thrasymachus' position is quite crude and not very satisfactory itself. The "me" of "What's in it for me?" does seem to be uneducated (as Aristotle, e.g., emphasized), insensitive (see Mill), not very rational (see Kant), and possibly imprudent (see Hursthouse). If we take into account what is most plausible in the various theories we have looked at in this book, then it is still possible that we will remain cynical; but I think our cynicism is likely to be reduced, which is why I believe the kind of study undertaken in this book is worthwhile. I can only hope that you agree. In the concluding chapter that follows, we will look back at exactly what has and what has not been proved and consider in more detail the value that this might have.

Questions for Further Thought

1. Should we change our attitude toward animals in the light of modern biology?
2. Do you believe that women and men tend to think differently about ethics? What follows for ethical theory?
3. Does traditional Western moral philosophy have a masculine bias? If so, what might we do about it?
4. Could philosophy as practiced by people such as Derrida have moral value?
5. Are happiness and virtue inseparably connected?

Notes

1. Martin Heidegger, "Letter on Humanism," in *Basic Writings*, ed. David Farrell Krell (San Francisco: Harper, 1977), 228.
2. Actually, Anscombe invented the word "consequentialist" in order to distinguish between the utilitarianism of people such as Mill and what she saw as a new development that occurred after his death. Many people today, however, read Mill as no different from the consequentialists she criticized.
3. Immanuel Kant, *Metaphysics of Morals*, trans. and ed., Mary Gregor (Cambridge: Cambridge University Press, 1996), 189.

4. Philippa Foot, *Natural Goodness* (Oxford: Clarendon Press, 2001), 97.
5. Ibid.
6. Rosalind Hursthouse, *On Virtue Ethics* (Oxford: Oxford University Press, 1999), 185.
7. Ibid., 186.
8. Foot, *Natural Goodness*, 90.
9. Hursthouse, *On Virtue Ethics*, 193–194.
10. Ibid., 265.
11. Richard Kearney, *Dialogues with Contemporary Continental Thinkers* (Manchester, UK: Manchester University Press, 1984), 124.
12. Simon Critchley, *The Ethics of Deconstruction: Derrida and Levinas* (West Lafayette, IN: Purdue University Press, 1999), 4.
13. Emmanuel, Levinas, "Ethics as First Philosophy," in *The Levinas Reader*, ed. Seán Hand (Oxford: Blackwell, 1989), 75–87, esp. 86.
14. As Anthony Rudd says, in his *Kierkegaard and the Limits of the Ethical* (Oxford: Oxford University Press, 1993), 46, footnote, "Derrida is a very obscure and very elusive writer." To be safe, Rudd presents Derrida not as he really is, necessarily, but as he has been widely understood. For this Derrida, "language is to be understood on the model of a solitary reader of a 'literary' text following up various trains of association that strike him" (p. 49). Rudd goes on to refer to "a Derridean vision of an infinity of possible interpretations, with no means of deciding between them, a semantic anarchy in which meaning disappears," (pp. 51–52). One popular conception of Derrida is nicely captured here by Rudd, who, like others, suspects him of sometimes "making outrageous claims so as to seem radical and exciting" (p. 46, footnote).
15. Wendell Berry, *Citizenship Papers* (Emeryville, CA: Shoemaker & Hoard, 2003), 183.
16. Critchley, *The Ethics of Deconstruction*, 22.
17. Richard Kearney and Mark Dooley, eds., *Questioning Ethics* (London: Routledge, 1999), 68.
18. Ibid., 71.
19. Jacques Derrida, "Psyché: Invention of the Other," in *Reading De Man Reading*, trans. C. Porter, ed. L. Waters and W. Godzich (Minneapolis: University of Minnesota Press, 1989), 36.
20. Immanuel Kant, *Prolegomena to Any Future Metaphysics that Will be Able to Come Forward as Science*, trans. and ed. Gary Hatfield (Cambridge: Cambridge University Press, 2004), 114.
21. Carol Gilligan, *In a Different Voice: Psychological Theory and Women's Development* (Cambridge, MA: Harvard University Press, 1993).
22. Annette Baier, *Moral Prejudices: Essays on Ethics* (Cambridge, MA: Harvard University Press, 1995), 1–17.
23. Alison Jaggar "Feminist Ethics" in *Encyclopedia of Ethics*, ed. L. Becker and C. Becker (New York: Academic Press, 1992), 363–364.
24. See "Boy Finds Two-Headed Snake" Friday October 17, 2003. http://www.cnn.com/2003/TECH/science/10/17/offbeat.twoheaded.snake.ap/.

25. Nel Noddings, *Caring: A Feminine Approach to Ethics and Moral Education* (Berkeley: University of California Press, 2003), 152.

Suggestions for Further Reading

Anscombe's paper "Modern Moral Philosophy" is published in both *The Collected Philosophical Papers of G. E. M. Anscombe: Ethics, Religion and Politics*, vol. 3 (Oxford: Basil Blackwell, 1981), and Mary Geach and Luke Gormally, eds., *Human Life, Action and Ethics: Essays by G.E.M. Anscombe* (Exeter, UK: Imprint Academic, 2005). After Anscombe, the classic early book of the recent virtue ethics movement is Alasdair MacIntyre, *After Virtue: A Study in Moral Theory*, 3rd ed. (Notre Dame, IN: University of Notre Dame Press, 2007). Rosalind Hursthouse, *On Virtue Ethics*, 2nd ed. (Oxford: Oxford University Press, 2002), is another important addition to this school of thought.

A useful collection of work on ethics by so-called continental philosophers is Matthew Calarco and Peter Atherton, eds., *The Continental Ethics Reader* (London: Routledge, 2003). An important, but difficult, book on the subject is Simon Critchley, *The Ethics of Deconstruction: Derrida and Levinas* (West Lafayette, IN: Purdue University Press, 1999).

To learn more about ethics and psychology, see Carol Gilligan, *In a Different Voice: Psychological Theory and Women's Development* (Cambridge, MA: Harvard University Press, 1993), and Louise Barrett, Robin Dunbar, and John Lycett, *Evolutionary Psychology: A Beginner's Guide* (Oxford: Oneworld Publications, 2005).

For more on the ethics of care, I recommend Nel Noddings, *Caring: A Feminine Approach to Ethics and Moral Education* (Berkeley: University of California Press, 2003).

Conclusion

So what have we learned? Why be good? Plato collects a variety of answers: to avoid punishment from God, to avoid punishment from the state, to avoid making yourself unpopular, and because it is in your self-interest to be rational and the rational part of you loves truth and goodness. The first three reasons, though, are problematic. God might not exist or might forgive rather than punish bad deeds, and we might not know what he wants us to do. The state might not be very good at catching people who break the laws, and its laws might not be very good in the first place. Certainly, some laws are regarded as regulatory rather than ethical, and not every unethical deed (betraying a friend, say) is actually illegal. Finally, popularity and moral goodness do not always go hand in hand. Even if they often do, what matters for the sake of being popular is surely seeming to be good, not actually being good. Popularity is based on people's perceptions, not reality independent of these perceptions.

So, again, what reason does Plato offer for actually being good? He sees all the problems mentioned above and tries to avoid them by arguing that you have a three-part self and that it is in the best interest of this self for you to be morally good. This is because it makes sense to be virtuous in several important ways. The four cardinal virtues are said to be courage, temperance, wisdom, and justice. It is in your own interest to be courageous because, roughly speaking, if you are too afraid to gamble, then you will never win. It is in your interest to be temperate because that simply means having self-control. Those who lack this virtue are at great risk of going off the rails and suffering embarrassment, poverty, disease, addiction, and an early death. And wisdom is obviously good since it basically means the ability to make good decisions.

So far so good. But what about justice? What about other people? Why should I ever do things that are not directly in my self-interest? Why should I care about such things as fairness, honesty, and integrity? Because, Plato seems to believe, these things are good. They are not just said to be good or thought to be good by some people. Goodness is real, objectively so. In fact, there is an object that we might call goodness. This is what Plato calls the form of the Good. And he thinks he can prove that it exists. But few people agree with him. He does not appear to prove that any forms exist as he understands them. Indeed, he does not even present a clear, consistent account of what these forms are meant to be. Nor does he prove that the form of the Good is one of the forms that exist, if any do. Nor does he prove that this form, if it does exist, corresponds to conventional, traditional ideas about what things are good and what things are bad. In the absence of proof, what we are left with is a series of powerful images, such as the image of the cave and the form of the Good as the sun. These images have real power to move and inspire, but they are not quite the rational arguments that we were supposedly looking for.

It might come as a relief, then, to find that Aristotle rejects Plato's idea of the form of the Good as irrelevant to ethics. According to Aristotle, you should be good because it is your nature to be rational, so irrational acts will be unsatisfying to you; because it is your nature to be social, so antisocial acts will make impossible the only kind of life that could satisfy you; and because, if you were raised well, you will want to be good and find badness unpleasant.

There is something to all of this, I think; and we have seen already that the idea that rationality is good would be accepted even by Thrasymachus. The tricky question is what exactly being rational means. And Aristotle does not even claim to answer that question. Something similar goes for being social. All human relationships involve some measure of give and take. How much take is right, best, or acceptable? Aristotle does not pretend to be able to tell us. Finally, how can I know whether the way I was raised is good or bad, perfect or imperfect? And it is surely too late now to do anything about it. There are probably limits to what can be regarded as rational and social behavior, so we probably should be somewhat good in this sense. That is, in saying that it is our nature to be rational and social and that only a certain range of lives will ever satisfy us, Aristotle appears to make a good point. The question then is whether we can narrow this range down at all usefully.

The idea that education and being raised a certain way are important in shaping our desires—in shaping the self that asks "What's in it for me?"—is also a good one. Thrasymachus' position is not straightforward. He seems to treat what he wants or what is good for him as being given, ignoring the way our desires and interests can be shaped by education and experience. If we care about self-interest, then we need to pay attention to what this self is. But philosophers have still not reached agreement on what the self is, nor do any scientists know exactly what part of our characters is a result of nurture and what is simply given by nature. It seems possible that some people might have natures that will not be satisfied by the Aristotelian good life. Might they be better off pursuing a dictatorial career or the life of the crafty criminal? We still do not seem to be in a position to judge.

Another problem with Aristotle's idea of the good life is that his list of virtues, of character traits that would benefit each of us, is controversial, even among people who agree that some such list can be drawn up. Christian virtues, for instance, are not the same as Aristotelian ones. We could turn to religious texts to try to find out how we ought to be, but then how can we know which such texts, if any, we should trust? And then, if we do pick one to follow, there is always the problem of interpretation. It seems that we cannot prove that God exists, let alone that one kind of religion is the true kind. That need not be a problem, of course. Many people are happy to rely on faith. But for the faithless, this provides no guidance as to what they should believe in. And there are some very bad doctrines out there waiting to be accepted with blind faith. Aquinas suggests that nature can guide our reason to the right kind of belief. But there is no proof that we should follow nature, and it too can be interpreted in a variety of ways. This is not to say that Aquinas' natural law theory has no value. Many of us do feel that certain things are unnatural and bad on that account. These intuitions might not be proof of anything, but if ethical thinking depends on intuitions as much as it seems to, then we should not simply deny or ignore this important class of intuitions in our thinking about what we should do. Still, we have not at all proved that the moral way of life is better than all others. So we move on from the medieval age of faith to the modern age.

Thomas Hobbes tries to show that even Thrasymachus has good reason to agree to behave morally. It is doubtful, though, whether acting moral and being moral are really the same thing. Moreover, self-interested agreements between amoral agents will probably not protect anyone who has little to offer at the bargaining table. The handicapped, the very young, and the very old are likely to be left out of the deal. So some of the most important aspects of a moral life, such as caring for those in need, might be absent from the version of moral life that Hobbesian agents would agree to.

According to David Hume, being good means being useful or agreeable to yourself or to others. It is usually beneficial to you to be useful or agreeable to others. If it isn't, then you still might care about others out of natural sympathy; and if you don't, then you are to be pitied. Hume brings out well the cost involved in living the Thrasymachean life, but that is about all he can give us on that question. He cannot prove that the cost is not worth it for anybody. Indeed, in some ways, Hume can be read as offering just a theory of how we happen to think about ethical questions, not a particular view on what we *ought* to think or do.

This kind of scientific approach to ethics is rejected by Kant. If ethical judgment were a matter of having certain sensations in the mind, then anything at all might conceivably be or become morally good or morally bad. If our brains were wired in such a way that cutting toenails set off our disapproval centers, then cutting toenails would be bad. Not on the utilitarian grounds that it made people unhappy but simply by definition, if we define evil as whatever causes this reaction in a certain type of person. This is rather implausible though, and it gets worse. If any act could be good or bad, then it would be possible to approve or disapprove of any act you can think of. But it is scarcely coherent to say "I disapprove of defending the innocent from unprovoked attacks" or "I approve of theft from people in need purely for personal gain." It makes sense to *like* or *dislike* such things, but moral approval and disapproval cannot be attached to just any kind of act. Hume presumably thinks that such thoughts (of approval and disapproval) are merely very unlikely to occur. Our minds do not work like that, he believes. Others think that there is something other than chemistry or physics going on here, that there is something illogical about the thought "Oh good, I'm being murdered." It seems to be part of the very concept of murder that it is a bad thing, so there is a kind of self-contradiction involved, making the "thought" in question quite meaningless and not something that one could really think (i.e., mean) at all. Someone might be glad that he or she were being unlawfully killed, if he or she was suicidal to begin with, perhaps; but one cannot say and mean anything like "Oh good, my will is being thwarted."

Kant picks up on this connection between reason, will, and ethics. Whatever cannot be willed, he says, cannot be good. Your rational self values reason, and rational acts are morally good acts. Irrational acts are slavish, driven by the unchosen desires of the body, peer pressure, etc. But logic does not appear to solve our ethical or existential dilemmas. Many things can quite meaningfully be willed and yet are still clearly immoral. People choose to commit murder, rape, theft, and so on all the time. Kant's categorical imperative tries to show that there is a kind of incoherence in such apparently meaningful (though still clearly bad) choices. But he does not prove that when we act on our will, we will that all rational beings act in the same way. Like Plato, he gives us a way of look-ing at action, of thinking about how we choose to live our lives, but he does not prove that this is *the* correct way to look or think, however compelling his vision might be.

Mill points out that we cannot separate ideas about what is good from what we actually desire or think of as good. We cannot, that is, do ethics in a purely rational or logical way, without reference to what we happen, empirically, to value. This is an Aristotelian point, that what we value depends partly on how we happen to have been raised. It does not follow, though, that anything goes and that anything at all can be valued. I cannot *morally* value red paint any more than I can *disap-prove* of cutting toenails (unless some significant explanation is added to this bare fact). But the range of meaningful, of possible, values is still disturbingly large, as Nietzsche recognized.

According to Mill, good acts maximize the general happiness. The better you are, the more you will want this. And one of the main reasons for unhappiness is narrow selfishness, so you have reason to want to become a more altruistic per-son. This might be true, and it is the kind of thing that Philippa Foot and Rosalind Hursthouse hope is true. Foot, though, admits that it has not been proved as a scientific fact. It is optimistic speculation, no more. Nietzsche seems to have seen quite well through the faults in the ethics of Hume, Kant, and Mill but admits that he is in much the same boat as I have said Plato is in. He offers a poetic vision, not proof.

Plato's vision is quite similar to Kant's, but Nietzsche's is very different. He does not value reason as highly as they do and does value individual taste and will. He values passion, which has been thought to be missing from much of mod-ern life. But when we think of the passion of a Hitler or a religious fanatic pre-pared to kill innocent people, we might not be so sure that Nietzsche's values are ours. And a compromise between Nietzsche and Kant, say, would be satisfactory to neither, nor true to their visions. It would lack any rationale.

The late twentieth century saw a blossoming of interest in ethics, but this has not provided any significantly new answer to Thrasymachus. If poetry does not work, then perhaps changing the subject will. Indeed, if we think of the subject of ethics as being the heir to the ostensible project of the *Republic,* that is, to answer Thrasymachus and Glaucon, then perhaps the subject simply is a dead end and needs to be changed. That, at any rate, seems to have been the view of Wittgenstein and Heidegger. There are few Wittgensteinian philosophers left today, though, and his analytical heirs generally consider themselves to have moved on to more scientific work, with no explicit link to questions about the meaning of life. This work is no doubt valuable, but attempts to base ethics on science, particularly psychology, have not proved that we should be more or less caring, or anything else of the sort. Heidegger's heirs have moved on too, but some would say that no movement can be discerned in the fog that their kind of philosophy generates. I will leave you to explore it and decide for yourself. Wittgenstein and Heidegger themselves led interesting lives but hardly ones you would want to emulate. There is little biographical evidence that either of them ever found the answer to the question of how to live. Indeed few, if any, philosophers are exemplary; perhaps philosophy cannot tell us how to live.

I do not mean to be overly pessimistic though. The visions of Plato, Kant, and Nietzsche are genuinely great and moving. They really might convert Thrasymachus to a better path. Whether this kind of conversion is what was originally intended is arguably beside the point. The insights of Aristotle on the role of education and upbringing, Hume on the price a real Thrasymachus would pay, Kant on the limits of empiricism in ethics (some principles simply make no sense and so, a priori, cannot be endorsed), and Mill on the need for an empirical element in ethics (what makes sense depends on what we happen to value or desire) are also genuinely significant. They might not tell us *exactly* what we ought to do. Indeed, they might explicitly deny that philosophy can ever do that, as Aristotle does. But they are still true and important. The history of ethics might show a tendency to fail to answer the questions directly asked, but it hardly shows a failure to produce vision and insight, guidance and truth. We might still have no answer for Thrasymachus, but we can thank him for his question and everything it has given us.

Is that it? I have suggested that we might not have seen much progress in the history of virtue ethics but that much that is valuable has come out of it all the same. The question remains, though: How should we live? What can we say directly about this question?

The Algerian-born novelist and philosopher Albert Camus (1913–1960) famously said that the only question that really matters is whether to live at all. Those of us who have never seriously considered this question or who have decided to keep on living presumably have other questions too, but they still might be related to the question of suicide. Hamlet, for instance, even more famously, said

To be or not to be—that is the question:
Whether 'tis nobler in the mind to suffer
The slings and arrows of outrageous fortune,
Or to take arms against a sea of troubles
And, by opposing, end them.[1]

This is generally taken (with good reason) to be about suicide, but we can also interpret it as being about ways of living. The stoical thing to do, which might also be thought of as the Christian or Buddhist thing to do, is to suffer life's pains nobly and uncomplainingly. It is to accept what happens and the way things are as God's will or fate or at any rate as something not to be interfered with. One's own will is not to be imposed on the world or on life but to be denied, perhaps even to be willed out of existence, to be unwilled. This can be thought of as a form of suicide, a refusal to be in the world or of the world, but also as a way to attain a different kind of life, perhaps even eternal life.

The problem, apart from the suicidal aspect of such a life choice, is that the world as we find it can truly be outrageous. No doubt petty wrongs from friends, colleagues, and enemies should be risen above and forgotten. Noble suffering has something to be said for it. But is all suffering, all putting up with wrongdoing, genuinely noble; or is it sometimes foolish, cowardly, or ignoble? Gandhi achieved great things through his heroic passive resistance to British imperialism in India, but all he could recommend to the Jews in Germany was mass suicide, which hardly strikes many people as the best possible response to the genocidal Nazis.[2] Nightmares threaten not only the sleeping or the dead, as Hamlet imagines. And to sleep through them hardly seems noble or even very prudent.

On the other hand, the idea of ending a whole sea of troubles by opposing them with arms—that is, not quitting but sticking around and fighting—sounds like the story of King Cnut sitting on his throne on the beach and commanding the waves to stop. Inevitably, he got his feet wet. We can respond to problems, whether natural disasters, human evils, or unpleasant facts of life such as cancer, but never hope, surely, to erase them all completely. So there can seem to be something foolish, something hopeless or pointless, about this kind of life too. And the twentieth century especially provides plenty of examples of attempts to make heaven on earth that ended up producing something closer to hell. At least some Nazis and communists had good intentions. It would be false, not to mention tasteless, to say that the roads to Belsen and the Gulag were paved with good intentions. But organized horror takes more than a few psychopaths or bad apples to get off the ground. It requires the assistance at least of people who sleep through life (for an illustration of this, see Shusaku Endo's novel *The Sea and Poison*) and quite possibly also of those who honestly believe that what they are doing is at worst a necessary evil. When we are tempted to impose our will on the world, to remake things in accordance with our own image of how things should be, we should remember Pol Pot's bloody efforts to return Cambodia to an "innocent" square one by killing, among others, anyone who wore glasses.

It is not my place to tell you what to think, but it may well seem to you at this point that you cannot simply withdraw from the world and "let it be," but neither can you play God. Some compromise or third way must be found, presumably letting be whatever is good or at least OK and imposing only a *good* will on things otherwise. Fair enough.

But what is good? This question sparks many others. Let us start with what is good for you. Now, what are you? Are we talking about your body only, your soul, both, or something else as well or instead? If you think of yourself as a purely physical being, presumably you will also want to take your brain into account and the various feelings associated with its chemistry. What we normally think of as health (physical fitness and freedom from illness) is not the only good of the body. There is mental health too, and by this I mean not only freedom from mental illness but also well-being or happiness. There are no such things as pills or machines that simply make people happy, so even if life could be meaningful if it revolved around physically induced feelings of happiness, this is not an option for us. There is no drug we can all take that will make us high but still capable of functioning as individuals and as a society. We need to find satisfaction some other way. Certainly, for most of us, this way will involve other people. It will also involve our consciences. So we have reason right there to be polite, friendly, loving (assuming a measure of tit-for-tat can be expected from the other people in our lives), and morally good, however our particular consciences happen to define moral goodness.

If you think of yourself as your soul, then things are more complicated. Wittgenstein seems to have conceived of ethics as the care of one's soul, as, in different ways, have Ayn Rand and some religious believers, not to mention the great Greek philosophers Socrates, Plato, and Aristotle. It is a problematic kind of view though. Rand ends up promoting selfishness as a virtue and rejecting thoughts of the greater good almost completely, as if altruism and utilitarianism, for instance, had no real appeal. Her view, in other words, is quite counterintuitive, which is a problem for any philosophy whose appeal is primarily intuitive in the first place. (This is why her novels, not her philosophical essays, are the best way for her to get her ideas across in a way that makes their intended appeal clear.)

Wittgenstein's approach to life faces some similar problems. He tended toward the stoic kind of ethics that we discussed above and so, for instance, went off to fight in the First World War rather than willfully refuse to do so, as his philosophical mentor Bertrand Russell did. There was no just cause here, and Wittgenstein was not much of a patriot; but when fate brings war, the stoic fights. So concerned was he to test and toughen his soul that Wittgenstein deliberately sought out dangerous, frontline positions. He must have known that such postings might have involved killing soldiers on the other side or at least helping to get them killed, but this appears to have been something that Wittgenstein simply accepted. On the other hand, he knew how terrible hand-to-hand trench warfare would be and decided to let himself be killed if he ever found himself in such a situation. It is almost as if the rights and wrongs of matters of life depend, in this view, not at all on who lives and who dies but solely on the psychological effects on whoever is deciding what to do.

I am speculating rather a lot here based on just a couple of points from Wittgenstein's life, so it would hardly be fair to condemn him on these grounds. But if one adopts what we might call "soul-selfishness" as an ethic, then there does seem to be a danger of getting what intuitively appears to be the wrong perspective on things. Isn't the best thing for one's soul to do what is right? And isn't the way to see what that is, to perceive what is right, to think about others or justice or God rather than oneself alone?

These might seem to be rhetorical questions that cry out for the answer yes. But I do not think that it is quite so simple. It is one thing to praise self-sacrifice when the self in question is someone's life (or body). The soldier who throws himself on a grenade in order to save the lives of his comrades is surely a hero. But what might it mean to sacrifice one's *soul*? Is it merely a selfish kind of squeamishness if there are limits to what I am prepared to do in order to combat Nazis or Al Qaeda terrorists, say? Modern torturers seem to enjoy moral sadism that makes such questions more than mere philosophical hypotheticals. Imagine any act of evil depravity you can think of, and there is a fair chance that some sadist has tried to make a decent person feel that he or she had to do it in order to prevent an even greater evil. What I have called "soul-selfishness" might equally be called integrity or a commitment to virtue. And it is not obvious that such a commitment is misguided, especially prior to finding oneself in the kind of nightmare I have in mind. It might be unwise to put oneself in such a dilemma, even if only in imagination, precisely because of the effect it might have on one's commitment to some important values.

In other words, we seem to need to avoid two extremes. If your *only* concern is with your own soul, then you might end up being a little too unconcerned about other people's bodies, as may have been the case, for example, when Wittgenstein was apparently prepared to machine gun others but not to stab them. On the other hand, if you have no concern for your own soul or integrity, then you might lose your grip on an essential ingredient of humanity. Perhaps in some circumstances it might be necessary to kill one person to save many or to torture a suspected terrorist to find a ticking bomb, but the decision to do so should surely never be easy. Our respect for the rights of others should not be easily overcome. Our integrity should not be compromised lightly. This is the kind of problem with consequentialism that Anscombe and Bernard Williams have identified. Yet many philosophers still believe in consequentialism. Others are skeptical about the value of integrity, especially if it just means sticking to whatever values you might happen to have. Philosophy seems to have few really solid answers to the questions of why we should be good or how to be good.

So should we just stop thinking right now? I do not think we can. Certainly, some people think about these things more than others, but those of us who do have such thoughts cannot simply shut them off at will. They can be redirected though. And perhaps they should be. Our tourist trip through the history of philosophy has shown us again and again that questions about how to live bring up all kinds of other questions too, questions not usually thought of as ethical. For instance, we might find ourselves asking now whether we have souls, what souls might be, what emotions are, or how (psychological) feelings and thoughts relate to the (physical) brain and nervous system. These are all questions within the branch of metaphysics known as the philosophy of mind, one of the most active areas of philosophy over the past 50 years.

These questions lead to still others. Thoughts have meaning and can be true or false. So questions about the mind and its contents can lead to questions about meaning (of the linguistic, not the existential, kind) and about truth. This leads into the philosophy of language, another very active area and one often rejected as being remote from real-life problems, when in fact we can see how it is connected to them. Perhaps, indeed, we can get nowhere in ethics, in trying to work out how we ought to live, until we have solved the problem of what we are; and perhaps that cannot be done until we have really understood what kind of beings we are. And perhaps, in turn, that cannot be done properly without working out the nature of reason, of thought, of language, and of logic. These questions might be somewhat remote from the meaning of life, but if they are fundamental to discovering what the meaning of life is, then surely they are worth taking seriously. They might not be fundamental in this way, of course; but it is hard to say one way or the other without taking a good look at them, which is precisely what many contemporary philosophers are doing.

Alternatively, if Thrasymachus' question cannot be very well answered, even by the greatest minds that have addressed it, perhaps we should challenge the question itself. Why ask "Why be good?" Maybe there is something inherently wrong with doing so. In attempting to give Thrasymachus an answer that will satisfy him, are we buying into some presuppositions that we would not accept if we saw them clearly? We might want to analyze his question further or set it aside and try to answer some other question instead. As well as answering questions, philosophy can question them, bringing out their full meaning and helping us decide which ones are really worth answering. I said that *perhaps* we can get nowhere in ethics, but perhaps we can. The only way to find out is to keep trying.

In short, I think we have seen that philosophy can shed light on important problems, even if it cannot completely solve them, and that, if you are not quite satisfied, the solution is probably more philosophy, not less. Good luck.

Notes

1. William Shakespeare, *Hamlet*, eds. Barbara A. Mowat and Paul Werstine (New York: Washington Square Press, 2003) 127. Act 3, scene 1.
2. For more on this, see George Orwell, "Reflections on Gandhi," in *The Orwell Reader* (San Diego, CA: Harcourt, 1984).

Suggestions for Further Reading

If you enjoyed this book and want to read more about ethics, you might try some of the following: Stephen Darwall, *Philosophical Ethics* (Boulder, CO: Westview Press, 1998); James Fieser, *Moral Philosophy through the Ages* (Mountain View, CA: Mayfield Publishing Company, 2001); Alasdair MacIntyre, *A Short History of Ethics: A History of Moral Philosophy from the Homeric Age to the Twentieth Century* (London: Routledge, 2006); Richard Norman, *The Moral Philosophers: An Introduction to Ethics* (Oxford: Oxford University Press, 1998); Donald Palmer, *Why It's Hard to Be Good: An Introduction to Ethical Theory* (New York: McGraw-Hill, 2006); Louis P. Pojman, *Ethics: Discovering Right and Wrong* (Belmont, CA: Wadsworth, 2005); James Rachels and Stuart Rachels, *The Elements of Moral Philosophy* (New York: McGraw-Hill, 2006); Mark Timmons, *Moral Theory: An Introduction* (Lanham, MD: Rowman & Littlefield, 2002).

The agenda for modern philosophy was largely set by René Descartes, who focused on questions about the mind and about what we can know. If you want to explore areas of philosophy other than ethics, therefore, you could begin with one of these: William Lyons, *Matters of the Mind* (London: Routledge, 2001); D. Z. Phillips, *Introducing Philosophy: The Challenge of Scepticism* (Oxford: Blackwell, 1996). I also like William H. Brenner, *Logic and Philosophy: An Integrated Introduction* (Notre Dame, IN: University of Notre Dame Press, 1993).

Index

9 780195 325058